FIGHTING TANKS

Ian Hogg

Grosset & Dunlap
A Filmways Company
Publishers • New York

in association with Phoebus

CONTENTS

Illustrations: John Batchelor
Designers: Richard Brookes   Keith Russell

© 1977 Phoebus Publishing Company/
BPC Publishing Limited
169 Wardour Street London W1A 2JX

First Grosset & Dunlap edition 1977

Library of Congress Catalog Card
Number: 77-78749

Made and printed in Great Britain by
Beric Press

ISBN 0-448-14459-X

IWM

INTRODUCTION

"The armored fighting vehicle represents a combination of three basic elements of warfare – mobility, protection and firepower" – so writes Ian Hogg in his opening chapter. These three basic elements were first displayed in the war chariots which raced into battle in the Middle East in 1700 B.C. Armored fighting vehicles evolved slowly through the centuries from hide-covered war carts and the dreams of Leonardo da Vinci to the tracked and armored gun carriers of the First World War – vehicles which were nicknamed "tanks" to conceal their identity from German intelligence.

Tanks first saw action in 1916, but though they scored local successes they were not used in significant numbers or on suitable terrain. It was not until Colonel J. F. C. Fuller presented "Plan 1919" that the British began to envisage a role for tanks wider than mere wire and trench crossing vehicles. Plan 1919 anticipated the deep penetration tactics of the Blitzkrieg of the Second World War between 1939 and 1943. Tanks, motorized infantry and dive bombers were used by the Germans to rupture the static defenses of Poland, France and the Balkan states and then take the war deep into the Soviet Union.

The race for technical superiority and a constant struggle to improve the three basic elements of the AFV produced war winners like the Russian T-34 and monsters like the German *Maus* and a range of "Funnies" to assist the conventional gun tanks. Since 1945 wars in Korea, India and the Middle East have shown that many of the lessons and doctrines of the Second World War are still valid.

Ian Hogg and John Batchelor trace the tank story from its origins in prehistory through the first experiments in the First World War to the Second and subsequent postwar developments. Line drawings and diagrams are combined with the text to record the men and machines that make up the tank story.

FIRST PRINCIPLES
the armoured fighting vehicle

The armoured fighting vehicle represents a combination of three basic elements of warfare – mobility, protection and firepower – and to a great extent the shape of an AFV is governed by the relative degrees of importance attached to these three features. And since all three have been appreciated by commanders since war began, it is no surprise to find that, throughout recorded history, there have been attempts to bring them all together into some sort of fighting machine.

The first fighting vehicle was, of course, the war chariot. Originally developed in western Asia as a form of transport, the chariot was introduced into Egypt by the Hyksos people some time between the XII and XVIII Dynasties, or around 1700 BC. The mobility given by the chariot was complemented by the firepower of well-trained archers carried aboard, and from its beginning the cult of the war chariot spread rapidly throughout the Middle East. Solomon is said to have formed a 'mechanized division' of 1400 chariots built from materials imported from Egypt and the Greeks and Romans adopted the idea in their turn; while the Persians, under Cyrus, are generally credited with introducing the idea of mounting a scythe blade at each end of the axle, an offensive device which soon spread, to appear in Britain at the time of Julius Caesar's invasions.

The third element, protection, was gradually added to the other two. The original chariots were light – accenting mobility and manoeuvre – and offered little or no protection from arrows or spears other than the driver's ability to dodge. Gradually, however, the superstructure became harder, the use of treated hides being a common measure. Shields hung over the vehicle side served both to protect the occupants and to be readily available in case dismounted action was called for.

But to every weapon, as we will see, there is a counter-weapon, and after a period of supremacy the war chariot fell from grace as more and more men became adept at archery and discovered that the chariot could be stopped in its tracks by concentrating the fire of arrows on to the horses rather than the occupants of the chariot.

Attempts to counter this move by placing protection upon the horses merely added to the weight and reduced the mobility.

In order to regain the lost impetus, the chariot was abandoned and the armies based their mobility on the individual horseman who, with superior manoeuvrability, was a much more difficult target for the foot archer. The only effective counter to a horseman was another horseman bearing an edged weapon – a sword or lance – and this one-to-one combat brought about the development of body armour for the rider and, later, horse armour to protect his mount.

This addition of protection had its inevitable effect: weight went up, and mobility went down. The weight of the armour slowed the horse and led eventually to the abandonment of fast horses and the adoption of heavy farming and cart horses, types more able to bear the weight but, on the other hand, more vulnerable to the foot soldier by reason of the reduction in speed and the lesser ease of manoeuvre.

The arrival of gunpowder, in the fourteenth century, brought about far-reaching changes. Firepower had now, it seemed, mastered mobility, since the gun-propelled ball could penetrate the armour of horse or man, and as a result the armoured rider completely disappeared from the battlefield. Moreover, the ponderous cannon, which became the anchor of the army, restricted manoeuvre. The cannon was difficult to move and took a long time to load and fire, and as a result it was unable to move during a battle so as to try and influence the course of the action.

Action was now restricted to a formal line of troops with the cannon in the centre. Once the cannon had spoken, the cavalry rolled past to perform their charge; when that was over the cannon might have been re-loaded and would fire another salvo, after which the foot soldiers fought each other with pikes and swords. The advent of the musket as the foot soldier's armament made very little difference to this system of battle.

Not all commanders were satisfied with this, however. Insofar as artillery is concerned Gustavus Adolphus, Marlborough and Frederick the Great all made attempts to lighten the cannon and move them about the battlefield, and this eventually led to horse artillery and paved the way to more mobility. But advances in war machines were less in evidence, though there is enough left on record to suggest that, if little was done, there were at least some people giving the matter thought.

Throughout the Middle Ages there are references to 'war carts'. The Chinese emperor Sun-Tze apparently used four-wheeled carts armoured with hides at about the same time as the Egyptians and Assyrians were producing their war chariots, and the idea kept recurring through the centuries. The basic principle seems to have been a heavy vehicle packed with archers who could move about the battlefield with some degree of protection, firing as they went and finally dismounting to give battle. In modern parlance, these have more in common with the armoured infantry carrier than they have with the tank. More-over, of course, the horses were still vulnerable.

The first proposal to use some other agency to propel a war vehicle appears to have come from an Italian, Guido del Vigevano, who, in 1335, produced a drawing of a wheeled strong-point propelled by the action of a windmill carried on the superstructure. His drawings rather gloss over the actual question of how the power was to be transferred from the vanes of the mill to the wheels of the vehicle, but he has to be given credit for trying. His idea was brought up afresh by Roberto Valturio in 1472, who proposed a rectangular box supported on four wheels and driven by wind vanes on each side, through intermediate gears. On the face of it, the idea is workable; at least the gears are in the right places and there is a discernible train of mechanical effort. But one is inclined to feel that the result in practice may not have been so happy. It is extremely doubtful if any arrangement of gearing could have derived sufficient mechanical advantage to allow wind power to propel the device, and, moreover, from the practical viewpoint one is inclined to suspect that the gears of the driving wheels would have become clogged with dirt and mud quite quickly.

It would be impossible to describe this period of history without reference to Leonardo da Vinci, that jack of all trades and master of few. Da Vinci was prolific at putting ideas on paper, but when it came to devices of war he was sadly lacking in practical values, as his fortification theories will demonstrate if studied. Da Vinci has been put forward as the putative inventor of the tank by virtue of a drawing of a 'battle machine' which resembles a flying saucer more than a tank. But it certainly has some elements of worth: for the first time we are presented with all-round protection, gun power and a self-contained method of propulsion – men operating cranks to drive the wheels by gearing. One of the most intriguing features is the choice of shape; by current standards this ex-tremely angular form would be highly thought-of, since it would deflect armour-piercing projectiles with great facility. Whether da Vinci had the thought of deflecting cannonballs, or whether he was simply concerned with the aesthetic appearance of his device (which is more likely) he certainly was several hundred years ahead on that score.

The first practical combination of mobility and gun power was put together by the remarkable Johann Ziška of Bohemia. Ziška, believe it or not, began as a page in the palace of King Wenceslas – for all we know to the contrary, *the* page, of whom we sing every Christmas. He then went forth into the world to become a soldier of fortune, fighting with the German, Hungarian and English armies of the late 14th century, until he returned to Bohemia in 1419. Bohemia, at that time, was seething with resentment after the burning of one John Huss, an early Protestant martyr, and this resentment was fanned into war by the death of King Wenceslas and the accession of his brother Sigismund, the man who had been responsible for handing Huss over to the ecclesiastical authorities for burning. The 'Hussites', as the protestant rebels were known, were soon brought into an organised force by Ziška, aided by an outstanding soldier-monk called Prokop.

Since the Hussites were largely labourers and peasants with little military background, Ziška had to think of some original tactical ideas in order to be able to counter the professional armies which Sigismund was able to put into the field, and he hit upon the idea of 'battle carts'. These were ordinary four-wheeled farm carts, strengthened and with the sides built up to give protection to the occupants. Some were used to carry archers, up to 18 men being able to ride inside and fire arrows through slits in the wooden sides; others were reinforced and used as beds for banks of small-calibre cannon.

So far, Ziška had done little that was new; cart-mounted cannon had been used

This fourteenth-century design by the Italian Guido del Vigevano was an attempt to improve on the medieval war carts by using wind power for propulsion and dispensing with vulnerable horses

Leonardo da Vinci's design for a 'battle machine' contained all the basic components of a fighting vehicle – gun-power, all-round protection and self-contained propulsion unit – plus sloped armour which would have been extremely good at deflecting projectiles

before, as had wagon-loads of archers. What he now had to do was to bring a new system of tactics into being, and since his scratch army had nothing to forget, this task was relatively easy. He trained his force to manoeuvre quickly – moves of up to 25 miles daily, a prodigious figure for the time, have been recorded – and, having moved, to bring the wagons together so as to form a prefabricated fortress which could be rapidly assembled on any suitable ground. The wagons were brought into a circle, guns and archers facing outwards, and the gaps between were filled by prepared barriers of thick wood and iron strapping. Once inside this, Ziška could provoke a careless enemy to attack and then destroy him, a tactic which he repeated time after time.

Having mastered this essentially defensive form of fighting, Ziška then moved to the offensive form by drilling his warriors to fight while the carts were on the move. The archers would rove the battlefield, while the gun carts would move to a suitable point, fire, and then move off, reloading as they went, to bring their firepower to bear on some other point of the battle. With combinations of these two features the Hussites defeated the Germans at Prague in 1420 and at Deutsche Brod in 1422. By this time Ziška had been blinded, but he continued to lead his unique armoured force from one victory to another until his death in October 1424. After this, Prokop took up the leadership until he was killed in battle at Lippau in 1434. Finally, peace was arranged between the Emperor Sigismund and the Hussites in 1436, after which the farm carts returned to more peaceful pursuits and armoured warfare on wheels ceased to exist.

In subsequent years, ideas for mechanically propelled vehicles continued to crop up. They were inevitably impractical, however, since the means of propulsion always came back to either manpower or wind power. One of the more remarkable ideas, and one of the few which ever got beyond a drawing, was that of Simon Stevin who, in 1599, produced what amounted to sailing ships fitted with wheels for the use of the Prince of Orange. It is recorded that these devices worked, but the references are somewhat sketchy and it seems likely that what actually worked was a light craft such as a ship's gig or dinghy, and the fanciful full-rigged men-of-war on coach wheels depicted in some old documents were figments of the designer's imagination. Even if some two or three hundred tons of oak could have been supported on four wooden wheels, the unit pressure would have driven them into the ground like tent-pegs before the ship could have moved.

And the wind as a source of motive power is a capricious thing. It is one thing to sail across the oceans in the beneficent flow of a trade wind, but a vastly different matter to try and manoeuvre a box-like wagon across the countryside, surmounting ditches and ploughed fields, with the wind eddying and re-eddying from buildings, woods and hillsides. What was needed was controllable power, and it was not until the arrival of the steam engine that such a thing existed.

One of the first applications of the steam engine was to the propulsion of a road vehicle, Cugnot producing a steam-driven three-wheeled vehicle in 1769. Cugnot was a Captain of the Corps du Genie, a military engineer, and it is therefore not surprising to find that the second steam vehicle which he built was intended as a tractor for heavy artillery. One of the greatest bugbears of the artillery commanders of that time was the practice of hiring civilian teamsters and their draft horses to move the heavy cannon in time of war, since they were too expensive a luxury to maintain in times of peace. Not unnaturally, the teamsters averred that the terms of their contract were limited to transporting the guns from place to place, and that there was no obligation upon them to stand still and be shot at. Consequently, when battle was joined the teams and teamsters disappeared over the nearest horizon and the artillery was immobile until they could be rounded up again – often at the point of a musket. Providing the gunners with their own mechanical traction would have been a great step forward, and it would probably have led to an armed vehicle in due course, but Cugnot's tractor was mechanically unreliable and its ponderous weight on three wheels cut the roads to pieces and caused it to sink into the ground if it essayed movement off the roads. The army would have none of it.

Had Cugnot but realised it, a partial answer had appeared in England in 1770 when one Richard Edgeworth patented a 'footed wheel', a wheel carrying flotation plates which spread the load and prevented it sinking into soft ground. This might have been a solution to Cugnot's problems, but Edgeworth's wheel appears to have had no success and Cugnot's steam tractor passed from sight.

The 'long peace' after Waterloo seems to have stifled military inventiveness in any field for many years, and the only major innovations seen in the 19th century were in the realms of naval engineering and heavy artillery. Similarly, there was little or no progress in the commercial field which could have pointed the way to an alert soldier; in 1883 the Holt Tractor Company of Stockton, California managed to produce a steam-driven agricultural tractor, and in 1888 the Batter Company of England marketed a steam tractor which moved on caterpillar tracks, a prerequisite in muddy farming conditions.

The steam engine, though, was a cumbersome method of propulsion, particularly in the somewhat inefficient forms used in agricultural machinery. Something more compact and delivering more power for its weight was needed before the self-propelled vehicle could become a reality, so when, in 1885, Gottlieb Daimler designed the high-speed internal combustion engine, the last piece of the jig-saw puzzle was out of the box and waiting to be assembled.

As the 19th century drew towards its close, the world seemed to take on a more

Less fanciful and more practical than many earlier designs were Johann Ziška's battle carts. Although the basic idea of using strengthened farm carts to carry squads of archers and small cannon was far from new, his tactics of bringing them together to form instant strongpoints or using them to deploy his troops rapidly on the battlefield enabled him to run up a series of victories

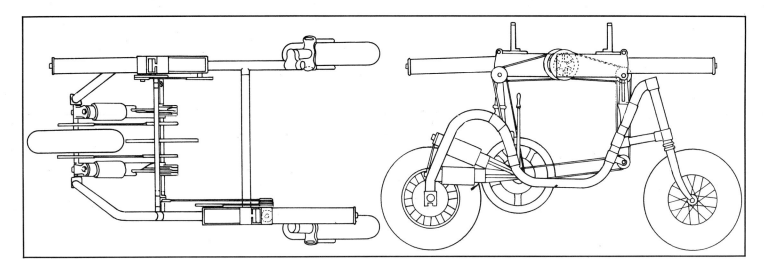

One of the first applications of the motor vehicle to the machine-gun was E J Pennington's 'Field Cycle' (above) of 1896. The tricycle is powered by two engines which also, through a series of chains, drive the two mechanical machine-guns, one of which points in each direction

One of the more exotic ideas for self-propelled machine-guns, this 1904 patent by S B Apostoloff would probably have been difficult enough to control and steer without the operator having to fire the machine-gun as well

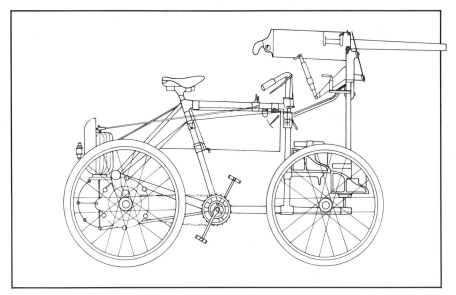

F R Simms was among the few inventors of mobile machine-guns who managed to see his ideas in the flesh. This 1899 patent covers his 'Quadricycle', with a Maxim gun at the front and a petrol engine at the back. The gun could be dismounted for use or fired from the cycle. Under the title of the Simms Motor Scout it was demonstrated widely in 1900

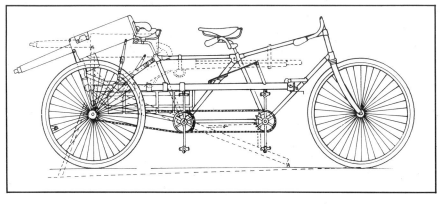

Sir Hiram Maxim did not rest content with inventing the automatic machine-gun but also put forward some novel ideas on how to use it in the field. This 1895 design, the 'Maxim and Silverman Tandem Cycle', carried two guns: steadying bars could be lowered to support the machine when stopped while the two riders jumped off and began firing the guns

belligerent hue. It hadn't been particularly peaceful since 1854, when the Crimean War broke out, to be followed by the Prussian wars with Denmark, Austria and France, the American Civil War and the Sino-Japanese War, but now the tempo seemed to be getting faster, and the South African War seems to have triggered off a sudden upsurge in military awareness on the part of people who otherwise might never have given warlike things a thought. Inventors vied with each other to produce every form of armament – machine-guns, new cannon, automatic pistols, rifles – and it was inevitable that some of them struck upon the possibility of allying the new automobile to the new types of firearms.

The gun and the modern wheel had, in fact, already come together in the form of armoured trains. The railway train was the 19th century's premier technical achievement, and the idea of putting guns on trains had occured as far back as the American Civil War. In the beginning it was simply a matter of mounting a cannon on a flatcar and pushing it to where it was needed, but with the growing importance of railway lines as arteries of communication and supply it became necessary to guard them against depredations by cavalry raiders. Soon the flatcars were reinforced by sheet-iron armour against small arms fire, with cannon sticking out of loopholes in the side. A similar makeshift was employed by the British in Egypt in the 1880s, and the South African War saw one or two more armoured trains brought into service. But for all their utility in keeping the supplies flowing, armoured trains were, of course, tied strictly to the ribbon of steel on which they ran, and their influence extended no further than gunshot range from the track. The armoured train, as we shall see, managed to survive for another fifty years or so but it cannot be considered as part of the development of the tank.

The Franco-Prussian War and the South African War demonstrated that warfare had moved on since the days of set-piece battles, with serried ranks meeting head-on and exchanging vollies until one or other caved in. Now mobility was the thing: skirmishers moved about the battlefield, artillery was light and mobile, and the battle tended to ebb and flow. There was scope for a method of moving firepower rapidly from one place to another, and in 1898 Mr F R Simms, a well-known motor enthusiast of the day, produced a De Dion Bouton Quadricycle, a four-wheeled motorcycle, with a Maxim machine-gun mounted over the front wheels so that it could be controlled by the rider as he sat in the quadricycle saddle.

There is a well-known contemporary photograph of Mr Simms crouched behind the small shield of the gun, grasping the pistol-grip with one hand and the cycle handle-bar with the other, giving the impression of pedalling (or motoring) smartly toward the enemy while spraying them with fire. But on second thoughts one begins to wonder. Controlling a Maxim gun was a full time job, without the added responsibility of piloting a quadricycle, and the imagination recoils at the prospect of attempting to control this machine across a bumpy stretch of grassland while trying furiously to fit a fresh ammunition belt into the gun and re-cock it. But as a means of getting a machine-gun rapidly from place to place there was some merit in the idea,

though the operator of such a remarkable contrivance (for its time) would doubtless have been the aiming point for every firearm in the district. For all that, Simms deserves his place in history as the man who first allied the firepower of the modern machine-gun to the mobility of the internal combustion engine.

In that same year, however, a more practical alliance between the two devices appeared in the United States of America. Major R P Davidson, Commandant of the Northwestern Military and Naval Academy at Lake Geneva, Wisconsin, designed a lightweight vehicle to carry a machine-gun and, in concert with the Charles E Duryea Motor Company of Peoria he built a three-wheeled gasoline-engined car which carried a Colt Potato-digger machine-gun. Little is known of this original car since Davidson, from all accounts, spent much of his time repairing it, and after having second thoughts he re-designed it as a four-wheeled vehicle. The machine-gun was mounted at the front, on its own tripod, and fired on the move by the co-driver while the driver gave his full attention to controlling the car; two men were carried at the back of the car, so that having arrived at a suitable spot the three-man gun crew could dismount with their gun and go into action while the driver could remove the vehicle to some place of safety. While the Davidson car had the facility to fire on the move, its primary purpose was that of a weapons carrier, and it reflects Davidson's military training that he separated the functions of driving and fighting.

Davidson continued to experiment along these lines. In 1899 he produced two steam-driven cars armed with machine-guns and used them with some success in Academy field days and exercises, but for all his connections with the military he was unable to generate any degree of interest in the War Department.

So far mobility and firepower had come together; in 1900 the third element of the formula, armour protection, was added. In Russia, the Imperial Artillery Commission instructed an engineer named Lutski to build an armour-protected steam car to carry a light quick-firing gun; Lutski duly built the vehicle, but after completion it was found that the engine was too feeble for the weight of the vehicle and the project was abandoned as unworkable. Meanwhile a Mr E J Pennington in England had proposed an armour-protected gasoline-engined car which was to carry two shielded Maxim guns in an open superstructure. The War Office evinced no interest in the machine and the idea was dropped. (Contrary to many statements made in the past, there is no evidence that the Pennington Car was ever built, even in prototype form.)

But F R Simms appears to have taken some notice of Pennington's ideas and in 1902 he produced his 'War Car' which used the same upturned-bathtub type of all-enveloping armour as had the Pennington and the same open-topped superstructure mounting guns in swivel mountings. Five men operated the vehicle: one in the centre, driving; two manning a Maxim 1-pdr pom-pom cannon at one end of the body and two manning a Maxim machine-gun each at the other end. Protected by $\frac{1}{4}$-in plating, the War Car weighed $6\frac{1}{4}$ tons, was 28 ft long and could move at 9 mph, a quite respectable performance for the time. But in spite of displaying the War Car at various motor

and other exhibitions throughout England in 1902–3, Simms could raise no interest in the machine and finally scrapped it.

The Russians, having failed to achieve anything with Engineer Lutski, now turned to a French motor-car company and asked them to devise a motor-gun-carrier. The Charron, Girardot et Voigt company were already making light automobiles with some success, and they simply took the chassis of their 16-hp car, removed the passenger tonneau and placed a round armoured barbette on the rear of the chassis, arming it with a Hotchkiss 8-mm machine-gun. This wasn't what the Russians had in mind and they turned it down, so the car was sold to the French Army who used it with some success in Morocco in 1902. The Russian General Staff now laid down some specifications, passed them to the Charron company, and asked them to build 36 machines.

The result of this Russian design was the prototype of all subsequent armoured cars: a four-wheeled box-like structure of steel plate with a revolving turret on the roof in which was fitted a Maxim machine-gun, with its water-jacket carefully shrouded in an armour trough. Steel channel-iron sections were carried in racks above the wheels to allow an extempore bridge to be thrown across ditches, and the whole vehicle gives evidence of some sound thinking on the part of the designer. The effect is, however, slightly diluted by the addition, by Charron, of an acetylene headlight devoid of any protection and a somewhat incongruous bulb horn mounted on the roof.

The Charron car weighed just over three tons and was propelled by a 30-hp engine. The first one was delivered to Russia in 1904 and was used for riot control in St Petersburg. But for some unknown reason the Russians now renegued on the contract and no more cars were delivered. The second car was taken by the French Army, and that was the end of the Charron production.

The Russian Charron car aroused the interest of the Austro-Hungarian army and in 1904 they approached the Austro-Daimler company with proposals for an armoured car. The resulting vehicle had a high-set armoured bonnet concealing the 35-hp engine, a square driving cab with vision ports and an elevating seat so that the driver could raise himself so as to see out of a hatch in the top of his cab when conditions allowed, and a wide body which carried a revolving turret in which was mounted a Skoda M1902 machine-gun. Weighing $3\frac{1}{2}$ tons, the Daimler car could travel at 28 mph, and it was demonstrated at the Imperial Manoeuvres in 1905 and 1906.

During the next five or six years a number of armoured car designs appeared, all more or less copies of the Charron and Daimler layout. But at the same time a new feature had arrived on the military scene – military aviation, using the lighter-than-air balloon, the airship and the aeroplane. And no sooner were the daredevil aeronauts aloft than the earth-bound soldiers began figuring out ways of getting them down again.

The airship was the prime craft of the time, and since it seemed to be a fairly substantial target, a fairly sensitive target, and a slow-moving target, the idea rapidly sprang up that the best way to shoot at it would be to have a gun mounted on a motor chassis which could chase the airship, shooting as it went. Alternatively, since the

11

airship had an infinite number of lines of approach to a potential target, it seemed a logical idea to have a motor-mounted gun or two in strategic locations near large cities and turn them out like fire-engines to rush into the path of the approaching raider and open fire, chasing him thereafter.

Whatever the reasoning, wheels under anti-balloon guns seemed a good idea, and at the Frankfurt International Exhibition in 1909 two German gunmakers displayed their solutions to the new threat. The Rheinische Metallwaren und Maschinenfabrik of Dusseldorf showed the Erhardt 5-cm quick-firing gun mounted in a turret on top of an armoured car, while Krupp of Essen displayed a 7.5-cm high-angle gun inside an armoured circular shield mounted at the rear of a truck chassis and with an armoured cab and ammunition racks at the front end. Strictly speaking, these two equipments belong to the line of development which eventually led to the self-propelled gun, but they also exhibited affinity with the armoured car and they undoubtedly influenced armoured car design by demonstrating that a machine-gun was not the most powerful armament which could be carried on wheels.

By 1911 then, the armoured car was moving along fairly well-defined lines. It had been accepted in small numbers by several armies and it had been used occasionally in action. But it was a long way from universal acceptance. As an example, in 1905 the US Chief of Staff, General Miles, had proposed converting five cavalry regiments to armoured cars, an idea so revolutionary that it was violently opposed by the horsemen and finally abandoned. Nevertheless, approved or not, the armoured car was an accepted fact and it was to be only a matter of time before improved reliability and design, allied with a more receptive frame of mind on the part of the soldiers, would turn it into a standard piece of military equipment. But there were one or two people who were not entirely convinced that the armoured car was the full answer to the old question of mobility, firepower and protection. On roads they were fine, but once off the road and on to soft earth, they were at a grave disadvantage with their narrow, high-pressure tyres, and the smallest ditch or obstacle stopped them.

By 1911 there were a number of track-laying agricultural tractors in existence, notably those of the Holt Company. Some of these had found their way to the more technically-conscious farm owners in Europe, and in 1911 a young Austrian officer, Leutnant Gunther Burstyn, saw one of these Holt tractors at work. Burstyn was familiar with armoured cars and appreciated their cross-country limitations. He was also a man with an enquiring and inventive mind, and he immediately realised that the alliance of the Holt Caterpillar Track with an armoured car would produce a vehicle which overcame this fundamental drawback. He set to work to design such a vehicle, and in October 1911 he submitted a set of drawings to the Austro-Hungarian War Department.

After three months deliberation, they sent the drawings back: a clever idea, they said. Perhaps Leutnant Burstyn would care to have one built by a commercial automobile company so that the idea could be tested? At his own expense, of course. Burstyn, an impecunious young officer, was in no position to have such a prototype built, nor could he interest any commercial company in taking a chance on it. He sent the drawings to the German General Staff, but they also turned the idea down. He then tried to patent it, but his application was refused on the grounds that the vehicle was driven by a gasoline engine and the idea of such propulsion was already patented, while the other features were so impractical as not to be worthy of a patent. And so, in spite of enthusiastic comments by one or two military periodicals to whom he had shown his idea, Burstyn's tracked gun carriage never got beyond a set of plans. Disillusioned, he turned to other things, producing plans for a simple trench mortar which was also well ahead of its time and met with no better response than had his tracked armoured car.

At much the same time, on the other side of the world, a young Australian civil engineer, L A de Mole, was pondering the problem of moving heavy loads across rough country. He designed a tracked vehicle, with sprung suspension, and then, struck by the possibility of using it as a military device, he submitted drawings to the War Office in London. After some months they were returned, together with the intimation that the War Office were not interested in experimenting with 'chain rails'. The idea was forgotten in Whitehall,

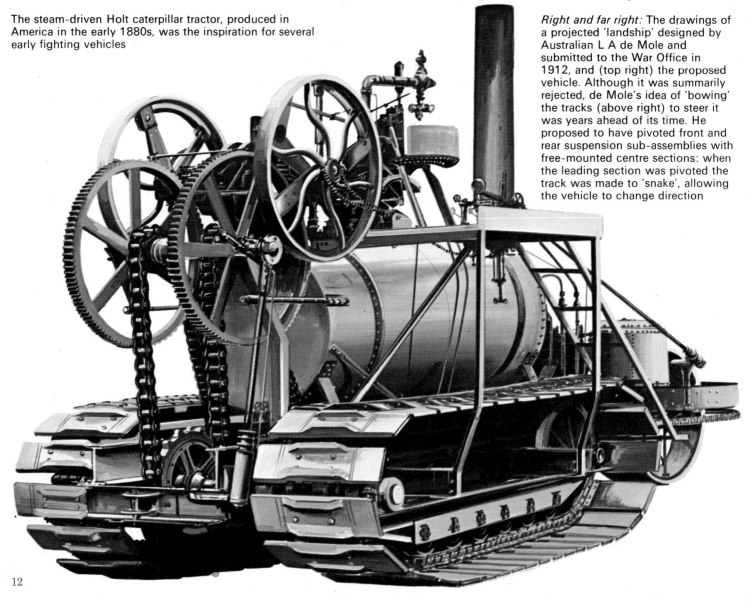

The steam-driven Holt caterpillar tractor, produced in America in the early 1880s, was the inspiration for several early fighting vehicles

Right and far right: The drawings of a projected 'landship' designed by Australian L A de Mole and submitted to the War Office in 1912, and (top right) the proposed vehicle. Although it was summarily rejected, de Mole's idea of 'bowing' the tracks (above right) to steer it was years ahead of its time. He proposed to have pivoted front and rear suspension sub-assemblies with free-mounted centre sections: when the leading section was pivoted the track was made to 'snake', allowing the vehicle to change direction

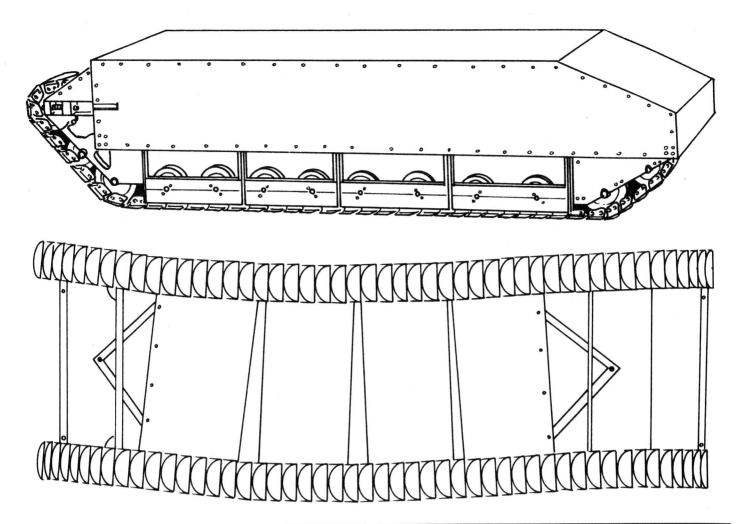

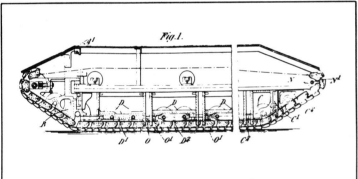

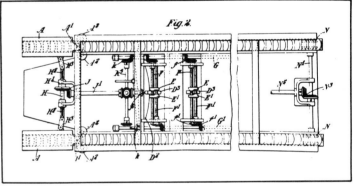

and it was not until de Mole laid a claim for the prior invention of the tank before the Royal Commission on Awards to Inventors in November 1919 – by which he was suitably rewarded – that those soldiers who had actually been concerned in the development of the tank found out about his proposal.

One interesting feature of his idea was that he proposed steering the vehicle by 'bowing' the track. The suspension wheels were carried on pivoted sub-assemblies at the ends of the tracks, while the centre sections were freely mounted so as to be able to swing in any direction. By pivoting the leading suspension unit, the track was induced to 'snake' and the free-mounted centre units automatically adapted themselves to this so that the track pattern assumed a curved shape and the vehicle could move to one side. Bowed track steering was not to make its appearance on a tank for many years, but again, de Mole had got there first.

And so, as the war clouds gathered over Europe, the various nations prepared their armies according to their own faiths. The Germans tightened up the Schlieffen Plan

and pinned their hopes on a rapid outflanking movement round the French Army to take them to the gates of Paris. The French relied on the *rafale* of fire from the revolutionary 75-mm gun allied to the spirit of offensive action in their infantry to carry all before them in an irresistible advance to the Rhine and beyond. The Russians had so many men they would smother any invasion with bodies. And the British relied on impeccable marksmanship, rapid rifle fire, discipline and fieldcraft. One thing they were all quite certain of; once war came it would all be over in a matter of weeks. To give but one example of the mood: the French Army were so convinced of a rapid war that they had only 1400 shells per gun in reserve and no mobilisation plans for the manufacture of artillery or ammunition.

They would all have done well to have read the forecast of Bloch, the Polish banker who had written, in 1899: 'Instead of war fought out to the bitter end in a series of decisive battles, we shall have as a substitute a long period of continually increasing strain upon the resources of the combatants . . . . Everybody will be en-

trenched in the next war. It will be a great war of entrenchments. The spade will be as indispensible to the soldier as his rifle . . . . All wars will of necessity partake of the character of siege operations . . . .'

But Bloch was derided by the professional soldiers. He was, after all, only a banker, what could such a man know of war? The fact that he was an economist capable of sound and logical reasoning was ignored, as was his prophecy.

And so in 1914 the warring nations threw themselves into the war in accordance with their doctrines. And when the manoeuvering and sparring for position was over, there were two lines of entrenchment across Western Europe, from which the soldiers peered at each other in frustration. The men at the top were less disheartened. This, after all, could be considered, technically speaking, as a siege, and the techniques of siegecraft were well known: you dug trenches closer to the enemy, pounded him with artillery, and then jumped out of the trenches and carried the enemy line with cheers and acclamation. Send for the engineers; send for the heavy artillery; it will all be over by Christmas.

CUTTING THE WIRE
landships and tanks

The war, however, failed to be over by Christmas. By the time autumn had set in there were quite a few people who appreciated that it wasn't likely to be over as quickly as had been thought. The Allies and the Germans moved rapidly westward, each trying to outflank the other in a race to the sea until there was a solid line of entrenchment stretching from the Swiss border to the North Sea, a line which was getting deeper and stronger every day. And with the forming of this line came two new weapons which, although seen in small numbers in the Russo-Japanese War some ten years previously, had largely been ignored. These were the machine-gun and the barbed wire entanglement.

Ignorance of the machine-gun's powers was inexcusable, since guns had been in use since the 1880s and their capabilities were well enough known. What was not appreciated was their devastating effect in the defensive role – although in the early days of the Gatling Gun the British Ordnance Select Committee had pointed out that they would be at their best when used in a fortress to protect the flanks. But the word fortress conjures up visions of granite and steel, and applying the machine-gun to a hole in the ground did not seem quite the same thing. Nevertheless, the German army soon demonstrated the value of a well-sited and protected machine-gun in denying ground to enemy infantry: to move above ground was instant death. Bad as the machine-gun was, it became infinitely worse when allied to barbed wire, for the wire held up the advancing infantry and fixed them in position so that the machine-gun could take its toll. The guns were carefully sited so as to sweep the length of the wire – 'in enfilade' was the technical phrase – giving each bullet a better chance of striking a target.

Moreover, the barbed wire was not simply a matter of a few strands. Most people with no experience of military wire think of the homely barbed-wire fence of the farmer and multiply it by five or so. But the truth was a good deal worse than that; vast belts of wire forty and fifty yards thick protected some strongpoints in later stages of the war, belts which defied gunfire and wirecutters alike. Nothing on feet could cross these belts and the attack had perforce to go into lanes where there was no wire – and, of course, where an overpowering number of machine-guns were sited for just that event.

So by the end of 1914 the wire, thin as it was in the beginning, and the machine-guns, few as they were, had begun to dominate the battlefield, and the only way to attack them was to pound away with artillery in order to hack the wire to pieces, then bombard the machine-guns, and then, with sheer intestinal fortitude, get the infantry, with rifle in hand, to walk forward in the high expectation of sudden death. It was no wonder that a few of the more thinking types of men began to wonder if there wasn't some better way of doing things.

Few thought to such good and far-reaching effect as did Lieutenant-Colonel (later Major-General Sir) Ernest D Swinton, of the Royal Engineers. He had fought in South Africa, written books (one of which, *The Defence of Duffer's Drift* was to become a classic text on military tactics and be studied for fifty years), edited the official history of the Russo-Japanese War and been Assistant Secretary of the Committee of Imperial Defence, and on the outbreak of war he had been sent to France with a roving commission as the one and only official war correspondent. In this position he saw at first hand the results of the combination of wire, trench and machine-gun, and it reinforced opinions on the tactical worth of the gun which he had formed as a result of his own combat experience and of his study of the Russo-Japanese War.

The germ of an idea was already in his head. In July 1914, before the war began, he had received a letter from a man called Marriott, a South African mining engineer whom Swinton had met during the South African War. Marriott, like de Mole, had been confronted with the problem of moving heavy machinery across rough country, and he had acquired an American Holt tractor with caterpillar tracks. He wrote of this to Swinton, expressing the opinion that such a machine might well have military applications for transport; Swinton agreed that it seemed a good idea and passed the

British troops advancing through German barbed wire. It was the need to find a vehicle that could break through the wire – vast belts of it, up to 50 yards deep – and cross the trenches behind that provided much of the incentive for the development of the tank

suggestion on to the various parts of the War Office concerned with transportation. Two months later Swinton went off to France and put the Holt tractor at the back of his mind.

On October 19, 1914 Swinton was driving across France en route to England for a conference and was mulling over in his mind the problem of beating the wire and the machine-gun. What was needed, he concluded, was 'a power-driven, bullet-proof, armed engine capable of destroying machine-guns, of crossing country and trenches, of breaking through entangle-ments and of climbing earthworks'. And while he was considering the difficulties of such a machine, he suddenly remembered Marriott's letter and the Holt caterpillar tractor.

On the following day, in London, he put the idea of using the Holt tractor as an armoured cross-country vehicle to Sir Maurice Hankey, Secretary of the Committee of Imperial Defence. Hankey recognised the value of the idea and recommended Swinton to discuss it with Lord Kitchener, the Secretary of State for War, but Kitchener was too busy to see Swinton and the latter had to return to France without being able to put his idea in front of 'K'.

Swinton afterwards said that had he been able to talk with 'K', the whole affair might have gone much faster, but there is room for doubt here. Kitchener was a difficult man to convince where any new idea was concerned, and when he finally saw the tank he scathingly declared it to be a 'pretty little toy' which would never be of any use in war.

Fortunately, though, Kitchener's approval or disapproval was never germane to the issue, since the whole idea now went out of the army's hands by a strange chain of events. A few days after Swinton's conversation with Hankey, the army did, in fact, take delivery of a number of Holt tractors for use as artillery prime movers and ammunition tractors, but that was as far as the army were interested in going at that time.

After Swinton's return to France, Hankey put the idea to Kitchener who, predictably,

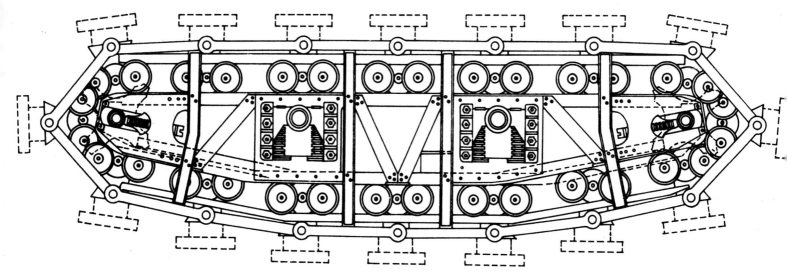

The Diplock Pedrail (right), invented by Englishman Bramah Diplock, consisted of a wheel with loosely slung feet which adjusted to enable it to cross uneven ground. It was later developed into an elongated continuous track (above) which was used on agricultural tractors and was demonstrated to Winston Churchill in 1915

would have none of it. Undaunted, Hankey turned in another direction. As well as being Secretary to the Committee of Imperial Defence, he was also secretary to the newly-hatched War Council, and in this latter capacity he had the duty to place before the Prime Minister any matter which appeared to be of importance to the war effort.

Accordingly, over Christmas 1914 Hankey wrote a memorandum on the subject of 'Land Cruisers' and sent it to the Prime Minister, Mr Asquith. Not confining himself to the plain matter of the invention, he expounded on the problems in France and then, having, as it were, laid the ground, he proposed 'Numbers of large heavy rollers, themselves bullet-proof, propelled from behind by motor-engines, geared very low, the driving wheel fitted with caterpillar driving gear to grip the ground, the driver's seat armoured, and with a Maxim gun fitted. The object of this device would be to roll down barbed wire by sheer weight, to give some cover to men creeping up behind, and to support the advance with machine-gun fire.'

Hankey's memorandum was circulated among the members of the War Council, most of whom appear to have regarded it as one more of the interminable pieces of paper they were expected to read. But one of the Council members was the First Lord of the Admiralty, Winston Churchill, and Churchill had some peculiar responsibilities as well as an urge to do something significant against the Germans.

As will be explained later, the Royal Navy operated an armoured car squadron in France, and they were also responsible, by a chain of devious reasoning, for the anti-aircraft defence of England. These two tasks gave the Navy an interest in land warfare, a foothold in France and a number of experts on motor transport, all of which were to prove useful. Furthermore, Churchill was anxious to promote the war

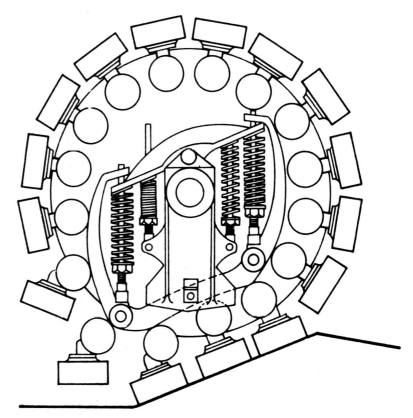

in every way possible. He had already raised a battery of Royal Marine gunners and sent them to France with a 15-in howitzer and was contemplating putting naval guns on to railway truck mountings, all with the idea of spurring the army into more action. By the New Year of 1915, when the memorandum came his way, Churchill had already authorised experiments in designing a wheeled and armed vehicle which would carry portable bridges so as to be able to cross trenches.

Fired by Hankey's paper, Churchill prepared a memorandum of his own, in which he expounded the idea of armoured vehicles and explained that 'Forty or fifty of these machines, prepared secretly and brought into position at nightfall, could advance quite certainly into the enemy's trenches, smashing away all the obstructions, and sweeping the trenches with their machine-gun fire and with grenades thrown out of the top.' A copy of this went to Kitchener,

where it met a dead end, but Churchill was in no mood to wait for the army and in February he set up the Admiralty Landships Committee to investigate the problem and prepare designs of a vehicle.

The only English pattern of track available at that time was the Diplock Pedrail. Bramah Diplock had invented his first Pedrail in 1899, and it was no more than a wheel with loosely-slung feet. During the intervening years his wheel had become elongated until it was now a form of endless track but still having the principal feature of a number of prominent plates to act as supporting feet. The Diplock Transport company made a moderate success of an agricultural trailer fitted with this track, and in February 1915 the company demonstrated this trailer to Churchill, pointing out its advantages in overcoming rough ground. Churchill was sufficiently impressed to order the construction of 15 armoured cars to be fitted with track

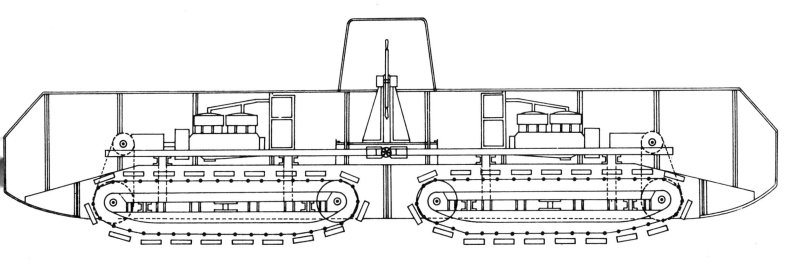

The Pedrail track was developed by the Landships Committee – so called because it was set up by Churchill under the auspices of the Admiralty – into an articulated monster intended to carry a storming party of 50 infantrymen. The engine was to be mounted on the centreline, leaving gangways along the sides for the men

Above and below: The Daimler-Foster tractor, built by Foster's of Lincoln as an artillery prime mover for the Western Front, and basis for the Tritton Trench-crossing Machine

assemblies in place of the normal wheels. This idea was passed across to the Landships Committee, they conferred with Mr Diplock, and the first design of an armoured vehicle was drawn up. It was to be an armoured box 38 ft long, 12 ft 6 in wide and 10 ft 6 in high to the top of the turret. Inside the turret was to be a 12-pdr gun. The vehicle was to weigh about 28 tons and was to be driven by two Rolls-Royce engines.

Meanwhile the Committee was considering another proposition, which had come from Commander Hetherington of the Naval Armoured Car Squadron. This was to be a massive platform carried on three gigantic wheels of 40 ft diameter and armed with a 12-in naval gun. The Committee scaled this grandiose idea down, though only slightly, turning it into an armament of three 4-in guns each in a turret, the whole vehicle to be 100 ft long and propelled by a submarine diesel engine at 4 mph. Once a mock-up of this device came to be made, it was obvious that it could never work and the idea was dropped.

The Committee now altered the Pedrail machine, lengthening it to 40 ft and giving

it an articulated joint in the middle. The engine, transmission and track supports were to be in the centreline of the vehicle, leaving gangways along each side on which a trench-storming party of fifty men with machine-guns could be carried. The two separate sections were to be joined in the centre by hydraulic rams which would allow the vehicle to be steered by bending in the middle.

Another move made by the Committee was to send a young naval officer, Lieutenant Field, to the United States in order to investigate types of track. He ended up at the Chicago factory of the Killen-Strait company, there to supervise the construction of a machine of his own design.

Construction of the Hetherington 'Big Wheel Machine' and the Pedrail-fitted cars had been entrusted to the agricultural engineering company of Foster, in Lincoln. Sir William Tritton, the director of the company, had already begun working on a design for a tracked tractor as an artillery prime mover, and this, under the influence of the various Landships ideas and contracts, now turned into the Tritton Trench-crossing Machine, more or less a lengthened

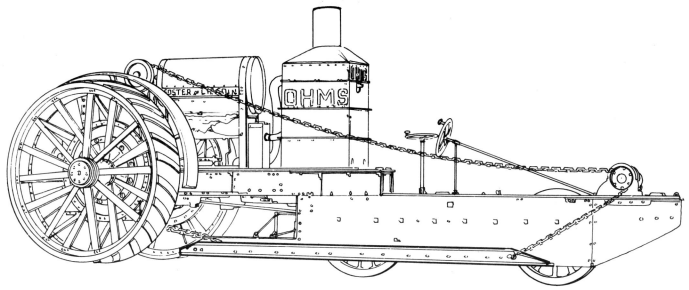

The Tritton Trench-crossing Machine, developed by Foster's under the direction of Sir William Tritton, was an elongated version of their artillery tractor. It was abandoned after demonstrations when, although successful against barbed wire, it failed to cope with trenches

agricultural tractor with Holt tracks. This was demonstrated at Aldershot on May 19, where it crossed barbed wire with success but nosed over and stuck in the specimen trench. It had originally been ordered with a bridging device, but this was not available for the demonstration. But in the following month, fitted with the device, it failed to cross a double line of trenches and was rejected.

As the month of May drew to its close, so did the abortive Gallipoli campaign begin its slow collapse, and in the political aftermath of this affair Winston Churchill left the Admiralty. With him went the driving force behind the Landships Committee, and his successor largely ignored the matter. But Churchill remained a member of the Cabinet War Committee and from this position he managed to exert sufficient influence to ensure that the problem was not completely shelved.

Colonel Swinton, during this time, had no idea that the Landships Committee had been formed, other than occasional rumours that the Navy were showing some sort of interest, and he had continued in his post of War Correspondent in France. But at the same time he was constantly thinking about his idea for a land cruiser. He had put his idea forward to the Inventions Committee of the Ministry of Munitions, who reported favourably on it (but who apparently did not know of the existence of the Landships Committee) and on June 15 Swinton produced another memorandum, complete with specifications of what he considered to be the ideal machine. This was forwarded by Sir John French, then C-in-C of the British Army in France, to the War Office. A week later the War Office finally woke up to the need for some sort of armoured vehicle and, rather belatedly, joined the Landships Committee.

So far the development of a vehicle had been made more difficult by one peculiarity of military etiquette of the day. The fact was that the Landships Committee were trying to design a machine without having any precise idea of what the machine would have to do. True, they had some idea that

it had to cross ditches and surmount wire, but there seems to have been nobody who actually appreciated how much wire and how deep a ditch – in short, the exact nature of the obstacles formed by the German trench line. On the other hand, the soldiers in France knew perfectly well what the problem was, but etiquette laid down that the army in the field could not presume to tell the War Office in London what was needed. Sir John French finally cut through this when he sent Swinton's specification home. And now, with Swinton's assessment of the obstacles and estimate of what was needed to overcome them in front of it, the Landships Committee could, at last, begin to make some useful suggestions to the designers.

While this was being considered, the Killen-Strait tractor, which Lieutenant Field had seen built in Chicago, had arrived in England, and was demonstrated to the Committee in the area of Wormwood Scrubs in London. It was a simple chassis with three track units disposed in tricycle form, one at the front for steering and two beneath the rear, supporting the engine and driver. Tests soon showed that it was quite useless as a wire-crusher or trench-crosser, but it did have some value as a practical demonstration of the value of tracks for those people who had never seen them before.

Next, the Metropolitan Carriage and Wagon Works, who were building Colonel

Crompton's articulated Pedrail, asked to be released from their contract. They had little faith in the idea and it was proving vastly more complex and expensive than they had expected. The contract was duly terminated and renegotiated with the Foster company, but when they came to examine the machine and the specification, they too had second thoughts. By some unrecorded piece of sleight-of-hand it was finally unloaded on to the infant Trench Warfare Department, who were convinced that it would be just the thing for carrying a massive multiple flame-thrower. They managed to have the machine completed by some other factory, but in the end the flame-thrower was considered far too complex for the limited tactical benefit it achieved and the whole idea was abandoned.

Another delivery from America was two 'Creeping Grip' tractors made by the Bullock Company. These were sent to Foster's factory with instructions to take them to pieces and use the components to make one larger tracked vehicle. Before this could be done, Colonel Crompton (he of the articulated Pedrail) proposed a similar machine, 60 ft long, using the two Bullock tractors as

After the Killen-Strait tractor had been demonstrated in May 1915, the RNAS mounted this Delaunay-Belville armoured car body on it, creating what has been claimed to be the first completed tank

a basis. In order to waste less time, Foster's simply tied the two Bullock machines together with a simple chassis frame and demonstrated that the idea was not much good. Then they got on with the task of reconstituting the two tractors.

By this time Colonel Swinton's appointment as War Correspondent had been terminated, the authorities having finally seen the sense of allowing professional reporters to go to France, and he had returned to England to become Secretary to the Dardanelles Committee of the War Cabinet. This was a responsible task and one which gave him sufficient authority to ask questions in all sorts of places, and he soon discovered that the Landships Committee was functioning. He also discovered that there were three or four agencies concerning themselves with armoured land cruisers, all of whom were working very much on their own and without much consultation with the others.

So, late in August 1915, Swinton, with the authority of the Prime Minister, managed to organize an inter-departmental conference with the Director, Royal Engineers in the chair. Here the Admiralty, the Army and the Ministry of Munitions all sat down around a table and discussed the whole question, laying their cards on the table and describing what they were doing or what they hoped to do. And the conclusion they came to was that the Admiralty should continue to develop the machines, since they seemed to have a well-working organisation, but that the actual requirements should be laid down by the War

Office. The Ministry of Munitions would give any assistance needed in the supply of material or equipment but otherwise, for the time being, hold a watching brief. Once the design had been finalised, then it would be the job of the Ministry to organise large-scale manufacture.

Manufacture of the Bullock Track machine was going ahead at Foster's. After work had begun on this, Sir William Tritton, together with Lieutenant Wilson, one of the naval armoured-car men seconded to the Landships Committee, had set about designing a somewhat different model known as the Tritton or Lincoln No 1 machine. Both these designs were little more than armoured boxes with Holt-pattern track units underneath, but, mindful of what Colonel Swinton had told him of the dimensions of German trenches, Wilson now began to toy with the idea of running the track completely around the tank, sloping the front section so as to approximate to the operating arc of a 15-ft wheel.

On September 6 the Bullock Track machine was tried out for the first time. It was a boiler-plate rectangle, surmounted by a turret with an automatic 2-pdr gun and provided with numerous ports for firing machine-guns from the body. (It should be said that the boiler-plate was because it was the prototype – armour plate was not necessary for trial purposes.) The engine was a 105-hp Daimler, giving a speed of 2 mph, and the vehicle could be steered by a two-wheeled tail unit behind the hull controlled by cables from a handwheel. The track units were located in recesses

beneath the sides of the superstructure.

Several defects made themselves apparent during the test. The biggest difficulty was in the tracks, which were of soft steel and soon stretched so that they came off the rollers. Moreover, the wheelbase was too short. It could cross a 4-ft trench, but the War Office had just issued a revised specification calling for the ability to cross a 5-ft trench and climb a 4-ft 6-in parapet. So the Bullock machine was not acceptable as it stood, though it had provided a good deal of useful information. Most important of all, it had pin-pointed the weakness of the tracks, and within a week a completely new type of steel track plate had been designed, developed and tested.

Late in October 1915 work began on building the all-round-track Wilson machine, which was nicknamed the Centipede. A wooden mockup had already been made and approved by the Landships Committee, and the method of arming had also been settled. Centipede was to carry a 6-pdr quick-firing gun in a sponson – or projecting armoured bay – at each side, together with five machine-guns. It is interesting to note that Swinton, in his memoirs, says that the decision was to use one machine-gun and four automatic rifles, and it is unfortunate that no other confirmation or explanation of this has ever come down to us, for at that time the British Army had no automatic rifles. Indeed, the only people who did were the Germans and the Mexicans. What Swinton probably meant were what later came to be called light machine-guns. The only machine-gun known to most people at

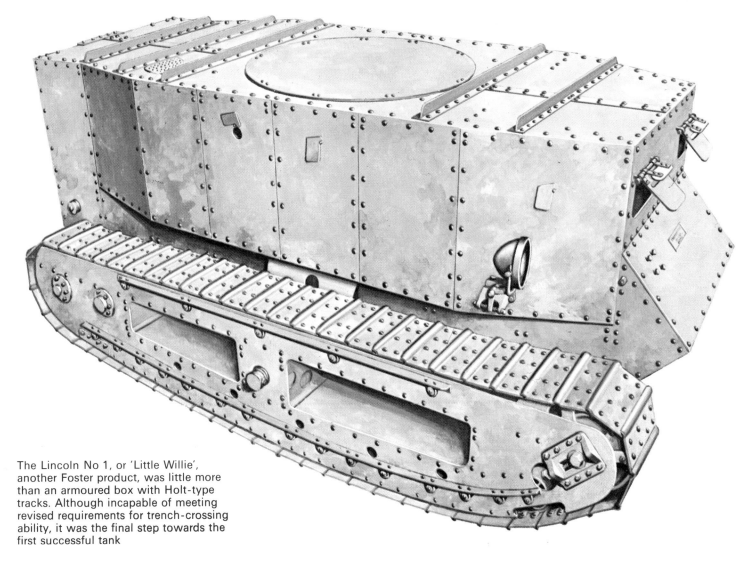

The Lincoln No 1, or 'Little Willie', another Foster product, was little more than an armoured box with Holt-type tracks. Although incapable of meeting revised requirements for trench-crossing ability, it was the final step towards the first successful tank

that time was the Maxim or Vickers, heavy water-cooled weapons vulnerable to damage when used in a tank. Eventually the Hotchkiss, an air-cooled gun less easily put out of action by stray bullets or splinters, was adopted for tank use.

By early December the Lincoln No 1, which was nicknamed 'Little Willie', was ready for testing. Since it was little more than an improved Bullock, it was not capable of meeting the War Office demands for trench crossing, but it furnished more useful data on track construction, steering and other mechanical problems which helped the team working on the Centipede.

Eventually Centipede was ready; it ran under its own power for the first time on January 12, 1916, and on the evening of January 28 it arrived on a railway flatcar at Hatfield railway station. It was off-loaded in conditions of great secrecy during the night and driven to nearby Hatfield Park,

to be carefully shrouded and guarded until its first demonstration on the following day.

'Centipede' was Foster's registered trade name for their pre-war tracked agricultural machines, and it was desirable that some innocuous cover name should be given to the new device which would conceal its purpose. Names like Landship and Land Cruiser were too obvious; during the construction of Little Willie the running gear had been called a Demonstration and Instructional Chassis, while the hull section was hinted as being a water carrier for

Mesopotamia, which led to the workmen in Foster's calling it 'that tank thing'. On Christmas Eve 1915 Colonel Swinton sat down with his colleague Lt-Col Dally Jones to draw up a report on progress, and one of the items to be considered was this matter of a cover name. In view of the shape of the article, and remembering the workmen at Foster's, and after rejecting a few ideas such as 'cistern' and 'reservoir', they decided to use the word 'tank', and in the draft report this was the word used, for the first time, to describe an armoured land vehicle moving on tracks.

Hatfield Park had been turned, for the purpose of the demonstration and trial of the first tank, into a passable imitation of a section of the front line. Shell holes had been blown with explosives, trenches and dugouts prepared, wire strung and, to add the final touch of verisimilitude, a stream had been dammed so as to turn the 'No Mans Land' into a swampy morass of more-or-less genuine Flanders consistency.

On January 29 Big Willie, or Mother, was unveiled for its first trial. Rhomboidal in shape, 31 ft 3 in long, 31 tons in weight, 13 ft 8 in wide across the gun sponsons and 8 ft high, it was propelled by a 105-hp Daimler engine. The drive from the engine ran to a two-speed-and-reverse 'primary' gearbox and then to a large differential, from which cross-shafts ran to the sides of the tank. This differential could be locked, so that both tracks revolved at the same speed for straight-ahead driving, or un-

'Big Willie', or 'Mother' as it became known, was the prototype of the first production tank, the Mark I. First demonstrated on January 29, over a mock battleground, it performed well and an order for 40 was placed. Eventually 150 were ordered and the first Tank Mark I saw action on the Somme on September 15, 1916. *Above left:* Tank C19 of the Heavy Section, the Machine Gun Corps, waiting to go into action. *Below:* A Mk I abandoned near Bouleaux Wood

Imperial War Museum

locked so that the tracks could move at different speeds when one or other of them was braked to steer the tank.

The two cross shafts carried, at their outer ends, sliding pinion gears giving high and low speeds, and these were operated by levers controlled by two 'gearsmen' who sat at each side of the tank and operated the cross-shaft gears on signals from the driver. From these 'secondary' gearboxes, heavy chains took the drive back to the driving sprockets at the rear of the tank which engaged with the tracks. The whole arrangement thus gave a choice of four speeds forward and two reverse, but the business of shifting the secondary gears on signal from the driver, assisted by some extremely clever clutch manipulation on the driver's part, was a clumsy system and productive of much bad temper and missed changes.

On each side of the tank body were the sponsons, a term taken from naval architecture, in which a 6-pdr gun was mounted. These 6-pdrs were ex-naval weapons which the Navy was, quite honestly, glad to be rid of. A grave shortage of light guns at the beginning of the war had been alleviated by the development of the 6-pdr Single Tube gun, in which the barrel was bored out of a steel rod and turned to the final outside dimension instead of being built up from barrel, jacket, and breech ring and then screwed together. This construction made a very strong gun but it was a specialist job to build such weapons. The Single Tube gun, on the other hand, could be bored and turned by any competent engineering shop, so these guns could be made more quickly and cheaply.

The only trouble was they were less strong than the traditional type and had to fire a reduced charge, which meant complications in ammunition supply and also a less powerful gun. So the Navy were only too pleased to hand them over to the Landships Committee for use in the new tanks. Their performance was ample for this task, their recoil stress was lower than any other comparable gun, and by this time there were ample supplies of 'proper' guns for the Navy. The 6-pdrs were supplied with high explosive shell and later with case shot, a light steel envelope containing several hundred shrapnel balls. When fired from the gun the steel envelope split open in the bore and the balls were ejected like a giant shotgun charge, making a highly effective anti-personnel weapon.

Behind the tank was a two-wheeled 'tail' unit, intended to aid the steering. The

wheels were kept in contact with the ground by powerful springs, while a hydraulic lifting unit could be operated to lift the wheels clear of the ground when required. The steering was done by wire cables running from a steering wheel in front of the driver, and by using this system it was possible to swing the tank around a circle of about 60 yards diameter. The device was a mixed blessing: it was extremely hard to operate since there was no mechanical gearing to aid the driver; the hydraulic system frequently failed to work; the steering cables stretched; and, in action, the tail unit was vulnerable to damage. On the other hand, the addition of the tail allowed the tank to cross wider trenches than later models without the tail. But the disadvantages outweighed this, and once it was found that the tank could be steered

Below: French Schneider tanks in action
Left: Schneider on trials. The girder on the front was intended to guide barbed wire under the tracks to be crushed

perfectly satisfactorily by braking the tracks the tail unit was abandoned.

Other defects did not make themselves apparent until the tank was actually used in combat. One fault was that the engine exhaust had no silencer, and the noise and flame which shot into the sky above the tank became a grave problem when trying to move up to an attack in darkness. Another problem was that the chain drive units shovelled mud back into the tank until the floor was often awash with several inches of greasy slurry.

But all these things were in the future when Mother churned around the test course at Hatfield Park, taking all the obstacles in its stride. This was by way of a private run-through by the originators, just to make sure all was well, and on February 2 the official demonstration was held, in front of such luminaries as Lloyd George, then Minister of Munitions, Lord Kitchener, General Sir William Robertson, Chief of the Imperial General Staff, and other high-ranking officers. Once again Mother went through its repertoire, and as a result the representative of GHQ who had come across from France to see the new machine gave it their blessing and committed themselves to the extent of saying that 'they would ask the Commander-in-Chief to order some'. Others were more enthusiastic, though Lord Kitchener was sceptical about the whole thing – but at least he was good enough not to countermand the recommendation of the GHQ representatives.

Mother was now sent back to Foster's factory, and preparations began for placing the design in production. Two types were to be built, the Male tank armed with two 6-pdrs and four Hotchkiss machine-guns and the Female type armed only with six machine-guns. Eight days after the Hatfield demonstration came the formal request from GHQ France – for 40 tanks.

Swinton, who had filled in the intervening time by writing the first training directive on the use of tanks, was horrified. Allowing for casualties in training, mechanical break-downs and other probable hazards, making 40 tanks would leave precious little for use in battle, and he was already thinking in terms of hundreds, to be used in a decisive fashion and not in penny packets. He managed to get War Office approval to increase the number to 100. On February 12 Lloyd George signed the authorisation, telegrams were sent out to the various factories, and work began. The tank was, at last, a military fact; all that was needed now was people to man and operate them.

It would be foolish to think that only the British Army had been sufficiently moved by the wire and machine-gun problem to try and do something about it. The same problem faced the French, and within a few months of the outbreak of war suggestions began to flow into GQG, the French High Command, of how to defeat the obstacles in front of them. Among the first was a machine built by an M Frot. This consisted of an 11-ton roller propelled by a motor engine and protected by boiler-plate shielding. As a wire-crusher it was a success but it foundered as soon as it met a trench.

Slightly more practical was an 'Electric Torpedo' designed by Auriot and Gabe. This was mounted on tracks and driven by an electric motor, the current being supplied by a cable which it paid out as it went forward. Loaded with explosive, it was intended to be driven under the wire and there detonated. Although this was a good idea it was not considered practical, largely because of the problem of supplying electric power in the trenches, and it was rejected. (It is interesting to note that the Germans revived this idea in the Second World War and had some success with it.)

Most of the French ideas were concerned solely with cutting wire, including tractors with sawtoothed blades on the front, and even one with a circular saw mounted on swinging arms. The only people who appear

French tank crewman, with a leather combat jacket over the ordinary service uniform of a Heavy Artillery Regiment. Early tank uniforms were improvised to give crew members protection from the heat and machinery of a tank's interior

Julian Allen

The Schneider tank, designed by the French Colonel Estienne, was armed with a 75-mm gun and two Hotchkiss machine-guns. Weighing 13.5 tons, it was powered by a 70-hp Schneider engine giving it a maximum speed of 3.75 mph

to have seen further than the wire were the armaments company of Schneider. In May 1915 they obtained two Holt tractors and encased one in armour, fitting it with a wire-cutter in the front, a two-armed tailpiece to assist in crossing trenches and a machine-gun. But M Breton, Under-Secretary of State for Inventions turned the idea down; it was, he said, unnecessary to arm such a vehicle when only wire cutting was needed.

But as with the British development, the impetus which actually resulted in something practical came from a serving soldier, Colonel Baptiste Estienne. An artillery officer, his thought processes more or less paralleled those of Swinton in that he first thought of an armoured vehicle and then, having seen some Holt tractors used by the British Army for towing artillery, realised that their tracked drive was the only feasible method of propelling an armoured machine. He made proposals to GQG but received no answer, and on December 1, 1915 he wrote to General Joffre, Commander-in-Chief of the French Army, making proposals for the construction and use of armoured infantry carriers. These were to be about 13 ft long and weigh about 13 tons, cased in armour plate, and armed with two machine-guns and a 37-mm cannon. Moving at $5\frac{1}{2}$ mph, it would be capable of crossing a $6\frac{1}{2}$-ft wide trench, and Estienne proposed packing this machine with twenty armed men to act as storming parties once the vehicle had delivered them past the wire and into the enemy lines.

'Papa' Joffre reacted surprisingly well; he approved of the idea and instructed Estienne to go to Paris and consult with manufacturers. On December 20 Estienne met Louis Renault, the motor-car manufacturer, but Renault was not impressed by the idea. Estienne then went to Schneider, to find that they had already been working on similar lines, and, assisted by M Brille, Schneider's engineer, Estienne modified his

Imperial War Museum

The St Chamond tank carried a long 75-mm gun and four Hotchkiss machine guns, but it weighed 23 tons and was poor on soft ground where the 75 became clogged up with mud

The powerplant of the St Chamond (above), a 90-hp Panhard driving through electric transmission, gave it a top speed of 5.3 mph

design, incorporating some features which Schneider had already found suitable. The Schneider company then set to work to produce a prototype.

M Breton, the Inventions Secretary, was upset at Estienne's action when he heard of it – largely, one suspects, because Breton was trying to push one or two of his own ideas (like the circular saw carrier) and didn't like the idea of competition. Grudgingly, Breton agreed to order a few Holt tractors for study, and Estienne, scenting obstruction, went to Joffre to urge that the War Department put some weight behind his idea. Joffre agreed, wrote the necessary orders, and Estienne went back to duty at the front.

GQG (Grand Quartier General, or General Headquarters) under Joffre's prompting, ordered 400 tanks on January 31, but the Secretary of State for Artillery stopped the order, insisting on there being a demonstration of the proposed vehicle before he would approve. This, of course, had to wait for Schneider to build the prototypes, and it was not until February 21 that two track-laying vehicles, modified Holt tractors with armoured bodies much the same as Little Willie, could be tried. They successfully crushed wire and crossed trenches; the Secretary of State was satisfied, and on February 25 Schneider's were given an order for 400 tanks.

M Breton now returned to the fray. His department was the one concerned with inventions, and here was an invention which didn't belong to him. So, he sat down to design a different, larger model, placing contracts with the other main French armament company, St Chamond. And while the army, in its ignorance, thought that both companies were working on the same design, in fact the Schneider and St Chamond companies were working on totally different models, with no consultation or liaison between the two. Estienne, meanwhile, had been nominated as future commander of the *Artillerie d'Assaut* as the new machines were called.

There was good reason for such a name. The French have always had a great respect for artillery and its power, and both these

The most numerous tank of the First World War, the Renault FT 17 (above and left), shown here with 37-mm cannon, was designed by Louis Renault at the prompting of Colonel Estienne. The intention was to flood the battlefield with these lightweight two-man machines, restoring mobility to the troops on a grand scale. In the event some 3650 of the basic model were produced in France by the end of the war, Renault alone churning out 75 a week.
Top right: FT 17s in a victory parade in 1919

vehicles were going to be armed with 75-mm guns, larger and more powerful than the 57-mm 6-pdrs in the British tanks. The Schneider Char d'Artillerie or CA was a rectangular armoured box mounted on Holt track units. The nose was brought to a point and fitted with a wirecutter, while a short-barrelled 75-mm gun was mounted in a sponson in the right front of the hull and a Hotchkiss machine-gun on the left. Entrance to the inside was by double doors at the rear, a crew of six being carried, and the tank was 19 ft 8 in long. Weighing 14.6 tons, it was driven by a 70-hp Schneider engine and could reach about 5 mph.

The St Chamond was a much larger vehicle, 25 ft 10 in long and weighing $25\frac{1}{2}$ tons. It too was a rectangular armoured box, with the front formed into a triangular shape and with a 75-mm field gun centrally mounted. The vehicle had a considerable front overhang beyond the tracks, though this was counter-balanced by the extremely heavy transmission machinery further back in the hull. This was heavy because it was complicated: a four-cylinder Panhard motor drove a dynamo which in turn furnished electric power to two driving motors, one for each track. Complicated as it was, there were considerable advantages in control with this system – known as the Crochat-Collardeau Drive – since it allowed much finer mastery of the track speeds and thus, on paper at least, better agility for the tank. Rheostats were employed to control the track speed, and by reversing the polarity of the current the vehicle could be propelled backwards with equal speed and facility. The St Chamond tank required a crew of nine men and carried four machine-guns in addition to the 75-mm gun. This gun, it should be noted, was not the famous French 'Seventy-Five' 75-mm field gun M1897 but a slightly different model made by St Chamond and fitted to the first 165 tanks. Later versions, however, used the 75-mm M1897.

By summer 1916, then, the French army had placed orders for 800 tanks, 400 of each of the two competing types, which was a far cry from the somewhat hesitant order for 40 which the British had made. But in June 1916 Estienne was sent to England,

after official notification of what was going on, to see the new British tanks for the first time. He visited the British training ground at Elveden, watched the tanks in action and conferred with Swinton, his opposite number in so many ways. Greatly impressed with the British work, he suggested that since the British ideas obviously lay in the direction of heavy tanks, and the French vehicles were smaller and lighter, an equitable division of labour might be for the British to continue development of heavy models and the French to concentrate on light ones.

But whatever else was decided, Estienne was insistent to Swinton that the British should not reveal the existence of the tank to the common enemy until the French models were ready for action; then a combined offensive would swing the war in the Allies' favour. Swinton was, in principle, entirely in agreement with this, though in truth questions of policy were out of his hands and he knew it.

On returning from England, Estienne went once again to the Renault factory to suggest the design of a lightweight vehicle. His idea was to flood the battlefield with two-man machines each carrying a driver and a machine-gunner, acting just like an infantry skirmish line but armoured and more nimble. This cloud of machinery would be able to force its way past obstructions, swing round, take trenches from the rear, and, in fact, do everything the foot soldier used to be able to do before the siege conditions of the Western Front put an end to his mobility. Renault set to work – he seems to have had more faith in this idea than he had in the earlier one – and by November 1916 the pilot model was ready. Estienne urged that a thousand be ordered and GQG agreed, giving the necessary instructions to M Breton, whose department was still controlling the development of the tank.

The Renault design, which was to become one of the most successful and widespread, in terms of numbers, of any tank design, was a 6-ton, two-man machine, 13 ft 5 in long and with a sprung suspension. The driver sat in the nose, the gunner operated a Hotchkiss machine-gun in the revolving turret, and the 39-hp engine was in the rear. It could move at 6 mph and was provided with an angled tail-skid which allowed it to cross trenches almost as wide as itself.

Meanwhile, what of Germany, the nation against whom all this Allied effort was directed? When it is considered that Germany was the birthplace of the petrol engine, and that the Germans were invariably alert to the possibilities of any new type of weapon, it might be expected that something similar was being worked on, but in fact very little was being done. Shortly after the outbreak of war an engineer named Göbel had put forward a suggestion for a machine capable of crossing rough country, and actually produced a small-scale prototype model. Powered by a 4-hp engine, this device used six spiked rails connected to elliptical wheels in such a fashion that four of the six rails were always in contact with the ground while the other two were being lifted and moved forward. For the want of a better description, it could be said that the Göbel machine 'skied' along the ground. But while it was capable of crossing rough ground, it was wholly incapable of negotiating wire

entanglements and crossing trenches, and the army lost no time in rejecting the idea.

Nothing daunted, Göbel came back early in 1915 with a fresh design which he called his armoured land cruiser. This was little more than an improved version of his six-ski system of propulsion allied to an armoured superstructure. The Weapons Test Office examined the proposal, could see no practical application for it, and were petrified at the thought of what it would cost to manufacture. For the second time Göbel was shown the door, but he came back a year later with a working prototype which he had built at his own expense. This was tested, but owing to an oversight – or perhaps incompetence – there was no means of steering the machine, and it ran itself into a ditch and stalled. Thereafter Engineer Göbel did not trouble the Commission any further.

But early in 1916, from some source which has never been tracked down or explained, rumours began to spread throughout the German soldiers on the front of monstrous Allied machines which would flatten all before them. Efforts by the German intelligence to discover more information failed completely, largely because there were, at that time, very few people in France with any knowledge of the tanks. Outside GHQ, indeed, it is probably safe to say that only a handful of senior officers knew of the project, and even they knew very little of it. So the rumours were discounted, and as week after week went by without the monsters appearing, the soldiers gradually came to accept that it was just another latrine story.

The basic reason why the German High Command never pursued any sort of mechanical device, however, was simply one of philosophy. It is a matter of record that

Above: A column of FT 17s *Right:* The Hotchkiss machine-gun-armed FT 17. Powered by a 35-hp R Renault engine giving it a speed of 4.8 mph, the tail skid enabled it to cross trenches as wide as the vehicle was long

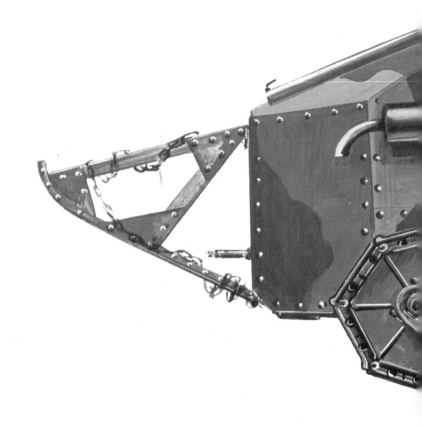

'The German High Command decided, from the very outset, not to fight a battle of materiel' (extract from a German GHQ Document of 1918). Men were what the German High Command relied upon, not machines, and by drafting in half-trained recruits they were able to point to a paper strength of 250 divisions by the middle of the war, a total strength which, unless examined too closely, appeared to guarantee success. So no machinery was needed; soldiers would do all that was necessary. Even after the tank had arrived on the battlefield, it took a long time for the High Command to change its opinion and begin the study of mechanised warfare.

Back in England Colonel Swinton was hard at work trying to train and organise the manpower to operate the tanks. The new unit was first called the Armoured Car Section, Motor Machine-Gun Service, but the name was soon changed to Heavy Section, The Machine-Gun Corps, this being considered a suitably obscure name which would conceal the purpose of the unit. Swinton had managed to get the total number of tanks on order increased to 150, 75 Male to act as machine-gun destroyers, and 75 Female to act as escorts to the destroyers and, by using their machine-guns, keep infantry away from them, since the supply of case-shot had been delayed and without this the 6-pdr was no use for protecting the tank.

National Archives

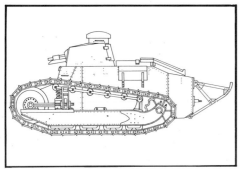

The original (37-mm gunned) French model of the Renault FT 17

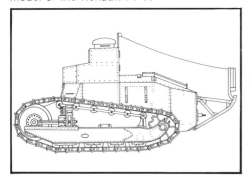

French TSF (telegraphie sans fils, or wireless) unarmed command version of the FT 17

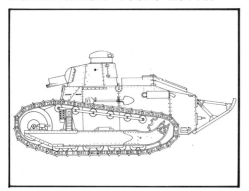

US M1917 model of the FT 17, of which over 1000 were ultimately produced

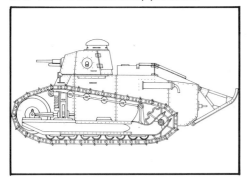

Soviet Lenin tank, based on an FT 17 captured from the White Russians

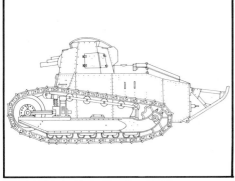

Later French FT 17, up-gunned with a short 75-mm gun and christened the BS

The next task was to calculate the establishment for the new unit: the exact number of officers and men of each rank and speciality, the scales of spare parts, tools, weapons, ammunition, cooking equipment – any and every thing which an active service unit might require. Establishments for infantry, cavalry and artillery were cut-and-dried affairs, worked out over years of experience, but to dream up a completely new establishment for a totally new kind of formation was a daunting job. The size of the tank unit was finally settled at six companies of 25 tanks each, plus a Headquarters Company and a Park Company, a total of 184 officers and 1610 men. Recruits were obtained, some by transfer from other units and many by direct enlistment of men familiar with motor vehicles, officers were brought in from other corps and regiments, and training began – hampered somewhat in the beginning by the fact that there were no tanks on which to train.

In April 1916 Sir Douglas Haig, C-in-C of the British Army in France, came to England and in the course of his visit found time to look at the tank men. At that time Haig was much concerned with planning for the forthcoming offensive on the Somme, and he asked Swinton whether he could have some tanks in France by June 1. Since Swinton's men had never yet seen a tank, let alone trained on one, the answer had to be 'No', but Swinton held out the hope that, provided the factories delivered on schedule, there might be a chance of getting some out by August 1, but he restated his firm conviction that there was nothing to be gained by sending the tanks into action in dribs and drabs, and that it would be better to wait until the whole unit was trained to concert pitch and then throw it in en masse, in cooperation with the French.

In the event it was the middle of June before the first tanks arrived at the training area at Elveden. Not surprisingly, there were numerous small defects which had to be rectified, but by the end of the month the strength was building up and the Heavy Section was beginning to find its feet.

More important was the fact that the 150 tanks ordered were now approaching completion, and the end of the contract would pose a logistic problem: what to do with the plant and workforce which had been assembled to build them? If there was to be a delay before further orders were placed, then the workforce would be dissolved; some would undoubtedly be called into the army, others would move to other factories. One way and another the only body of men trained to assemble tanks would be dispersed and the machinery put to other uses. GHQ France, on the other hand, were reluctant to order any more until they had seen some in action, and this was the thin end of the wedge which Swinton had feared.

GHQ wanted to put twenty tanks or so into action just to see how they performed. There was also the fact that the Battle of the Somme had begun, and begun badly. As every Englishman knows, the first day of the battle cost 60,000 British casualties, 19,000 of them killed by machine-guns and wire. Things had reached a sticky impasse and there were those at GHQ who felt that a handful of tanks might well turn the scale and get the whole operation moving. Swinton tried arguing, but it was no use and, eventually, like the good soldier he was, he saluted and got on with what he was told

to do. One company was to be sent to France in the first half of August, a second, if sufficiently trained, by the end of the same month.

But even this proposal was watered down: it was finally arranged that one section of six tanks would be sent to France at the end of the first week in August, followed by lots of twelve at weekly intervals. GHQ had decided upon the new tank tactic, and in spite of Swinton's insistence, the tanks were to be used in sections of six at a time.

On August 14 the first tank section moved to France. A tank centre was established at Yvrench, near Abbeville, while Swinton made his way to the GHQ at Beauquesne to find out what Sir Douglas Haig had in mind for the tank's first battle. In his memoirs he later said: 'The official atmosphere was not very helpful. In many quarters there was amused tolerance or contemptuous scepticism towards the new arm, in some a tendency to place too much reliance on the influence of a few tanks to make up for the recent disappointment of the offensive. There seemed to be little inclination to make allowance for the imperfections of a brand-new weapon or for the difficulties of those who were handling it in strange surroundings after very little practise'.

What was worse was that the few tanks which were in France were being paraded as some sort of circus for the amusement of the troops. Instead of being allowed to train and perfect their techniques, the Heavy Section were forced to wear out their precious vehicles by giving daily displays to crowds of officers, for no better reason, it seemed, than to keep the latter amused. One infantry brigade actually notified their units in orders that 'The tanks will perform daily from 9.0 to 10.0 am and from 2.0 to 3.0 pm', rather as if the whole unit was there as some sort of concert party. Protests by Swinton and by the commander of the tank unit did no good – indeed, the only result was that GHQ had the commander removed and replaced, and the ill-feeling generated at this time undoubtedly played a part in Swinton's later departure.

But eventually 50 tanks and their crews, trained to the best of their ability were ready for action.

Renault FT 17 in front of the Arc de Triomphe in Paris, taking part in a 1968 parade to mark 70 years of Renault history

THE SOMME TO CAMBRAI
armoured battle

Belgian Minerva armoured car, armed with a Hotchkiss machine-gun and used as a reconnaissance vehicle by the cavalry

Although it was 1916 before the tank appeared on the battlefield, armoured vehicles had, in fact, been in action ever since 1914, though like so many other aspects of the story of the tank, the original impetus had come from the Royal Navy.

The British Expeditionary Force in France had been augmented by a Naval Landing Brigade which found itself involved, with the Belgian Army, in the defence of Antwerp. To assist this force Winston Churchill had sent a squadron of the Royal Naval Air Service to Belgium late in August 1914, and a few days later he issued orders for the expansion of this force and its stationing further inland.

On September 4 a Captain Murray Sueter RN, then Director of the Air Department of the Admiralty, suggested that a force of

fifty cars, armed with machine-guns, should be provided to serve as an airfield protection unit and, if need be, to conduct lightning raids into German territory to rescue pilots and observers shot down. In true Churchillian fashion, this figure was doubled and every available Rolls-Royce car was bought up for shipping to Belgium.

Once arrived there, the first few cars and some trucks were given rudimentary protection comprising mild steel plates with 1-in wood planking between. The driver was enclosed in a box, while the rear part of the car was simply an open-topped tonneau with a Maxim gun on a pedestal.

At much the same time similar cars were being produced in France and Belgium. The Belgian vehicles were based on Minerva chassis and the French on Peugeot and

Renault touring cars, all carrying machine-guns and some with 37-mm Hotchkiss cannon. These were issued to cavalry formations for reconnaissance tasks and as long as there was some chance of movement in the battles, they found employment. Once the siege phase set in though, there was less for them to do.

The RNAS cars soon proved their worth. They were able to screen the advanced airfields from German cavalry scouts and they frequently made forays past the German outposts to rescue aircrew, but it didn't take long before both sides realised that the combination of mild steel and wood was no sort of protection against short-range machine-gun fire. Experiments were put under way, in England and a number of Rolls-Royce cars were built with 8-mm armour plate protection. Although more resistant to bullets, they were otherwise little of an improvement since they were still open-topped.

Captain Sueter visited Belgium in October and appreciated the overhead protection problem. On his return to England he had a design of turreted car drawn up, approached the Beardmore Engineering company to have the armour plate made, and began negotiating for contracts with Rolls-Royce, Lanchester and Wolseley for the assembly of armoured cars. The first of these turreted cars were delivered on December 3.

The Rolls-Royce car retained the characteristic Rolls radiator and bonnet shape, although it was now encased in armour plate. The wheels were exposed, double wheels being fitted to the rear axle, and the turret, with bevelled top, carried a single Maxim gun. The Lanchester design was similar except that the bonnet was sloped and the body, beneath the turret, was more cylindrical.

For heavier support a number of Seabrooke trucks were armoured and provided with dropdown sides at the rear end, behind which a naval 3-pdr quick-firing gun was mounted. A Maxim gun was also carried.

But just as the designs were finalised and the armoured cars began to roll from the factories, so the front line stabilised, the trenches came into being, and the scope for wheeled warfare was severely curtailed. The naval cars were able to assist in the First Battle of Ypres in May 1915, but after that there seemed to be little prospect of employment for them.

Two alternatives presented themselves; either the armoured cars could be sent somewhere else, where there was scope for their activities, or the car could be transmuted into something else, something capable of cross-country operation. It was this latter side of the options which led to the development of the Landships Committee and, eventually to the tank. But this didn't do anything for the cars which were now standing around in some numbers. So the Naval Armoured Car Squadron was packed off to Egypt and Mesopotamia where there was some scope for its operations. One detachment of this force later went into Turkey, then to Russia and Lapland.

With the exception of the unit then in

Rolls-Royce armoured car, 1914 Admiralty pattern, as used by the RNAS in Belgium.
Above: Rolls-Royce armoured car with naval crew flies the White Ensign

1 Tripod for machine gun (stored)
2 Tools
3 Swing seat for optional fourth crew member
4 Lee Enfield ·303-inch rifle (one of three)
5 Can of water for machine gun cooling
6 Vickers ·303-inch machine gun
7 Ammunition feed box
8 Ammunition boxes slung round turret rim
9 Straps for passenger back rest
10 Rolls-Royce engine
11 Armoured radiator doors (controlled from inside car)
12 Magneto
13 Rolls-Royce Silver Ghost chassis
14 Steering box
15 Handbrake
16 Gear lever
17 Driver's seat
18 Gear box
19 Wooden floor
20 Armoured petrol tank
21 Locker for chains, ropes, personal items
22 Cooker
23 Blankets
24 Tow rope
25 Fire extinguisher

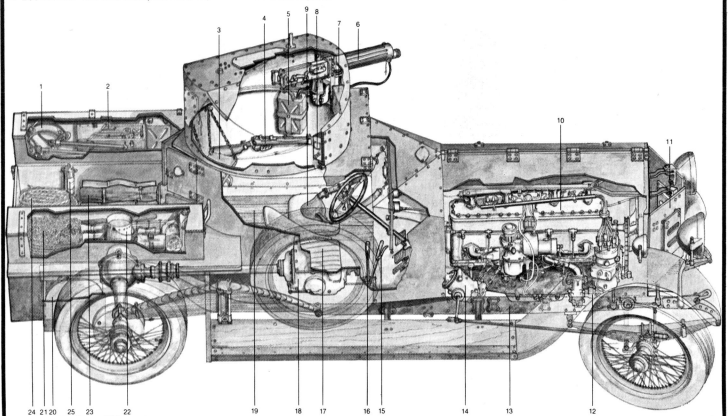

Russia, the naval car squadrons were disbanded in September 1915 and handed over to army control, becoming 'Light Armoured Motor Batteries', and they were employed to good effect in the Middle East for the rest of the war.

The Russian Army, doubtless because of the enormous distances it had to cover, was alive to the possibilities opened up by the motor car and had formed an Automobile Corps at the time of mobilisation for war. As soon as reports of the British and Belgian armoured cars reached them, the Russian Army requested a design from the Austin company of England, and Austin produced a robust vehicle based on a truck chassis. Four-wheeled, with boiler-plate armour, its most noticeable feature was the fitting of two separate turrets, side by side on the roof, each turret carrying a Maxim gun. This was in response to a Russian demand that the vehicle had to be capable of engaging two targets at once; it was felt that with only one turret there was a danger that while the sole gun was occupied with one target, another might pop up in the rear.

Another innovation which the Russians added to these cars after delivery was to provide for them to be steered from either end. It was not always possible for a car, when confronted with trouble, to turn off the road, and turning the car around in the width of the road in the classic three-point turn was no sort of manoeuvre to perform in the face of the enemy. So an auxiliary steering wheel was provided at the rear of the car, later to be augmented by auxiliary gear controls as well.

The difficulties of supply soon stopped the Austin company from sending complete cars but they were able to continue to furnish chassis to Russia for some time, and these were given armoured bodies in Russian workshops. The principal change was the arrangement of the turrets diagonally instead of side-by-side. Placing one turret at the left front and one at the right rear of the roof gave each turret a wider arc of fire and allowed both guns to be brought to bear on a single target at almost any angle. In addition to armouring the Austins a wide variety of other car and truck chassis to be found in Russia were taken and modified, so that White, Packard, Sheffield-Simplex, Pierce-Arrow and Jeffrey cars were produced. Some of the trucks were provided with 57-mm Obuchov quick-firing guns removed from fortress armament.

The Russian cars saw wide use against German troops in 1915, and one of the greatest problems which arose was that of using the cars in the deep snow of the Russian winter. A M Kegresse, engineer and manager of the Czar's garage in St Petersburg developed a tracked suspension unit to replace the normal rear wheels of an ambulance, a device which proved successful in allowing the vehicle to propel itself through deep snow, and after seeing a demonstration the War Ministry promptly ordered 300 such assemblies to be fitted to armoured cars. Unfortunately, before many

of these could be produced the Revolution broke out, so none of the half-track devices was ever used in action. M Kegresse wisely fled from Russia and later allied with Citroën of France to improve the half-track idea, as we shall see.

Useful as the armoured cars were, it was a limited usefulness in most cases, and it remained for the tank to make the full impact of the armoured vehicle on tactics. And it made its first move on September 15, 1916. There were two reasons for its unveiling on this particular day. Firstly, the insistence by GHQ that the tank had to be tried in action before any orders could be given for manufacture of more, and secondly the rather more fundamental fact that the Somme offensive was faltering and needed a stimulus. It was to be given this stimulus by a fresh attack, and it seemed likely that the new tanks would be able to earn their keep by clearing out some notably obstinate German outposts.

And so at 0520 on September 15, Lieutenant H W Mortimore of the Heavy Section, the Machine Gun Corps, in command of Tank D1, assured his place in history when he ordered his driver to start up and move forward against the German line. Following D1 were two companies of the King's Own Yorkshire Light Infantry and their joint task was to clear the Germans out of the corner of Delville Wood, the two trenches known as Ale Alley and Hop Alley. The German defenders in Hop Alley were petrified by the sight of the armoured monster

This early model of armoured car was based on a Ford chassis and armed with a Vickers machine-gun. It served with the British forces in Mesopotamia

33

straddling their trench and they surrendered without much further persuasion. Then the infantry rushed ahead of D1 to take Ale Alley . . . and were promptly shot to ribbons by machine-guns sited in shell craters which took them in enfilade. Assisted by D1 these craters were bombed and taken, Ale Alley was cleared, and this advance raiding party then turned back to rejoin the main force. In doing so D1 was hit by shell fire and halted. Two of the crew were killed, but the remainder jumped clear and made their way back to the lines safely.

At 0540 the main offensive began, with the usual mighty artillery barrage and, at 0620 the advance by the infantry. Six tanks, with one in reserve, were attached to the 2nd Canadian Division, their task being to parallel the main road to Bapaume and support the capture of an objective known as the Sugar Factory. In fact, the artillery barrage so smoothed the way for the infantry that they could move faster over the ground than could the tanks, and the Sugar Factory was taken without the aid of armour. Of the six tanks one broke down before the start line, one was bogged in soft mud in the first German trench, two others were bogged near the Sugar Factory and the remaining pair trundled along in the wake of the infantry. They were, however, extremely useful in this position, their appearance alone being enough to encourage the surrender of numerous Germans who had remained in strongpoints behind the Canadian advance with the intention of making life difficult for the reinforcing troops as they moved up in support.

One of the most critical features of the German position was High Wood. Situated on a ridge, its position allowed it to command the line of advance, and clearing it had a high priority. Four tanks were allotted in support of the infantry, but their value was eroded by the order, from the Corps Commander, that the tanks had to pass through the wood. In vain did the tank commander protest that the jagged stumps would impede the path of the tanks. As a result the three tanks which moved off – the fourth having broken down at the start point – lost their sense of direction after dodging through the wood. The first managed to rectify matters and found the first German trench, raking it with machine-gun fire until a German medium gun shell set it on fire. The other two completely turned about, came out of the wood back into their own lines, and opened fire on the first troops they saw who were, unfortunately, men of the London Regiment.

In the centre of the line seven of the ten allotted tanks managed to cross the start line, and among these were the tanks destined to become famous. The village of Flers was the prime objective and the infantry, once again outdistancing the tanks, had managed to reach the outskirts of Flers before being pinned down by machine-gun and artillery fire and blocked by unbroken wire. Then four tanks of 'D' Company appeared. The tanks thundered across the wire, brought the German defences under fire, and while three moved against the outskirts of the village (or what was left of it) Lieutenant Hastie in D17 drove straight down the main street shooting up both sides. The infantry, heartened by the sudden appearance of the four armoured monsters, leapt to their feet and charged into the village, cheering. Overhead an aerial observer of 4th Brigade, RFC,

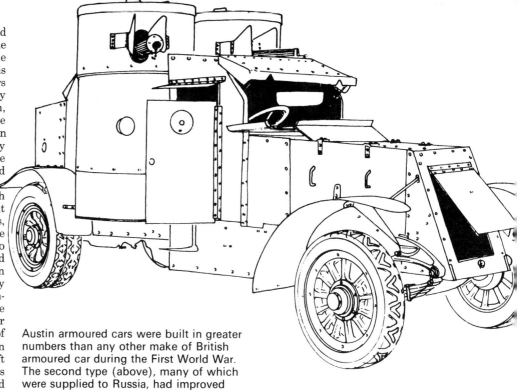

Austin armoured cars were built in greater numbers than any other make of British armoured car during the First World War. The second type (above), many of which were supplied to Russia, had improved superstructure layout and twin steering gear so that the car could be driven in either direction. The twin turrets mounting Hotchkiss machine-guns were demanded by the Russians, whose desire for multiple turrets was reflected in many of their early tanks

Below: An early pattern RNAS armoured car, based on a Talbot chassis and with a Vickers-Maxim machine-gun mounted on top of the driver's armoured hood. *Bottom:* Another primitive armoured car design, a Belgian Le Verguer, armed with a single Hotchkiss gun

wirelessed the immortal message, 'A tank is walking up the high street of Flers with the British Army cheering behind it.' Against the odds, a hole had been punched in the German lines.

However, it was soon plugged by the inevitable German counter-attack, artillery retaliation and the throwing in of reserves. Rain began to fall and the opportunity to break the Somme impasse had gone, never to return. The first armoured battle was over and the tanks were destroyed, bogged down in the mud or scattered.

The tanks had not been able to cancel out all the other drawbacks and guarantee lightning victory. That was too much to ask of 20 vehicles in their early stages of development, with crews learning their trade as they went along. But sufficient had been seen to show that they had a considerable potential. However, Rawlinson, commander of 4th Army, under whose nominal command the tanks had been, was far from enthusiastic. Tanks were no good, and that was that. He apparently expected miracles and was disappointed. Haig, on the other hand, who is often painted as a reactionary, was most pleased with the performance of the new arm. He told Swinton (who visited his Headquarters immediately after the battle) that the tanks, if not achieving all that was hoped, had nevertheless done well; that he wanted five times as many; and that the system of training and raising tank troops should continue as Swinton had begun it.

Haig's staff managed to have the last word; it was represented to Swinton that the command of the tanks in France ought to be by an officer who had experience of warfare on the Western Front. Swinton suggested Lt-Col Hugh Elles, an engineer who was familiar with both the fighting and, probably more important, with the personalities in GHQ. He was found accept-

able by the Staff and duly took up his post; they thought they had a pliable yes-man, but they were to find out differently.

Back in London a thousand tanks were now ordered, solving the problem of the labour gangs and the factory utilisation. More important, however, was to assess what changes in design seemed to be necessary, basing such changes on the reports made by the men who had actually taken the tanks into action. The first objection was that vision from the tank was poor; small slits were provided which, when examined in the peace and quiet of a factory floor might give a reasonable view, but when one was in a pitching and bucking tank were less practical. Moreover these slits were visible from the outside to become targets for German riflemen. The odds of getting a bullet through were fairly high, but close hits were enough to 'splash' hot lead through the slit into the eye of the observer.

The exhaust, too, needed silencing. Not only was it noisy for a night approach, but equipment carried on the tank roof was inevitably ignited by the flames from the exhaust stacks. The hatches for entry and exit were poorly thought out and too small, and rapid exit if the tank caught fire was impossible.

Fire was a particular hazard since the fuel tank was inside the vehicle, at the front. It was vulnerable to gunfire, and a hit meant that blazing fuel ran into the vehicle. Moreover, its position was such that feed to the engine was by gravity. Consequently, when a vehicle ditched nose-down the engine suffered petrol starvation and could only be induced to run by one of the crew pouring petrol into the air intake of the carburettor, a hazardous business in the heat of battle. All these defects, and many smaller ones, were now considered, and designs drawn up for improved models.

Above: D17 one of the tanks of D Company which were in action at Flers on September 21, 1916. On the left stand a group of Highland infantry, possibly men from the 15th (Scottish) Division. The group of officers by the gun sponson may be part of a team preparing the after action report of this first armoured victory

A conference in London on November 23 decided that 50 Mark II tanks would be ready for delivery to France by January; these were basically the Mark I with some of the major defects corrected. These would then be followed by 50 Mark III, a further improvement in design, by February 7. The major step forward was to be the Mark IV tank, deliveries of which were to begin in late February and continue at the rate of 20 per week until the end of May. By August a Mark V would be ready, and it was hoped that by Christmas 1917 a new light tank, the Mark VI, would be in the trials stage. Needless to say, this programme soon fell apart; very few Mark II or III tanks were made and it was June 1917 before any Mark IV models made their appearance.

What was more important than the materiel was the vexed question of how best to use it. Swinton had, in February 1916, written a most explicit paper entitled *Notes on the Employment of Tanks* in which he carefully explained the strengths and weaknesses of the new vehicle and suggested the best way of employing them in action. But when the time came to use the tanks, these notes were entirely ignored by GHQ, who substituted their own idea of tactics – if, indeed, their somewhat nebulous instructions could even be graced with the term 'tactics'.

As a result almost every precept laid down by Swinton was violated. The tanks were used in small packets instead of en masse; they were sent out into country totally unsuited to them, thick with mud and littered with tree stumps; they were given little or nothing in the way of communication; they were given no opportunity to reconnoitre the ground; and instead of leading the assault they were generally behind the infantry they were supposed to be protecting. Colonel Elles and his officers in France now sat down to try and bring some order and sense into the training schedules so as to try and get back to the simple rules laid down by Swinton.

But try as they might, they were up against the implacable assurance of GHQ that whatever was ordained by them must be right and must be obeyed. And so for another year the tanks were to continue being misused, and it speaks well for the individual tank commanders and the officers and crews of the new arm that in spite of GHQ they still managed to achieve some successes and eventually managed to convince the doubters that the tank was a formidable fighting machine.

Nevertheless, in *Training Note No 16*, issued in February 1917, the tanks were given a common doctrine and battle drill for breaking through a trench system which, given the same circumstances again, would be as valid today as it was then.

The first premise was that since the tank was, at that time, mechanically unreliable, no tank should operate on its own, Instead, they should work in pairs or fours for mutual support. Taking a pair as the basic unit, their task was seen as breaking the trench line and then rolling it back so as to make a gap through which troops could pass. To do this the basic manoeuvre was to cross the trench, swing to one side, and then drive down the length of the trench, shooting up the occupants and driving them back so as to open a gap. Obviously, with the labyrinthine trench systems of the day, some of the trench occupants would dive down into shelters where the tank's fire could not reach, and then return when the tank had passed, taking up their place in the trench again to deny passage to the following troops. In order to forestall this, the tanks were to be followed very closely by 'mopping-up' squads, bombing and shooting into the dugouts. And since this squad had to keep up with the tanks, it had to be followed by another, larger squad to occupy and hold the trench which had been gained.

With this as a basis, there were a number of combinations and permutations which could be worked. With four tanks two could move to the left and two to the right so making an even larger gap. Or two could move to a flank while two went straight ahead and dealt with the next line of trenches. The possibilities were numerous.

While the world was still talking about the unveiling of the tank in September 1916, the French Army had been accepting delivery of its first tanks. Both St Chamond and Schneider models were produced, and there were defects in both, but since the perfidious British had unveiled the new engine instead of waiting for the French, it was decided to put them into production, begin training crews and have them ready for action by Spring 1917.

On April 16, 1917 the first French tank attack took place, part of the 5th Army operation in the Chemin des Dames area. Eight companies of Schneider tanks were employed (128 tanks), and their employment was in accord with the French idea of

the tank's place – accompanying artillery. Three companies failed to get into action, coming under fire from German artillery while they were moving up to the start point and being shelled into immobility. The other five companies were not sent into action until some time after the infantry, were late in reaching their objectives, and eventually reached the third line of the German trench system. Here they managed to establish a degree of superiority, but the fire fight was so intense that the infantry could not follow, and as night fell the surviving tanks were pulled back.

On May 5 a company of St Chamond tanks and two companies of Schneider took part in a hastily-arranged operation with the French 6th Army at Laffaux Hill, but of the 16 St Chamond only one made it across the start line, the rest falling victim to a variety of mechanical breakdowns.

These two attacks pointed out the defects of the designs. The St Chamond, due to its forward overhang, tended to scuff dirt and mud ahead of it until the build-up jammed solid beneath the front end and prevented further movement. Moreover, the tracks were too narrow, giving too high a unit ground pressure, so that the tank bogged in ground which a British model would have crossed with ease. Also, the forward mounted 75-mm gun was vulnerable to enemy fire, particularly the hydro-pneumatic recoil system beneath the barrel.

The Schneider suffered from similar complaints regarding the tracks, the temperature inside was far too great, and, worst of all, the vibration level was so high that the gun mountings shook loose. Both tanks were exceptionally poor in the provision of vision slits, and, like the British tanks, carried their fuel inside and compounded this hazard by poor exit doors.

The *Artillerie d'Assaut* brought all these faults to the attention of the manufacturers, and at the same time they asked for 48 special command and supply tanks to be produced. The makers, rather gladly it seems, used these supply tanks as an excuse for delaying the modification of the fighting tank designs and it was not until late in the summer that improved tanks began to appear. To make matters worse, the makers were dilatory about the supply of spare parts, so that many of the tanks supplied to service units were ripped to pieces to provide spares for others and the fighting strength of the tanks never bore much relation to the paper strength.

But all this was of little importance in the eyes of GQG; like their British equiva-

lent they had little faith in the new machine, even though the limited actions in which the tanks had performed had shown that they had some value. Moreover, the tank men themselves were having doubts about these large tanks. In spite of modification they were still mechanically unreliable, owing more battle casualties to breakdown than to German fire, and they lacked the trench-crossing ability of the larger British tanks. Opinion in the French tank units was coming round to Estienne's idea of a horde of small tanks rather than a sprinkling of large ones, and when the initial order for St Chamond and Schneider tanks had been completed, no more were made.

Right: A British Mark I knocked out by a grenade attack during the fighting around Arras

ECP Armées

Early in April the British had fought the Battle of Arras, with 60 Mark I and Mark II tanks to assist. Analysis of the task indicated that there were three ways in which these 60 could be used: mass them for a drive against one objective and penetrate the German line; mass them against the left flank and turn the German position; or split them up and spread them across the front for minor mopping-up operations. Given GHQ's opinion of the tank and their peculiar idea of tactics, it comes as no surprise to find that they elected to take the latter course – eight tanks to the First Army to operate against Vimy Ridge, forty to Third Army subdivided amongst the

Above: A French St Chamond with infantry of the 6th Army during manoeuvres in the Chemin des Dames area, May 1917. Only one of the tanks managed to cross the start line the others fell victim to mechanical breakdowns and took no part in the fighting

various corps, and twelve to the Fifth Army.

Even this might have been a success, but for two things – firstly the inevitable preliminary artillery barrage and secondly the weather. A five-day artillery bombardment preceded the attack, cutting the wire and battering the trenches of the defenders but also churning up the ground into a sea of shell-holes. Then, on the night prior to the attack, it began to rain heavily. As a result the battlefield soon turned into a swamp. All the tanks with the First Army bogged down within the first 500 yards and never got into action at all, while several of the Third Army tanks suffered the same fate. Of the remaining tanks, many managed to struggle through the mud and perform useful functions, but in spite of their efforts the Battle of Arras failed to break into the German line. Or at least, it broke in, but with the usual ineptitude, GHQ failed to recognise the opportunity and the reserves

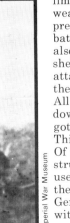

Imperial War Museum

were too far back to be of any use.

In a back-handed fashion, Arras did the Allies some good, insofar as the sight of British tanks waist-deep in mud convinced Hindenburg and many of the German High Command that the tank was a mechanical novelty of no practical value, and he discouraged any talk of developing a German equivalent. Men, not materiel, was still Hindenburg's credo.

Another result of Arras was less helpful. Two tanks were captured by the Germans, who lost no time in making experiments against them with a variety of munitions so as to develop some useful anti-tank weapon. They soon discovered that their armour-piercing bullet, devised for aerial warfare, could penetrate the sides of the Mark I tank, and arrangements were quickly made for supplies of AP ammunition to be made available to every machine-gunner on the front.

Arras was the last battle in which the Mark I or II tanks were used as combat vehicles. The Mark IV was now arriving in France in increasing numbers, and these were first used in the Battle of Messines, June 7, 1917.

The Mark IV was of the same general form as the earlier marks, subdivided into Male and Female types, the differences being matters of detail. The most immediately obvious difference was that the two-wheeled tail was no longer used, steering being by the tracks only, and the sponsons in which the guns were mounted were smaller and could be swung inside the tank for transport. (Those of the early tanks had to be unbolted and removed when the tank was being carried by rail, which meant a long and difficult job of re-fitting them at the journey's end.) The 6-pdr guns were no longer the single tube models but a completely new design, the '6-pounder of six hundredweight', specially designed for the job and only 5 ft long instead of the 8 ft of the single tube gun. This made them easier to operate, aided the design of the collapsible sponson, and made very little difference to the ballistics.

The engine was the same sleeve-valve Daimler but improved by the fitting of twin carburettors and aluminium pistons to give 125 hp. The tracks were improved so as to give better grip and an 'unditching beam' was provided; this was an iron-shod baulk of wood which could be fixed to the track, on top of the tank, by chains. As the engine was engaged and the track revolved, slipping through the mud, so the beam was drawn round and provided a massive grip as it came into the mud, heaving the tank out. As the tank gained hard ground and the beam came around to the roof once again, so two men of the crew, working through hatches on the roof, unchained it and fixed it to the roof ready for the next time.

Other improvements in the Mark IV included the provision of a silencer for the engine, the enlargement of the fuel tank to hold 75 gallons and its fitting outside the rear of the tank, and the supply of fuel to the engine by a positive system instead of by gravity. This was originally a pressure system but it gave so much trouble that it was soon changed to a vacuum system using the well-tried 'Autovac' device.

Messines saw a number of innovations. Supply tanks were used for the first time, these being Mark I tanks with the guns removed and the sponsons enlarged so as

to carry stores. The function of these was to carry forward one complete refill of ammunition and fuel for each of the combat tanks. 72 Mark IVs were to be the combat force, and they were brought up behind the line and camouflaged by special covers which resembled the normal sort of military hut. The marks left on the ground by these tanks as they took up their places in their 'hide' were carefully removed by dragging chain harrows across with horse teams, so that German aviation would not be able to detect the track marks.

The artillery barrage before Messines was probably the greatest barrage of the war; it began on May 28 and, continued until the attack on June 7; fortunately for the tanks the weather stayed dry. Finally, at dawn on June 7, 40 tanks were launched. Twenty-seven of them reached the first infantry objectives, and by 0700 the New Zealanders had taken Messines. North of Messines, one tank achieved immortality and became known throughout the army as the 'Wytschaete Express' for its exploit in leading the assault into the village of Wytschaete and covering the occupation there.

For once the planning of the battle had been performed reasonably well, and British artillery had been moved up into positions from which it could shell the farther side of the battlefield and keep the German reserves away while the gains were consolidated. Then at 1510 the attack was begun once again, with the still-active tanks in the lead. They performed their battle drills immaculately, cutting through wire and crossing trenches, then swinging left and right to cover the area behind the German line while the infantry dealt with the trenches. By evening the whole German line was in Allied hands and, with the tanks dug in to act as temporary pill-boxes, the infantry were wiring and digging as hard as they could go. The inevitable German counter attack on the following day was repulsed, and Messines was to stay in Allied hands until the German offensive of April 1918, and there was little doubt in anyone's mind that the tanks had contributed a very great deal to the day's success.

But while it looked as if the tank was at last beginning to show what it could do, back in England there was still a danger

Far left: A Mark II bogged in a roadside ditch during the fighting near Arras. A platoon files past as a group of their comrades awaits orders to assist in the recovery of the tank
Centre: A British advanced dressing station in the yard of a shell blasted farm
Above: British infantry pose in a captured German position. The man in the foreground has the typical dress and equipment of a front line soldier, leather jerkin, rifle swathed in sacking as protection from the mud, and ammunition pouches positioned to the side for easy access in the confines of the trenches *Below:* A German MG 08 machine-gun team take cover in a shell hole. Tanks were beginning to break up the static trench warfare

39

that it might be knocked on the head. The original tight-knit organisation which had produced the first tanks had now, naturally enough, expanded to deal with the manifold problems of equipment supply, design, inspection, accessories, signal communication, first aid equipment, guns, pigeons and dozens of outlandish ancillaries which had not been dreamed of in the early days. As a result of all this proliferation the organisation had been restructured several times and there was friction with the War Office, with the Ministry of Munitions, the Treasury and many other people. The whole story is extremely involved and cannot be told here, but there is no doubt, reading the memoirs of some of the contestants, that in the middle of 1917 it would not have taken much to have killed the whole tank programme.

But by dint of various shake-ups and re-organisations, and because there were still enough senior officers with faith in the idea, it staggered through this hard time. In October 1917 work began on the design of the Mark V tank, a design which would overcome some of the defects of the earlier models. The primary change was in the engine. Instead of the Daimler engine used so far, a totally new design by Harry Ricardo, one of the foremost engine designers in England, was used, allied to a new epicyclic gearbox designed by Major W G Wilson, the man who had been responsible for the basic design of the first tank. The combination of engine and gearbox allowed one driver to control the vehicle, improved the speed and made the vehicle more manoeuvrable. The fuel capacity was increased to 93 gallons, giving the tank a range of 45 miles, and the armour plate was increased to 14 mm thickness. All this improvement put the weight up by one ton, but this was less of a defect than the fact that for some reason never completely understood, the Mark V suffered from poor ventilation, and riding inside it was even less pleasant than riding in the earlier models.

At the same time a completely new design, the Mark VI, was put on paper. This was on the same general lines as the Mark V but was to carry a single 6-pdr in the front face of the vehicle instead of having two in sponsons. This reduction in firepower was not looked on favourably by the army, and by this time they were sure enough of what they wanted to be able to over-rule the designers. So the Mark VI never got off the drawing board. What the army wanted was a tank which would cross an even wider trench, since the Germans were digging wider and wider anti-tank ditches in their Hindenburg Line defence system.

Foster, the company who had built the first tank, solved this problem very neatly by what they called the Tadpole Tank, a standard Mark IV with the bodywork lengthened to give a long tapering tail which, to some extent, did resemble a tadpole.

Until now all the British tanks had been of the same rhomboidal shape and all of the order of about 28 tons. Their top speed, on good ground, was about 4 mph. But very early in the tank's life an opinion had been expressed that something faster and less ponderous might be advantageous, to move quickly to occupy ground and cut off an enemy force. Sir William Tritton, co-designer with Wilson of the first tank, set to work to produce an answer and came up

with the Tritton Chaser, which was first demonstrated at the Oldbury Experimental Ground, near Birmingham, on March 3, 1917. Weighing 12 tons, it could move at 8 mph, was armoured with 8-mm plate and carried a revolving turret mounting a single Lewis machine-gun. The most remarkable thing about the Chaser was that it was driven by two 45-hp Tylor four-cylinder engines, each driving, through a normal four-speed-and-reverse gearbox; one track. The engine throttles were connected to the steering wheel, so that steering was accomplished by altering the speed of the engines so as to slow down one track and speed up the other. Needless to say, this called for a delicate touch, especially at low speeds, and stalling the engines was by no means uncommon when attempting to negotiate some obstacle.

Nevertheless, the Chaser made a good impression, though some modifications were requested by the army, notably the removal of the revolving turret because of problems connected with the production of the device. The armour was increased in thickness to 14-mm, the fuel tank was given armour protection, and the armament changed to four Hotchkiss guns. The weight went up to $15\frac{1}{2}$ tons in the process, but it finally appeared in service in October 1917 as the Medium Mark A, though nobody ever called it that except the supply officers; to everyone else it was the Whippet.

Meanwhile, in France the war had been going on, and the tanks had been thrown into action in the Third Battle of Ypres, better known as Passchendaele. Here they floundered and sank in the bottomless mud, achieving very little except that they confirmed the German opinion that the tank was a mechanical aberration which they need not pursue. But the tank men in the British Army were still sure that if only they could manage to put enough tanks into action on a suitable piece of ground, then their critics would be confounded and their faith in the mechanised arm would be justified.

By this time the Heavy Section, Machine Gun Corps had become the Tank Corps, commanded by General Elles, and the Staff Officer was Lieutenant-Colonel J E C Fuller, the man who later came to be called 'The

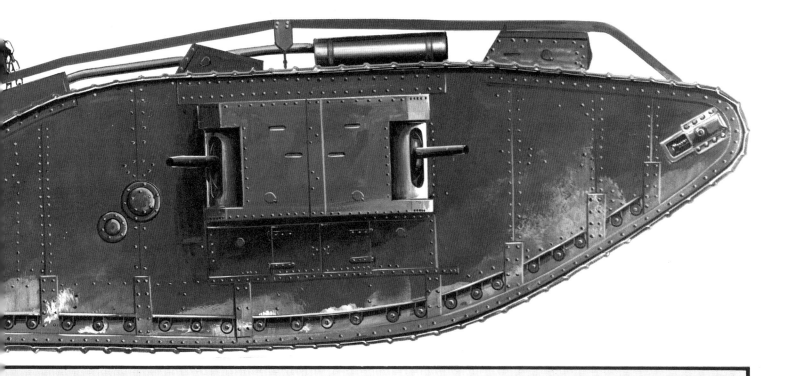

41

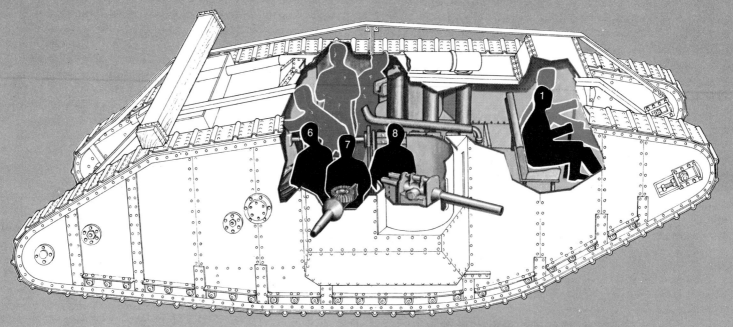

Peter Sarson

Above: The crew of a Mark IV tank:
1 Commander **2** Gearsman **3** 6-pounder gunner **4** Lewis machine-gunner (and loader for 6-pounder) **5** and **6** Brakemen **7** Lewis machine-gunner (and loader for 6-pounder) **8** 6-pounder gunner

Below: The cramped interior of the Mark V, looking forward on the right-hand side and looking behind the engine from left to right
Bottom: An exterior view of the same Mark V showing the camouflage painting

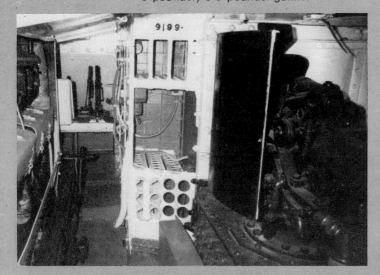

Right: British tank crewman. The main requirement of the tank crew was protection from the noise, vibration and high temperatures (up to 100° Farenheit) experienced inside a vehicle moving over rough ground without any suspension or shock absorption. Seconded from other units, tank crewmen were distinguished by their unorthodox clothing.
Far right: A Mark IV female with fascine.
Below: A diagram of the Tank Battle Drill devised by Lieutenant-Colonel J F C Fuller

Julian Allen

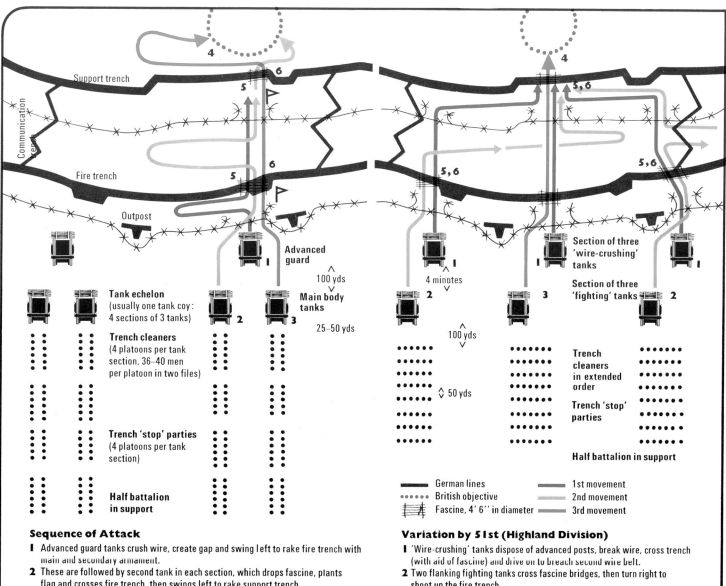

Support trench

Communication trench

Fire trench

Outpost

Advanced guard

100 yds

Main body tanks

25–50 yds

Tank echelon
(usually one tank coy: 4 sections of 3 tanks)

Trench cleaners
(4 platoons per tank section, 36–40 men per platoon in two files)

Trench 'stop' parties
(4 platoons per tank section)

Half battalion in support

4 minutes

100 yds

50 yds

Section of three 'wire-crushing' tanks

Section of three 'fighting' tanks

Trench cleaners in extended order

Trench 'stop' parties

Half battalion in support

━━━ German lines   ━━━ 1st movement
•••• British objective   ━━━ 2nd movement
╫╫╫ Fascine, 4' 6'' in diameter   ━━━ 3rd movement

Sequence of Attack

1 Advanced guard tanks crush wire, create gap and swing left to rake fire trench with main and secondary armament.
2 These are followed by second tank in each section, which drops fascine, plants flag and crosses fire trench, then swings left to rake support trench.
3 The last tank in each section crushes second wire barrier, drops fascine, plants flag and crosses the support trench towards the objective.
4 All tanks then rally in the vicinity of the objective.
5 Infantry 'trench cleaners' then clear the German lines (2 platoons per trench) from right to left, aided by 2nd & 3rd tanks.
6 Infantry 'stop' platoons secure trenches, set up blocks and improve wire gaps, through which the reserves then pass.

Variation by 51st (Highland Division)

1 'Wire-crushing' tanks dispose of advanced posts, break wire, cross trench (with aid of fascine) and drive on to breach second wire belt.
2 Two flanking fighting tanks cross fascine bridges, then turn right to shoot up the fire trench.
3 The remaining fighting tank passes straight ahead to bridge support trench.
4 General tank rally.
5,6 Infantry, deployed in extended order, carry out normal 'cleaning' and 'stopping' rôle (from left to right).

Prophet of Armoured Warfare'. Fuller was commissioned into the Oxfordshire and Buckinghamshire Light Infantry in 1898, served in South Africa and India, and eventually became a Staff Officer in GHQ. When the Tank Corps was formed in December 1916 he was given the post of Staff Officer and he took the job with no previous knowledge of tanks or commitment to tank warfare. Initially sceptical, his views rapidly changed and he became one of the foremost advocates of armour. Indeed in postwar years he became rather too enthusiastic and upset a good many senior officers, as we shall see.

But Fuller had a first-class analytical brain and he was, after all, a trained planner of high quality. And in 1917 he sat down to look closely at the situation on the Western Front in order to find some way to make the best of the tank force. His first idea was to stage a battle near St Quentin, in which two tank brigades, four infantry divisions and three cavalry divisions would be engaged, the object being to 'restore British prestige' after the disastrous Third Ypres and 'strike a blow against Germany before the winter'. There are suggestions

Above and top: Mark V Male, the first British tank that could be controlled by one man. Two hundred Male and 200 Female were produced, first seeing action at Hamel and serving until the end of the war

Below: Experimental version of the Mark IV with tadpole tail, an extension added to the rear of the tank which increased its trench-crossing ability to 14 ft. However, it was not sufficiently rigid, and the Marks V* and V** had properly lengthened bodies

here that Fuller's usual incisiveness had slipped and that he was more concerned with showing the tanks in a good light than he was with promoting a worth-while military exercise. The St Quentin area wasn't particularly profitable when closely examined, and, moreover, it was practically in French-held territory – and to get the number of troops he needed, Fuller wanted two French divisions.

Fuller placed his proposal in front of Elles, who promptly turned it down, largely on the grounds that it required French troops and therefore GHQ would be unlikely to agree to the idea. On the spur of the moment, Fuller looked at the map, pointed to Cambrai, and said 'Why not here?' Elles agreed, and the idea was forwarded to GHQ. And, as casually as that, the venue for the Tank Corps' most critical battle was decided.

In fact, a full-scale battle was not what Fuller really wanted: he embodied his Cambrai idea into a paper entitled *Tank Raids*, which suggested short and sharp raids by tanks on strictly limited objectives. But when his Cambrai suggestion reached GHQ it was worked over and modified by several other minds.

In the first place another plan for a battle in the Cambrai area had already been put up by General Tudor, commanding the artillery of the 9th Division. In this he suggested an attack by tanks under cover of smoke screens but without the usual preliminary artillery bombardment, the bombardment which invariably left the battlefield in such a state that the tanks were hampered in their movement. This, allied to Fuller's idea, would have been good enough, but these two notions were now to have a third one superimposed on

The 'Tank, Medium, Mark A', or Whippet, was based on the 'Tritton Chaser', designed in November 1916 by Sir William Tritton to provide a lighter and faster tank better able to co-operate with cavalry than infantry-paced heavy tanks

them. The Third Army commander, General Byng, was a cavalry enthusiast, and he was well aware that there were forty thousand cavalrymen champing at the bit and waiting for the long-promised break-through which would turn them loose in German territory. Now the plan became more involved: the tanks would smash a hole through the Hindenburg Line and the horsemen would sweep through, all-conquering, hopefully stopping before they reached the Baltic.

Fuller was horrified when he found how his original plan had been modified into a full-scale battle, but there was nothing he could do about it; when Generals were hatching plans, a mere Lieutenant-Colonel had no chance of arguing. Nevertheless the planning went forward, and it has to be said that the initial planning for Cambrai was among the best of the whole war.

At 0620 on November 20, 1917 1009 British guns opened fire with an earth-shaking crash and 216 tanks of the assault battalions moved off. The guns divided their attention between laying smoke screens to blind the flanks, bombarding gas on to known German artillery positions, and firing a complex rolling barrage of gas, high explosive and shrapnel 300 yards ahead of the tanks. Behind the armour came the infantry, running 50 yards behind and relying on their individual tank to crush the wire and protect them. The tanks were carrying fascines – large bundles of brushwood – on their roofs, and these were dropped into the trenches as they arrived at them so as to support their own crossing and act as a bridge for the following infantry.

This sudden onslaught in the misty dawn completely unnerved most of the German front line infantry, and the British success was overwhelming. By 1000 the first objectives, the 'Blue Line', had been taken and another 96 tanks were rolling forward to pass through and take over the lead. In addition 32 special grapnel tanks fitted with chains and grapnels had come forward to drag away huge sectors of the German wire and clear the way for the cavalry.

Unfortunately it didn't all go easily. In

the centre of the battlefield lay Flesquieres, the remains of a French village which now formed a fortified German position. The 51st Highland Division had to deal with Flesquieres, and their commander, having no experience of tanks, was quite convinced that Fuller's 'battle drill' was wrong. He took it on himself to modify Fuller's instructions, his principal change being that instead of having the infantry bunched tightly behind the tanks, they were strung out in long lines to each side. This meant that when the tank forced its way through the wire it left only its own width of gap; whereupon the strung-out infantry had to run inwards to cross the wire through the gap or else force their own way across, which was a ridiculous negation of the tank's primary purpose. This was the thin end of the wedge, and with the German's very tough resistance added in, Flesquieres was never taken and remained to threaten the flanks of the advances on each side. Here too was the famous 'gunner of Flesquieres', Unteroffizier Kruger of the 8th Field Battery, who manned a 77-mm gun single handed after its crew had all been killed, and personally knocked out seven British tanks before being killed alongside his gun.

After the first flush of success, Cambrai began to bog down. Due to misunderstandings, a flank attack against Flesquieres failed to get moving before darkness and rain overtook it. Then, because of an erroneous message the Cavalry decided to march up to the new front via Flesquieres, and in so doing got into a terrible tangle with the 51st Highland Division which took several hours to sort out. One or two minor cavalry units actually did manage to get into action, notably the Canadian Fort Garry Horse, but the principal drawback was a canal which was firmly held by the Germans for most of its length and of which all the crossings had been destroyed.

By the evening of November 21 the forward elements of the attack had shot their bolt: the tank men, and their machines, were exhausted, and there was a hold-up

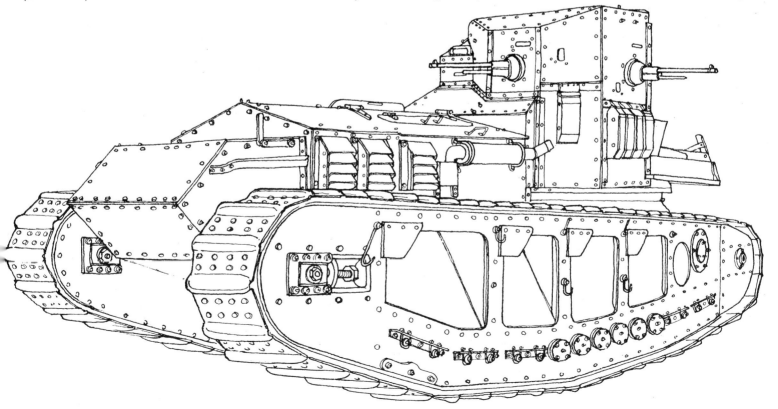

Above: A Mark IV brings in a captured German 5.9-in naval gun during the Battle of Cambrai. *Below and background:* Powered by two 45-hp Tylor engines, one driving each track, and armed with four Hotchkiss machine-guns, 200 Whippets were produced

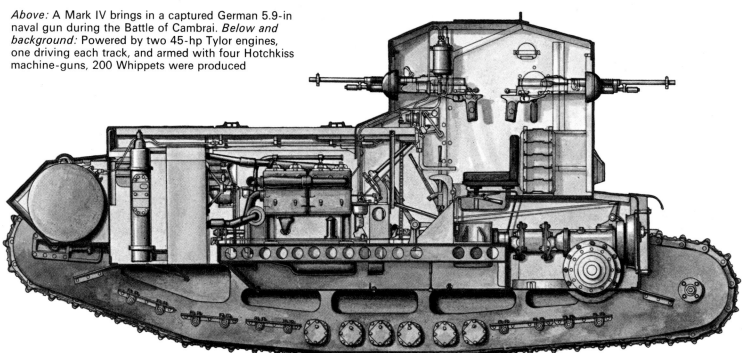

Imperial War Museum

Below: A pilot's view of a tank action, four tanks, two with fascines, approach the German trench lines

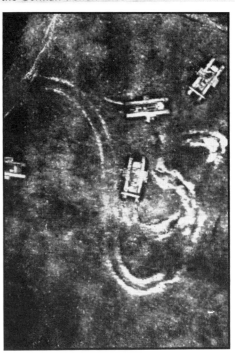

in the petrol supply. The infantry were also exhausted, the reserves having failed to come up in their proper time. So, of course, the big hole was never driven through to the rear, and the forty thousand horsemen turned round and went back. After allowing the British to hold their new positions for a week, the Germans returned with a smashing counterattack which drove the British line almost back to its starting point. Cambrai was over, and precious little to show for it, largely because it had been put into action without sufficient thought for what would be needed if it happened to succeed. It did succeed, exactly as the tank men had promised, but there were no worthwhile reserves to go in and keep the momentum of the initial assault going.

But in all the argument and finger-pointing which went on after Cambrai, one fact was indisputable: whoever had slipped up, it wasn't the tanks. Everyone was agreed on that. The Tank Corps had done a splendid job, they had shot the infantry through exactly on schedule, put them where they wanted to be and protected them there, precisely as advertised.

Whatever the future might bring, the Tank Corps was vindicated by Cambrai, and although it fought better battles afterwards, it was because of Cambrai that it was able to strengthen its place in the army, and it is by Cambrai that it will always be remembered. Cambrai was the turning point in the history of the tank.

The tanks were to fight a number of battles before the war ended, but probably the most significant and best-conducted— and least known—was that of Hamel, in July 1918. The commotion generated by the German attack in Spring 1918 had died down, and the Allies were beginning to think of a summer offensive; and among the people doing the thinking was Lieutenant-General Monash, commanding the Australian Corps in France. Monash was a very different man to most of the Allied generals; no fire-eating traditionalist he. His idea was to use the maximum effort of artillery, tanks, gas, aircraft and mortars to take the pressure off the infantry and allow them to walk forward with relatively little effort to occupy a position and keep it. No nonsense about cavalry breakthroughs

Left: Trees felled by the Germans in the Flesquières sector of Cambrai — one of the reasons for the checks which jeopardised the battle. *Right:* Lt.-General Kavanagh, whose cavalry were to follow the planned breakthrough. *Far right:* Major-General Harper, 51st Div. He substituted his own tank/infantry drill for Fuller's. *Below:* Mark IV Hyacinth ditched near the German second line at Ribécourt

Special Order No 6.

1. To-morrow the Tank Corps will have the chance for which it has been waiting for many months, — to operate on good going in the van of the battle.

2. All that hard work & ingenuity can achieve has been done in the way of preparation

3. It remains for unit commanders and for tank crews to complete the work by judgment & pluck in the battle itself.

4. In the light of past experience I leave the good name of the Corps with great confidence in their hands

5. I propose leading the attack of the Centre division

Hugh Elles.
B.G.

15th Nov. 1917. Commanding Tank Corps.

_____

Distribution to Tank Commanders.

Left: Brigadier-General Hugh Elles, commander of the Tank Corps at Cambrai, with (above) his Special Order, written on the day before his Tank Corps went into action. Cambrai was the first co-ordinated tank battle, planned with proper artillery and infantry support, and, initially at least, was a resounding success. *Above right:* A Mark IV crashes through German barbed wire. Tanks towed grapnels to hook up the wire and tow it out of the path of the supporting infantry. If however the tanks pushed ahead too fast they could leave the infantry unprotected from isolated machine guns that had survived the initial attack

or lines of men with fixed bayonets, rigidly dressed-off from the left, marching straight into the German machine-gun fire.

Monash now put forward a plan to take the village of Hamel and the surrounding area, a small ridge which would be advantageous for British observation, as, indeed, was every slight rise of ground on the flat plain of Flanders. He made it clear that he envisaged a tank operation, well supported by artillery and air, in which the tanks would actually effect the capture of the area and the infantry would simply follow up in order to consolidate the gains and mop up anything the tanks missed.

Monash had to do some arguing. Fuller, the tank man, wanted the tanks to press ahead; Rawlinson, who had commanded on the Somme and was less starry-eyed about tanks than Fuller, wanted them to trail along behind the infantry; while Monash wanted the infantry and tanks to act together. Moreover, the Australians were less than happy about working with tanks, since they had suffered considerable casualties in a previous attack when the tanks had failed to turn up at the right time or the right place.

Eventually all this conflict was resolved. Rawlinson gave way over the position of the tanks, as did Fuller, while the Australian troops were firstly appeased by the promise of an artillery barrage and then

actually turned into tank enthusiasts by a series of exercises. In these, tanks and infantry co-operated to the full and individual tanks were allotted to each company of infantry, so that the tank men and the foot-sloggers became working partners and fast friends.

Monash made even more innovations: every NCO had an air photograph of the whole battlefield, every man had a map and, by a series of lectures, was (probably for the first time in the war) fully in the picture about what was being tried and how he fitted into the scheme. And instead of burdening the infantry with every round of ammunition or other store likely to be wanted in the consolidation phase of the battle, the Royal Air Force were ready to fly machine-gun ammunition forward and drop it on pre-arranged signals, while a number of supply tanks were ready to bring forward wire, pickets, entrenching equipment, sandbags and more ammunition.

For some days before the battle, the German lines were desultorily shelled with a mixture of smoke and gas, and when the battle finally began the high explosive barrage was supplemented by smoke shells, the idea being to make the defenders put gasmasks on, fearing the usual smoke-gas combination, and thus further reduce their fighting efficiency. At 0310 on July 4 (chosen for its American connection, since

four companies of US Infantry were participating in the attack) the advance began, preceded by an accurate barrage. The noise of the advancing tanks was partially masked by the noise of aircraft as bombers flew across to bomb the German positions, and the troops walked forward with the tanks in relative comfort.

But the fallacy of putting infantry and tanks level with each other was soon shown when the assault actually reached the German lines. Small parties of German machine-gunners, missed by the tanks, were able to wreak havoc among the infantry as they picked their way through the gaps in the wire. This initial misfortune was redeemed by the initiative of the Australians who soon realised that their best course was not to advance in open order but to cluster close around their individual tanks, and use them as a combination of cover and retaliatory fire. As machine-guns were spotted, so the tanks either picked them off with the 6-pdrs or, more simply, lumbered across the nests and ground the machine-guns and their crews into the mud.

When daylight came, the work became easier and the tanks romped ahead, followed by their attendant infantry, until by 0600 the German positions were overrun and the ridge line was in Australian hands. The aviators now appeared on schedule,

dropping boxes of ammunition to the Vickers guns, while the supply tanks came forward to deliver 450 coils of barbed wire, 180 sheets of corrugated iron, 600 mortar bombs, 40 000 rounds of small arms ammunition, water, pickets for hanging the wire, and various other useful oddments; four tanks with 24 men delivered equipment that would have had to be carried by 1200 foot soldiers, always supposing they could have got forward on time.

The only cloud on the horizon was the appearance of a new weapon on the German side, a super-powered Mauser rifle firing a 13-mm armour-piercing bullet capable of penetrating the armoured sides of the tanks. Few casualties were, in fact, due to these rifles, but they were a pointer to the future.

As Fuller later said, 'In rapidity, brevity and completeness of success, no battle of the war can compare with Hamel.' For a loss of 51 officers, 724 men (including wounded) and five tanks, the Australians had captured 41 German officers and 1400 men, 41 mortars, 171 machine-guns and two field guns, plus several square miles of valuable terrain. More important than the material gains, though, was the knowledge that the tank was finally vindicated, finally accepted as a weapon which could not be dispensed with in any future operation. To quote Fuller once more, 'From Hamel onwards, the war became a tank war . . . .'

51

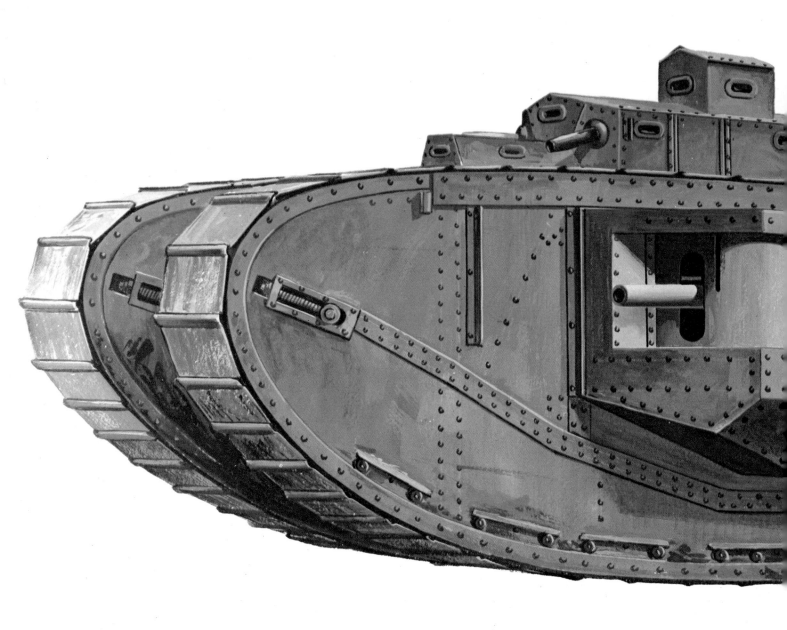

THE NEXT GENERATION

an accepted weapon

While Hamel had firmly established the tank from the soldier's point of view, the dyed-in-the-wool enthusiasts had already decided that the tank was the coming thing and the designers had been hard at work improving the machine. Hamel was fought with the British Mark V tank, which proved to be absolutely reliable, but even so, a Mark VII was already under investigation. At the same time, other people were beginning to think about tanks.

Before the American entry into the war the US Military Mission in Paris had been asked to report on the tank, but its initial reaction was not one of enthusiasm, stressing mechanical unreliability of the early Mark I and apparently failing to appreciate the tactical worth of the device. After the arrival of the American Expeditionary Force in France, more details became known and the American HQ came to the conclusion that a heavy and a light model of tank should be procured for American use. The heavy pattern should be that

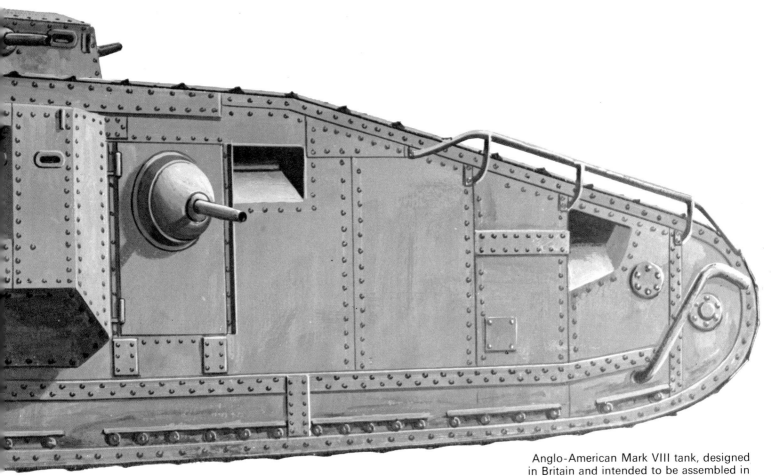

Anglo-American Mark VIII tank, designed in Britain and intended to be assembled in France using British hulls, guns and ammunition, and US-built Liberty aero engines, transmission and tracks

developed by Britain, while the light type, it was recommended, should be the French Renault. Allied Commissions were set up, in which various matters of design were argued, but very little was actually achieved. It was not until Cambrai had shown what the tank could do that American interest was really aroused.

By this time the prototype of the British Mark VII had been put together and was being tried. Little more than a Mark V with slight improvements, it was 3 ft longer and was fitted with a Williams-Janney hydraulic transmission, and – quite an innovation – featured an electric self-starter. Beyond that, though, there was little to recommend it over the Mark V, and since this latter was performing well and reliably, the Mark VII was dropped in favour of making some radical improvements in a Mark VIII design.

The newly-formed Mechanical Warfare Department set about designing the Mark VIII and, in the process, the Anglo-Ameri-

can Tank Commission were invited to give their views. Moreover, the reports of tank commanders in battle were studied so as to raise any useful suggestions which they might make. It was 8 ft longer than the Mark V, to enable it to cope with wider trenches; the power was increased to 300 hp and the engine mounted within a separate compartment; the interior was ventilated by fans; the sponsons were mounted on rollers so that they could be retracted into the tank for transportation by rail; and the track plates were made from armour plate instead of mild steel.

Arrangements were made to have the Mark VIII, now known as the Liberty tank, manufactured in a special factory to be set up in France by the Anglo-American Commission: Fifteen hundred were to be assembled from components made variously in the US and Britain. Britain was to furnish the hulls, guns and ammunition, while the Americans were to build the engines, transmission and tracks. In addition, an-

other 1450 were to be built in the US, and it was hoped that at least 1500 would be ready for the spring offensive of 1919.

Unfortunately, this programme never got off the ground. The failure of the American aircraft production programme prevented their using Liberty engines to power the tanks, as had been hoped, while British losses in the German spring offensive in 1918 meant that the available tank facilities were pressed into producing more Mark Vs to keep up the supply instead of cutting down on production in order to get the lines ready for the Mark VIII.

At the same time, drawings of the Renault light tank had gone to the US and preparations were made for manufacture. It was hoped that the first 100 American-built Renaults would be issued in April 1918, followed by 300 in May and 600 every month thereafter until 1500 had been delivered, plus an estimated replacement rate of 15%. But it turned out that American manufacturers were reluctant to undertake the

This unusual American design by the Pioneer Tractor company was intended to provide a tank long enough to have a useful trench-crossing ability and light enough to use existing powerplants. Two 50-hp engines, the two-man crew and a machine-gun were carried in an armoured box supported by a tracked tubular frame, 25 ft long. Seen here at Aberdeen Proving Ground, the Skeleton Tank's malleable iron tubing frame would not have survived long in battle

construction of something as radically different as a tank, while the French drawings, in metric style, had to be completely re-drawn to suit American manufacturing methods. Contracts for 4440 tanks were finally negotiated, at a price of $11 500 per tank, and a variety of sub-contractors were involved, supplying their components to three major assembly plants run by the Van Dorn Iron Works of Cleveland Ohio, the Maxwell Motor company of Dayton Ohio, and the C L Best company, also of Dayton. In spite of the promises, it was actually October 1918 before the first American Renault came off the production line, and by the November 11, 1918 only 64 had been completed, six of which had been shipped to France.

As always, private enterprise did its best to assist the war effort, and since the tank was a new and romantic aspect there was no shortage of people ready to produce tanks for the army. The trouble was that they were not in touch with anyone in France who could tell them precisely what a tank was supposed to accomplish, and

their designs were long on mechanical ingenuity and short on combat effectiveness.

The C L Best company, who were tractor makers, had demonstrated their CLB 75 tank late in 1916. This was no more than a commercial tractor chassis with a simulated armour hull and a revolving turret above. Apart from performing in some field day evolutions with the National Guard it never achieved any success with the military, and, indeed, it would not have survived two minutes on a real battlefield. Another prototype was the HA 36 one-man tank made by the Holt Tractor company, powered by a motorcycle engine and with tracks made of chain to which wooden cleats were bolted.

After the entry of the US into the war the government began to channel all these suggestions into one stream and to give some guidance on what was wanted. Moreover, of course, the arrival of war contracts and the need for priorities in obtaining steel and other vital materials soon gave the factories other things to think about. But under the guidance of the US Govern-

ment the Holt company, in collaboration with the General Electric company, began developing a 'gas-electric' tank. This relied on a pair of gasoline engines to drive two electric motors, one for each track, so that varying the current controlled the speed and a very fine and precise degree of adjustment could be achieved.

A similar system had already been tried on a specially built British Mark IV, but it was found that the system did not have sufficient power to haul a heavy tank out of a shell-hole. The Holt design weighed 25 tons, and mounted two machine-guns and a 2.95-in Vickers mountain gun in the front plate. While it worked well enough over good country, it suffered from the same defect as the British model – the only way to haul it out of a shell hole was to so ill-use the motors as to ruin them for further operation. Only the prototype was ever built.

Next came the Steam Tank, which arrived more or less by accident. The original demand was to produce a tank which could carry a powerful flame-thrower, and the

The Ford Three-ton tank, designed by the US Army Ordnance Department and based on standard Ford components to speed production and keep down costs. Fifteen thousand were ordered, but only 15 had been completed when the contract was cancelled after the Armistice

The A7V – named after the initials of the department by which it was designed – was the first tank to be produced in Germany. Its production was hindered by shortages of raw materials and manufacturing capacity, and in the event only 12 were built. Armed with a 57-mm Russian Sokol gun and six Maxim machine-guns, and powered by two 100-hp Daimler-Benz engines, it carried a crew of 18 men

only way to generate the necessary pressure to shoot out the flame mixture was by steam. It followed that, if steam had to be developed, it might as well be put to some other uses as well, so two automobile steam engines were geared to the tracks. The tank was actually a made-over British Mark IV, and the two engines produced 500 hp, so at least it was sufficiently powerful. Armed with the flame-thrower and four machine-guns, it appears to have been a success, being demonstrated in April 1918. But its subsequent career is unknown, and it seems likely that manufacturing difficulties held things up until the Armistice, after which the design was abandoned.

Another unusual device was the Skeleton Tank designed by the Pioneer Tractor company. As they saw it, the problem was to provide a tank long enough to cross trenches, but, on the other hand, not so heavy as to demand excess power. Their solution was to build the tank to the desired dimensions – 25 ft long – by means of a tubular frame, then insert an armoured box into the frame just sufficiently large to hold the crew of two men, a machine-gun, and two 50-hp engines. The all-up weight was thus kept down to about 9 tons, but for all its ingenuity it is doubtful if it would have survived for long in battle, since the tubular framework was of malleable iron pipe, held together by standard plumber's connections.

A somewhat more practical machine was the Ford Three-Ton Tank. This was designed by the US Army Ordnance Department along the lines of the Renault two-man tank but so as to utilize as many commercial Ford components as possible and thus hasten and cheapen production. Two Model T Ford engines and transmissions were used, one to each track, and the armament

was a single machine-gun in the front plate. Crewed by two men, it weighed 3.1 tons and could move at 8 mph. The Ford company estimated that 100 of these vehicles, costing no more than $4000 each, could be made every day, but by the end of the war only 15 out of the 15015 which had been ordered had been delivered. Ten were sent to France where they were tested in a number of roles, including field gun towing, but the balance of the contract was cancelled after the Armistice.

Tank development in Germany got off to a bad start. The difficulties experienced by British tanks in operating over the shell-torn and muddy ground in the Somme led Hindenburg to a poor opinion of the tank's worth, and it didn't seem as if the addition of tanks was helping the Allies very much. Nevertheless the General Staff were sufficiently interested to urge the manufacture of experimental vehicles and the War Ministry set up a special committee, the Allegemeine Kriegsdepartement 7, Abteilung Verkehrswesen (General war department 7, vehicle division). This group started work by examining a Holt tractor, found in Austria, in order to get at the basic facts about tracked vehicles.

A prototype tank was then built by Ing. Vollmer in Spring 1917. This used two separate sets of tracks, front and rear, very similar to the early British Pedrail machine, but it failed to make much of a showing on trial, and as a result Hindenburg was even more certain that the tank was useless.

Nevertheless, the special committee persevered, with the assistance of Vollmer, and by taking the Holt chassis as a basis, eventually produced a design of tank which they called the A7V. Demonstrated before the German General Staff at Mainz on May 14, 1917, it was moderately successful; at least, the defects looked as if they would be amenable to correction with a little work. So the A7V was approved, but approval was one thing and production was another. By the summer of 1917 raw materials and manufacturing facilities were short in Germany, and the current 'Hindenburg Programme' of munitions resupply, involving artillery, ammunition, motor vehicles and aircraft, was absorbing all the available facilities. The War Ministry refused to grant any form of high priority to

tank production, largely because of Hindenburg's opinion of the tank, and as a result it was not until the spring of 1918 that quantity production was able to begin. A small number were, however, available to troops from September 1917 onwards, and they were first used in action in March 1918.

The A7V was, in fact, a good design, and had sufficient experience been gained with it and some modifications made, it could well have been the best tank of the war. The tracks were concealed beneath the armoured hull, since the Germans had found the mild steel tracks of the first British tanks to be their weak link. The suspension was sprung, which gave better riding characteristics, and it carried a crew of 18 men, with the driver and tank commander perched in an armoured cupola in the centre of the hull. It was armed with a 57-mm Russian Sokol gun, stocks of which had been captured, and six Maxim machine-guns. Each track was independently driven by a 100-hp Daimler-Benz engine, steering being done by braking one track while accelerating the other, and it could reach about 8 mph on good ground.

After the Battle of Cambrai the Germans at last managed to capture a British tank, and, after examining it closely, their first suggestion was simply to copy it as it stood. This, though, was impractical for various manufacturing reasons, and plans for producing the A7V went ahead. But one prototype tank was built on the same general lines as the British, with all-round tracks and sponsons mounting 57-mm guns. This, known as the A7V/U (U for *umlaufende ketten* or all-round tracks) was tested and 20 were ordered, but only the prototype was produced.

Meanwhile Vollmer had been looking at the light tank question and had come to the conclusion that simple lightweight tanks were a better proposition for Germany than heavy and complicated models. He therefore produced a design for a 7-ton tank, using many standard Daimler automobile components in the chassis. In many respects it resembled the British Whippet, with a three-man body, engine at the front, turret at the rear, and low-set tracks at each side. The turret mounted either two Maxims or a 37-mm gun, while the 60-hp engine moved it along at about 7 mph.

The Special Committee examined Vollmer's prototype and, after some argument, devised a specification for a light tank which called for a weight of 8 tons, a speed of 9 mph, the ability to cross a two-metre trench, a 57-mm gun as main armament, and reasonable conditions of room and ventilation for the three-man crew. This led Vollmer to design the LKII which was little more than an enlarged version of his earlier LKI but without the revolving turret and with a 57-mm gun in a fixed cupola at the rear end of the hull. Two prototypes were built but although orders were given for the manufacture of over 500, none were built before the war ended.

As a result, the German tank forces came to rely on captured British vehicles, a number of which fell into their hands during the German offensive of 1918. A repair station was set up at Charleroi in Belgium to which these were shipped, and there they were made serviceable, re-armed with 57-mm Sokol guns and Maxims, had black crosses painted on, and then were returned to the front. The planned strength was to be three sections each of five A7Vs and ten sections of five captured British tanks by August 1, 1918, when the British tanks would be gradually replaced by new A7Vs. But in fact the new A7Vs never appeared, and when the war ended there were but three sections of A7Vs and six of captured Mark IV and V tanks.

As might be expected, there were those among the German committee who were in favour of bigger and better tanks – the same sort of thinking, in fact, which had been responsible for some of the grandiose 'landship' ideas put forward in the early days of British tank design. In response to this, Vollmer, assisted by a Captain Wegner, designed a 42-ft, 148-ton monster to be armed with four 77-mm guns and seven machine-guns and carrying a crew of 22 men. Two prototypes were begun in the Berlin factory of Reibe-Kugellager, but they were not completed before the war ended. Powered by two 650-hp Daimler-Benz aircraft engines, and designed so that they could be rapidly dismantled into four sections for convenient railway transport, it was estimated that they would achieve 5 mph and they were foreseen as 'breakthrough' tanks for use in the 1919 offensives.

The Italian army, as we have already seen, was early in the field with armoured cars, but they were less eager to experiment with tanks since the fighting in the mountainous areas of North Italy was hardly suitable ground for early armour. Nevertheless the FIAT company began thinking about tracked vehicles in August 1916 and, after

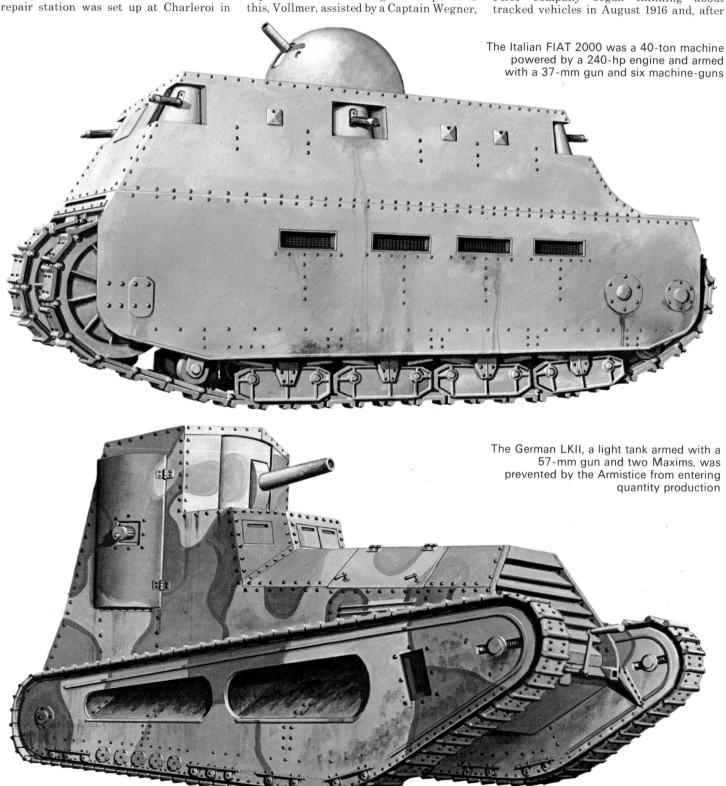

The Italian FIAT 2000 was a 40-ton machine powered by a 240-hp engine and armed with a 37-mm gun and six machine-guns

The German LKII, a light tank armed with a 57-mm gun and two Maxims, was prevented by the Armistice from entering quantity production

more information on British tanks had come to Italy, continued with a design known as the FIAT 2000. This was surprisingly modern in appearance, with the tracks set low and partly concealed, a hemispherical turret mounting a 37-mm gun, six machine-guns in the hull, and sprung suspension. Weighing 40 tons, it was powered by a 240-hp engine, carried a ten-man crew and could reach 4½ mph on good country. The prototype, which differed in having a cylindrical turret, was ready in June 1917 but the army showed little enthusiasm and the project was suspended. Eventually another four were built, being completed after the war.

The Italian army's lack of enthusiasm was simply because they could see no hope for such a heavy vehicle in the battles they were fighting against the Austrians; on the other hand, they were sure that the French Renault light tank could be of more use, and they ordered 100 from France in September 1917. They also asked for 20 Schneider heavy tanks, and, if the French could not deliver the Renaults, requested licenses so that they could be built in Italy. In the event the French were unable to provide the number requested and only a handful of Renaults arrived.

The Italians then decided to go ahead building a modified Renault design in Italy, and FIAT were given a contract to produce 1400 vehicles. The Renault design was modified to meet Italian requirements, largely determined by the terrain in which they were proposed to be operated, and this became known as the FIAT 3000. Similar to the Renault in appearance, it was lighter, due to improvements in the transmission and suspension, and armed with twin machine-guns in a rotating turret. But the war ended before many of these were made; about a hundred were actually completed, the balance of the contract being cancelled.

In France, the trend towards giant tanks had taken hold. The *Artillerie d'Assaut* were gripped with the idea of a massive breakthrough tank and examined a number of suggested designs. Among them was the Char C1, designed by M Jammy of the Société des Forges et Chantiers de la Méditerranée, La Seyne. Two alternate designs were to be built, one mounting a 105-mm gun and using petrol-electric transmission, the other with a 75-mm gun and

normal mechanical transmission, both weighing about 42 tons. This was not unreasonable, but the next proposal was for a Schneider design weighing 141 tons and mounting four 75-mm guns and nine Hotchkiss machine-guns in three turrets, the whole contrivance manned by 28 men. After toying with this idea for some time, sanity prevailed and it was thrown out.

But it was one thing to design heavy tanks; actually building them was an entirely different proposition, and the shortage of steel in France made it unlikely that much in the heavy tank line could be expected before the middle of 1919. In the middle of considering this problem, the French were quite relieved when the Anglo-American Tank Committee came along with their proposal to build Mark VIII tanks in France, particularly as all the French were being asked to do was to provide the factory, in return for which they would receive a proportion of the factory's output. The Char C1 programme received a lower priority in anticipation of the forthcoming Mark VIIIs, but when the Mark VIII programme in turn fell behind, the British had to make up the French deficiencies by supplying them with a number of Mark V* models instead of the promised Mark VIII.

The Char C1 was eventually built, the pilot model with electrical transmission being tested in December 1917. Armed with a 105-mm howitzer in the turret, it was driven by a 240-hp Renault aircraft engine at about five kilometres an hour. Although mechanically sound, the suspension design was faulty and gave a rough ride to the occupants as well as proving reluctant to make turns. So the design was dropped and work began on a fresh model, the Char 2C, using the same petrol-electric transmission system. This mounted a 75-mm gun in a forward turret, a machine-gun in a rear turret, and three machine-guns in the hull. It weighed 68 tons and carried a crew of 12. Due to technological problems, though, the prototype was still incomplete when the war ended.

In keeping with their conception of tanks as a means of carrying artillery to the enemy the French soon began to examine the possibility of mounting heavy ordnance on tracks. One of the most difficult aspects of artillery support in the First World War was that of bringing guns forward across

shell-cratered and muddy ground, and the caterpillar tractor had been brought into service as a towing vehicle in order to try and overcome this terrain difficulty. Even so, a wheeled gun carriage often sank into the mud over which its tracked tractor had passed, and defied the power of the tractor to unstick it. The Americans appear to have been the first people to take the logical step and put a tracked suspension unit underneath a towed gun, in place of the conventional wheels. This was done when they fitted 20 ex-naval 7-in broadside guns on to tracked carriages built by the Baldwin Locomotive company in 1917. But the French took the idea further by putting power on to the mountings to produce self-propelled guns.

The Schneider and the St Chamond companies both produced designs, which showed an interesting difference of opinion as to the best way to propel the chassis and which also foreshadowed the tactical dilemma which was to cloud the early days of self-propelled and even mechanically towed guns for several years. Schneider used a straightforward gasoline engine and mechanical transmission on the mounting, the driver sitting at the front, under the gun barrel, and the engine being mounted at the rear, driving the tracks through a rear sprocket. Thus each weapon was a self-contained unit; and, said the pessimists, if the engine breaks down you are stuck with an immobile gun and if the gun goes wrong you have a mobile ornament.

St Chamond were extremely enthusiastic about petrol-electric drives and, as we have seen, the idea had a considerable following among French designers. But putting the necessary engine and generators on to the gun carriage made the whole affair very crowded and extremely heavy, so their solution was to place only the electric propulsion motors on the gun mounting. A separate vehicle was built to carry the Crochat-Collardeau petrol-electric generator, plus a supply of ammunition for the gun and some of the gun detachment. This supply tractor was hitched to the gun mounting by a rigid connector and a power cable was plugged into the gun unit to carry electricity from the supply vehicle to the gun carriage motors. The supply tractor thus provided power to drive both itself and the gun mounting, the whole connected

The French *Char de Rupture* 2C, designed in the closing stages of the First World War as a breakthrough tank

assembly being controlled by the supply tractor driver while the gun carriage driver merely steered his section in the wake of the tractor.

The advantage claimed here was that once the assembly had arrived at the gun position, the ammunition was unloaded and the supply tractor disconnected, whereupon it drove off to some sheltered spot. When it came time to move, the tractor drove back, hooked and plugged up, and the unit drove off again. Should the gun be damaged by enemy fire, then the tractor could either tow away the remains or, if that was not necessary, it could go back and find another gun. Should, on the other hand, the tractor be damaged, then a spare tractor could be dispatched to team up with the gun and form a new unit.

Top: Bombed Char 2C. *Right:* The 68-ton Char 2C, armed with a 75-mm gun in the forward turret, a machine-gun in the rear turret and three hull-mounted machine-guns, was powered by a 240-hp Renault aero engines

On balance it would seem that the designer was more concerned with the mechanical aspects of the design, and claimed the tactical advantage as an afterthought; it was a very belt-and-braces way of going about things, and one is inclined to suppose that if equal numbers of tractors and guns were built there would rarely be a spare unit when the need arose. Moreover, when you come right down to it, all you have is a towed gun with some additional complications.

Nevertheless, both types were built in some numbers in 1918, mounting mainly 22-cm guns and 28-cm howitzers. A number were used on the St Mihiel salient in 1918, though there is no particular note of their effectiveness in the official records. But it was probably due to these early ideas that

the Americans, early in 1918, began to develop self-propelled mountings for their guns. The first to appear was a Holt caterpillar chassis carrying a 3-in anti-aircraft gun and propelled by a gasolene engine. The 3-in gun was then removed and a British 8-in howitzer fitted in its place. This was tested, both for firing and travelling, and was found so satisfactory that another three were ordered for trial. These, incorporating small modifications, were so good that orders were immediately given for another 50, together with a further 50 for mounting 155-mm guns and 250 for mounting 240-mm howitzers. The latter were to be of two types, a self-contained unit designed by the Ordnance Department and a two-piece unit copied from the St Chamond idea.

It might be said that ordering 250 carriages for the 240-mm howitzer was a piece of boundless optimism in keeping with the rose-coloured dreams of production seen by the Ordnance Department in those days. At the time of this order, early in 1918, the 240-mm howitzer existed only on paper; it was designed by the St Chamond company in France as a scale-down from a 280-mm weapon designed for the Imperial Russian Army and never delivered. The design was bought by America, drawings and technicians sent to the US. There was then the usual delay while the drawings were translated into American measurements and contractors were found; then the war ended before anything was built; and finally, in the early 1920s, the first howitzer was delivered, taken to the proving ground and fired, and burst on its first shot. By which time, of course, the self-propelled

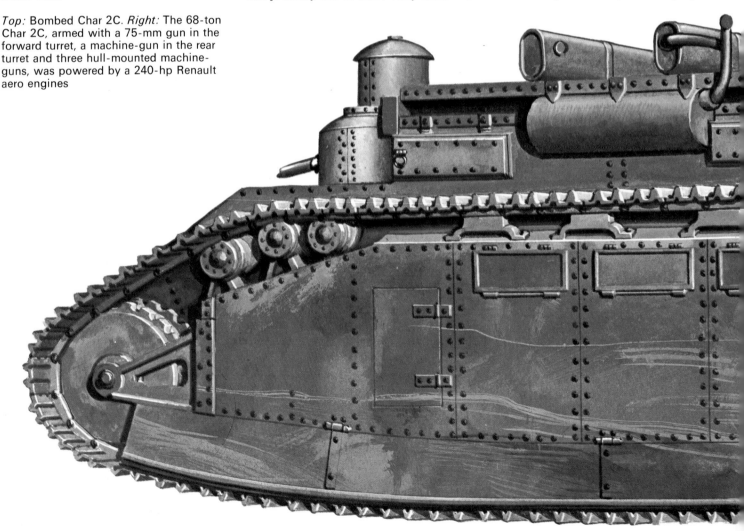

mounting contract had long since been cancelled and forgotten. Indeed, all the contracts were terminated at the Armistice, and only a handful of mountings for the 8-in and 155-mm guns had been built, which served as a useful basis for American development programmes in the post-war years.

But that was the fate of all the tank programmes in December 1918; the war to end wars had been fought and wholesale cancellation of armament programmes was the order of the day. The Germans had least to lose; their tank programme had produced about 20 A7Vs and a handful of pilot models of the LK series, plus the prototypes of the Krupp and K-Wagen designs, and those which were left at the end of the war were soon cut up for scrap on the orders of the Allied Disarmament Commission. Britain, France and the US closed down their programmes as soon as they decently could, allowing some tanks to be completed in order to run the factories down gently, and these were destined to be the main tank strength of the victorious armies for several years to come; some, indeed, soldiered valiantly on until the outbreak of war in 1939, mainly as training tanks though some actually appeared in a fighting role in 1940.

Top: Char 2C with its 13-man crew. *Above:* Ten Char 2Cs were completed by 1922, and in 1940 the six remaining models were recommissioned. Loaded on special rail wagons, however, they were all destroyed by a German bombing attack

All pics RAC Tank Museum

BETWEEN THE WARS 1

When the whistle blew on November 11, 1918 the regular armies of the world sighed with relief and looked forward to demobilising all the conscripts and 'getting back to proper soldiering'. And high on the agenda was the restoration of the proper peace-time pecking order, with the cavalry at the top of the pyramid.

The First World War had been a humbling experience for the horse soldiers who had seen their premier position taken over by other arms while they had spent most of the war waiting for the breakthrough which never came. As soon as peace prevailed they were quick to point out that the conditions in France had been an aberration, never likely to occur again, and they instanced the use of cavalry in Palestine as evidence that the day of the horse – the 'well-bred horse' as Haig once put it – was not over. And their principal target was the infant tank arm, firstly because the tanks threatened to usurp the cavalry's function and secondly, it seems, because many of the best tank officers were turncoat cavalrymen.

The United States Army had founded its Tank Corps in December 1917 as a component of the American Expeditionary Force, with an authorised strength of 14 827 officers and enlisted men. In February 1918 a second force, the Tank Service, National Army, for functioning within the continental United States, was formed with a target strength of 15 660 all ranks. On November 11, 1918 these two forces numbered 15 870 all ranks and in 1919, when the final deliveries were made on the war contracts, there were about 1200 tanks, 1163 of which had been built in the USA.

A year later the Tank Corps ceased to exist, manoeuvred out of existence by political pressure and the 1920 National Defense Act. This reconstituted the US Army as the Army of the United States, comprised of the Regular Army, the Organized Reserves and the National Guard, and in the consequent reshuffle of units the Tank Corps was abolished. The few tank units which had survived demobilisation and the rundown of the army were now designated 'Infantry' and parcelled out to act purely as support troops. It came down to one company of tanks to each infantry division, plus five battalions and a headquarters group under Army command; but still as support; they were denied any opportunity of independent action.

In France the *Artillerie d'Assaut* had succumbed before the end of the war and tanks had become solely an infantry support weapon, largely due to the vast number of Renault two-man tanks which had been produced. So that it was no surprise when, in 1920, this casting was given official backing and, in spite of objections by

Left: Liddell Hart the advocate of mechanised war
Below: A Mk I bogged down in mud

Above: Waiting for the breakthrough, British cavalry near Arras

General Estienne, the tanks were dispersed throughout the army in independent battalions attached to infantry regiments.

And yet in Britain, where the voice of the cavalry was probably the loudest, the Tank Corps survived intact, if rather battered. There was a strong argument that, like the French and Americans, the British Army should disperse the tanks, abolish the separate Tank Corps, and treat the vehicle purely as another infantry weapon. Another suggestion was that each infantry battalion should have its own tank company, manned by infantrymen. Liddell Hart, then a relatively unknown captain, suggested his 'New Model Division', a completely tank-mounted force with infantry in a supporting role, thus completely reversing what everybody else thought to be the natural order of things. And with all this argument going on the Tank Corps managed to survive until 1924, when it was finally placed on a permanent basis and became an element of the Regular Army in its own right. By this time its

strength had dwindled to about 150 tanks.

The basic dispute (and this was not confined solely to Britain) was over the method of employing the tank. Cavalry saw it threatening their traditional tasks of reconnaissance and flanking raids, and argued that the tank was so slow and unreliable that it could never replace the horse in such work. The infantry wanted it solely as a mobile pillbox and gun-carrier to accompany them at a slow walk across No-Man's Land and punch the necessary hole in the enemy trenches to allow the foot soldiers to do the rest. The cavalry were willing to accept this since, of course, the hole-punching would open the way for the Cavalry breakthrough. The tank men themselves, on the other hand, were quite convinced that they had the beginnings of something which could form a completely new weapon or arm of the service in its own right, could manoeuvre, take ground, occupy ground, defend ground, all on its own and without reference to any other arm.

There are none so devout as the newly-converted, and in their enthusiasm for their new concepts of war the tank enthusiasts often over-reached themselves and, in so

doing, made more enemies than friends. Perhaps this was no bad thing: if the infant tank arm could survive the enthusiasm of its supporters, it had little to fear from the attacks of its detractors.

Among the most fervent tank supporters was Fuller. In 1918 he had been profoundly impressed by the disorganisation which followed on the sudden German offensive in the spring. British and French troops were driven back and lost all coherence, communications failed, and the conduct of military affairs seemed to be, for a short time, completely paralysed. Fuller drew an analogy with the human body, pointing out that if the brain were affected then the limbs failed to function properly. From this he began to argue that the most decisive method of defeating an enemy would not be to batter away at the limbs – the front line troops – but to attack the brain – the headquarters – and the nervous system – communications and supply lines. There was nothing fundamentally new in this idea, but it had always been recognised as a policy of perfection which could never be achieved due to the limitations in speed and mobility of foot and horsed troops. But with the ability of the tank to cover long distances at relatively high speed, the idea, Fuller felt, was worth taking out and re-examining.

At that time a new design of tank was on the drawing board, the 'Medium D', a 20-tonner armed with either machine-guns or a 6-pdr and machine-guns, capable of a speed of 25 mph and with a range of action of 100 miles. This speed and range was a vast improvement on what had gone before, and if a sufficient force of Medium D tanks could be produced, then there was every chance that Fuller's idea of attacking the 'brain' might succeed. From this came his 'Plan 1919'; he called it 'a kind of military novelette' but it was so far-seeing that it became the bedrock of much of the theories of armoured warfare which followed.

Plan 1919 envisaged an attack developed on a 90-mile front; the enemy would be positively encouraged to stiffen up the defence of his front by allowing him to see sufficient of the build-up to convince him that an attack would take place in that area, and by this strengthening the adjacent

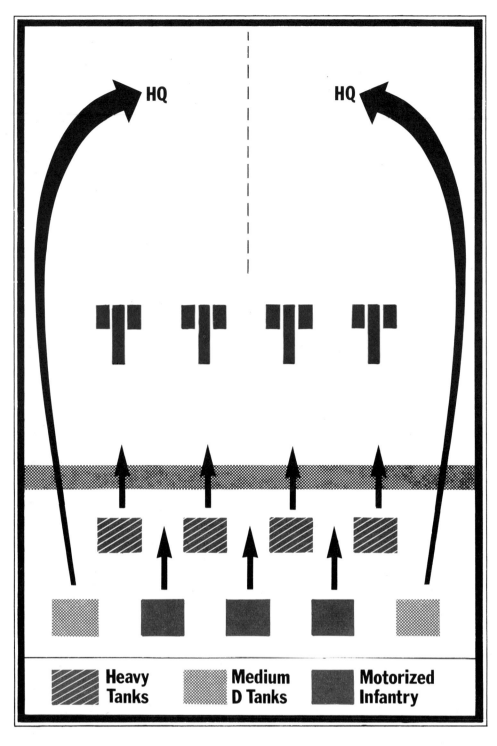

Heavy Tanks

Medium D Tanks

Motorized Infantry

zones would be weakened. Once everything was ready a concealed force of Medium D tanks some 800 strong, divided into two columns, would bypass the flanks of the selected front, crashing through the thinned-out sectors at the sides, and make a swinging pincer movement through the lines of supply and communication behind the front to converge on the headquarters area in the rear.

It was estimated that since these areas were generally about 20 miles back, the attack would reach there in two or three hours, since it would be slicing through a thinly-held zone, all the enemy strength being piled up in the front line. Some two hours after the tanks had moved off, at the time when the enemy headquarters would be thrown into confusion by the sudden appearance of the medium tanks and the communications and supply routes severed, the main attack of heavy tanks and infantry would strike the front line. Twenty-five hundred heavy tanks and another 400 medium tanks would make this attack in the conventional manner relying on the disorganisation and lack of control brought about by the severing of the enemy's 'brain' and 'nervous system' to render the 'limbs' incapable of much resistance. Once this force had broken through the front, a 'Pursuing Force' of another 1200 medium tanks would pour through the breach and fan out in the rear of the front, moving laterally to complete the severing of communication with the rear, destroy supplies and reserves, and generally round off the victory. Fuller estimated that 5000 tanks and 17 000 tank corps men would be needed to carry through 'Plan 1919'.

By the time the plan had been devised, perfected and circulated for comment, the war was coming to an end, and so it never got past the paper stage. Had it done so – and there was some high-powered support for it – the concept of an independent and strategic armoured force would have appeared twenty years earlier than it actually did, and the whole history of the tank, armoured warfare in general, and possibly the world, might have been a good deal different.

Although the proposals were too late, Plan 1919 was the seed planted in the Tank Corps officers which led them to argue for a completely independent force, a force capable of influencing the course of a war by its own efforts and without having to rely on other arms. Fuller was quite aware that such a plan needed infantry and artillery to support it and carry it through,

A 20 mph Model D Medium tank

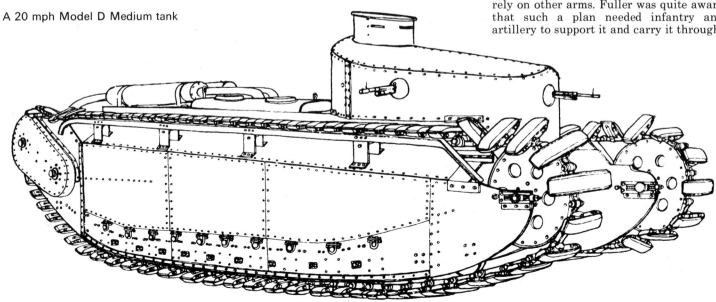

and he also relied heavily on air support in his Plan 1919, but during the 1920s he honed and refined his theories to the point at which he was advocating a completely self-contained armoured force, an army within the army, which in addition to its tanks would have 'Tank Marines' and 'Royal Tank Artillery' as component parts, thus arrogating to the tanks all the necessary fighting functions.

At the time he produced this theory the Royal Artillery were, in fact, experimenting with some self-propelled guns, but Fuller's 'Royal Tank Artillery' idea made it look as if they would lose control of half their force if it got on to tracks, and, as much as anything else, this sealed the fate of the self-propelled gun for the next ten years. Either the gunners fired the guns or they didn't; and if they weren't going to fire them, they were damned if they were going to go to the trouble of designing and testing them for other people to fire.

Fuller was backed up in his less outrageous theories by other able minds, notably that of Captain Liddell Hart. Liddell Hart was by no means a narrow-minded partisan of armour. His thoughts on warfare embraced every aspect, and indeed his early theories were solely to do with infantry tactics. It was not until after the war, and after he had met Fuller, that he began to take a closer look at the tank and its potential. Even then, his view was more to the total mechanisation of the army than solely concerned with the tank.

In an essay in 1922 entitled *The Development of the 'New Model Army'* he advocated firstly the mechanisation of supply transport for the division, followed by mechanisation of the infantry battalions, mechanical traction for the artillery, and finally armoured and tracked carriers to deliver the soldier to battle. With this degree of mechanisation, Liddell Hart contended, the army would have a balanced force, a brigade consisting of two tank battalions, three infantry battalions in carriers, a mechanised artillery regiment (or 'brigade' as they were then known) and the necessary supply, signal and service troops all mechanised. This was to form the first phase of mechanisation, and it was ultimately to be followed by a general assumption by the tank force of the infantry and artillery roles. In the end, he claimed, the ideal army would be a massive tank force supported by aircraft and heavy artillery, accompanied by a force of carrier-borne infantry. In essence he was ahead of Fuller in his allocation of the major role to the tanks and the subordination of the other arms to the tank force, but at least he had the grace to wrap it up in more circumlocutory language and didn't antagonise half the army by calling for 'Tank Marines' or 'Royal Tank Artillery'.

In the face of these and other persuasive arguments the conservatives and plain reactionaries fought back with some fervour, arguing the massive expense of such forces; the equally massive cost of maintaining them in time of peace; accusing the armoured school of failing to take into account the human element; and, of course, fighting to keep the cavalry. Many armies would have been torn apart by such strife – many have been torn apart by less – but the British Army always seems to thrive best in the presence of a good argument, and although voices were strident there was little animosity as a general rule. Much of

the argument was, indeed, quite good-natured – as in this extract from a poem published in the Royal Artillery Journal in 1931:

The dear old horse is going, you can see it in his eye.
As long as we have horses though, the Country will not die.
Off to your stinking petrol fumes; go to your grease and oil!
When engines cease to function – then the horse will start to toil.

And because of this attitude most of the arguments were traded back and forth and hammered out until some sort of a policy slowly began to emerge which was acceptable to everybody in some degree. The development of tanks continued. Even though it was at a low level, it was certainly greater than the development taking place anywhere else in the world, and in the 1920s Britain established itself as the foremost expert in the design and handling of tanks, poor as the results may now seem to be.

In 1926 the Secretary of State for War, in presenting the Annual Army Estimates to Parliament, announced that an Experimental Mechanised Force was to be assembled, the first such force in the world. It was to consist of a battalion of armoured cars, one of medium tanks, a brigade of field artillery and a battery of mountain howitzers, both with mechanical traction or self-propelled mountings (in fact one battery was self-propelled), an infantry battalion in half-tracked carriers, and an engineer company in trucks. The formation was to be commanded by none other than General Fuller.

Unfortunately when Fuller made enquiry into his new command he found it was not quite as advertised; instead of a coherent formation it was, in fact, no more than a normal infantry brigade 'to which, from time to time, certain mechanised units will be allotted'. Moreover, as well as commanding this force he was to act as Garrison Commander at Tidworth, then one of the largest military camps in England. He

protested that such a dual command allowed him neither the time nor the opportunity to do either job satisfactorily, and it would certainly prevent him using the experimental force to demonstrate his theories of armoured warfare to the rest of the army. His objections were overruled; he resigned; the job went to another; he was talked out of his resignation; his old job in the Staff had, meanwhile, been filled; and he found himself shunted off to a backwater. He resigned in 1933, seeing that he was to have no chance of furthering his ideas in the face of the opposition of Sir Archibald Montgomery-Massingberd, who became Chief of the Imperial General Staff in that year and who had a very low opinion of military theorists and writers in general and of Fuller in particular.

But before Fuller retired he managed to write a masterly study of the trends of future warfare entitled *Lectures on FSR II* (FSR II: Field Service Regulations Volume II, the standard British Army handbook on operations). This study was intended for use by Fuller's officers in the 13th Infantry Brigade, and in it he worked out, in great detail and in an unsensational manner, the exact method in which the various arms should co-operate in armoured warfare. The front line of 1914–18 would be replaced by an 'area' war, since the tank had made the penetration of static front lines possible; attacks might develop anywhere; an anti-tank base would have to be formed from which security the tanks could manoeuvre; the enemy was to be encouraged to attack and to expend his energy battering against the anti-tank base, and so on. By any standard *Lectures on FSR II* was a notable work, but when it is read in conjunction with descriptions of the tactics employed, particularly in the Western Desert, by the German Army during the Second World War, it begins to look like sheer clairvoyance.

The Experimental Armoured Force was assembled, in accordance with its planned composition, for the 1927 manoeuvres, where it performed with some ability, and it was then retained in being and appeared

A Vickers Medium
Mk III

again in the 1928 manoeuvres. It was given three basic tasks to perform; reconnaissance, co-operation with infantry, and action as an independent force, and in all three it was less than entirely successful, demonstrating that each of these tasks required a different approach and a different composition of forces.

Colonel Collins, who had assumed command of the force when Fuller refused it, suffered a great deal of criticism, most of it ill-informed; he was, after all, feeling his way into a new form of warfare and even when he felt sure of what he was doing the officers and men underneath him, who were actually translating his ideas into movement on the ground, were more in the dark than he was. As a result, he tended to move slowly so that the troops could get used to the simplest tactical moves before he tried something more advanced. Liddell Hart, writing as the military correspondent of the *Daily Telegraph*, was particularly caustic, accusing Collins of making war according to the motto of the Pawnbrokers Battalion – 'No advance without Security'. Indeed, his attack on the whole mechanised force idea – or, rather, the Army's interpretation of the idea – was so pungent that it led to extremely sour relationships with the War Office which were not to be sweetened for many years.

In spite of all this the exercises taught many lessons which were of value: the problems of controlling and manoeuvring large numbers of tanks; the problem of supplying them and maintaining them in

A British Light Tank Mk VI during manoeuvres in 1936. Light tanks were intended for scouting and reconnaissance work, but were often misused for other tasks

the field; questions of mechanical reliability and similar mundane but vital matters all came to light in 1927–28. At the same time, there were some wrong lessons there to be assimilated, such as the apparent superiority of light tanks. This arose because it was an exercise, and exercises are controlled by umpires, and in 1927–28 umpires had little or no idea about how to evaluate a tank-versus-infantry encounter. Indeed, from the reports of some of the participants, it seems that in many cases the umpires, on horseback, had been left behind by the tanks and were in no position to rule on anything. Since the infantry were not equipped with anything resembling an anti-tank gun, the light tanks were able to run rings round them, and even indulged in such fantasies as charging batteries of field artillery, and the upshot of this was a completely false opinion of the value of light tanks which was to take a very long time to eradicate – and not only in the British Army.

The principal lesson which appeared to come from the manoeuvres was that of the difficulty of operating tanks with other types of force, and as a result the Experimental Armoured Force was broken up in 1929 and the official policy turned to the idea of armoured forces composed entirely of tanks, to which elements of other arms could be attached as and when desired. In 1931 the 1st Tank Brigade was formed, consisting of four battalions of tanks. The formation was 'Provisional' – in other words, capable of being shuffled and cut until something like the right mixture was reached, and when that happened the brigade was made 'Permanent', in 1934.

At the same time, and also as a result of the 1927–28 experiments, a new manual was written, called *Mechanised and Armoured Formations* which, having a mauve cover, soon became known in the Army as the 'Purple Primer'. This laid down doctrines of employment at brigade level, but, probably so as not to antagonise the rest of the army, it was careful to include roles for cavalry formations, lorried infantry and mechanised artillery in support. The concept of the armoured division was mentioned but not stressed, while such matters as command and communication received their share of attention. While this document was being studied by the British Army, it was soon to be studied elsewhere: Captain Baillie-Stuart, the notorious 'Officer in The Tower', sold a copy to the Germans, together with plans for the latest Vickers tank. He was discovered, arrested and later served a term of imprisonment. But in the meantime the German Army had translated the Purple Primer and it became required reading for the officers of the nascent armoured force.

In Germany the provisions of the Treaty of Versailles had proved to be a mixed blessing. On the one hand the Army was restricted to 4000 officers and 96 000 other ranks, no armour and no anti-aircraft guns, among other conditions. On the other hand, the Disarmament Commissions had sliced away all but a nominal strength of guns and other equipment so that whatever the army may or may not have had, it was certainly not over-burdened with a crammed arsenal of obsolescent gear which had to be used up come what may, a situation in which all the victorious armies found themselves.

It is customary to point to the writings of Fuller and Liddell Hart and imply that these were the foundations upon which the German Army built its philosophy of armoured warfare; and, as we have seen already, their writing were certainly studied with greater care in Germany than they received in the country of their origin. But the beginnings of the 'Blitzkrieg' lie further back than that, and it would be unjust to suggest that the German Army received its inspiration second-hand.

The doctrine of mobile war was already implanted when von Seeckt was appointed Commander-in-Chief of the Reichswehr in 1921. Seeckt was a trained Staff Officer – he had been Chief of Staff to von Lochow in 1914 and von Mackensen in 1915, and had planned the Austro-German breakthrough in Galicia in 1915 and the over-running of Serbia – and his vision of the future, in his own words, was of the 'employment of mobile armies, relatively small but of high quality and rendered distinctly more effective by the use of aircraft.' He now had the chance to form that sort of army, 'relatively small but of high quality', from the 100 000 men allowed to him, and he concentrated on an extremely high quality of training so that he finished up with a hundred thousand potential instructors, the majority trained to one or even two ranks above their actual status, and all ready to form the nucleus for expansion when the time arrived.

To obtain the degree of mobility he wanted, von Seeckt looked to the motor vehicle, and an 'Inspectorate of Motorised Troops' was set up under General Tschischwitz, briefed to study both the tactical use of motorised formations and also the logistic problems they brought in their wake – supply, maintenance, driver training, route-finding and so forth. In 1922 a Captain Heinz Guderian was attached to this Inspectorate, after a three-months attachment to a Motor Transport Battalion in Munich to allow him to learn something about the practicalities of motor vehicles. On arriving at the Inspectorate, Guderian found himself landed with a desk job, studying the logistics of transportation and after an initial protest he buckled down to it, mastered the deskwork, and then began to take more and more interest in motorisation and its possible effects upon tactics.

While all this was going forward, von Seeckt had persuaded his political chiefs to sign the Treaty of Rapallo with Soviet Russia. Ostensibly this was simply a matter of economic co-operation between two countries who had emerged from the war looking decidedly worn, but clandestine clauses in the agreement provided for co-operation in the development of military equipment. The Germans were prohibited from developing weaponry, and the Russians were quite willing to trade their facilities for German know-how, setting up tank and aviation schools which the Germans stocked with instructors and equipment and in which both German and Russian troops were to be trained.

As a result of this agreement, Krupp set up an 'Experimental Tractor Factory' at Rostov-on-Don which was more concerned with tank design than it ever was with agricultural implements, and an 'Arma-

A British Light Tank Mk IIIA during a training exercise in 1934

ments Development Company' was financed by the German Government and set up in business in Moscow to control the provision of German technicians and equipment to Russian research establishments. In 1927 a combined German-Soviet tank testing station and armour school was built at Kazan, 500 miles east of Moscow, and almost immediately secret German prototypes began to appear there for testing and evaluation.

With the materiel side of affairs under control, the tactical side now had to be dealt with, and Guderian, together with others of the same frame of mind, were active in their studies, developing ideas, writing papers for military journals, arguing, and seeking to convert the rest of the officers of the Reichswehr. Many of them needed little urging, since there were plenty who thought that the tank's appearance in France had weighed the scales against Germany. On the other hand, there were still plenty of reactionaries, and they became more obstructive than ever when it became clear that Guderian and his friends

were agitating for the total dissolution of the cavalry and its conversion to tanks and armoured cars.

But there is no doubt that this period of argument served to cut away the loosely constructed theories and faulty reasoning and refine the arguments into the best possible form. Guderian and his friends were trying to convert the four thousand officers of the Reichswehr, and these four thousand were the cream of the military talent of Germany – had they not been good, they would never have been in von Seeckt's army. And any attempt to lull these men with specious argument was doomed before it began, since their brains were keen enough to demolish a bad case when it was put before them.

In 1927 Guderian was assigned to the transport section of the General Staff, his task being to develop the mechanisation of lorried infantry. But in 1928 this section was enlarged by the addition of a tactical

Mk VIB light tanks on Salisbury Plain in the background are Vickers Mk II

Imperial War Museum

department charged with studying the employment of tanks and their co-operation with other arms of the service, and Guderian was appointed Head of Department. There was only one slight difficulty; the apostle of the tank had never actually been inside one in his life. This was attended to by an attachment to a Swedish tank battalion where he learned to drive tanks and had a concentrated course in their employment from the soldier's angle. The tank he trained on was the Swedish M-21, little more than a locally-made variation of the German LK-II, specimens of which had gone to Sweden at the end of the war together with a licence to build from Vollmer's designs. It was by no means the best tank available at the time, but it was sufficient to convince Guderian that he was working along the right lines, and it appears to have convinced him that the tank working on its own, or solely in conjunction with a small force of infantry, was wasting his effort. Nothing but tanks in company, and in mass, could be effective, he realised, and his arguments and teachings began to reflect this idea.

When the stolen copy of the 'Purple Primer' landed on his desk, then, Guderian found in it a message close to his own, and had the work translated and issued as the basic textbook for all officers of the motorised forces.

In 1929 the first German exercise with armoured formations took place, though the armour was, in fact, no more than a collection of light cars and trucks with canvas and wood additions to make them look like tanks. In spite of rude remarks from the foot soldiers, who poked their fingers through the canvas and their bayonets through the wood, to the embar-

rassment of the 'tank' crews, enough good came out of these exercises to warrant the setting up of plans for an armoured command and the authorisation of design studies for bigger and better tanks.

In 1933 Hitler came to power and von Fritsch was made Commander-in-Chief. His Chief of Staff was General Beck, and Beck saw little future in armour except strictly as an infantry assault weapon, so the urgings of the armour school made little impression on him. Hitler however, always avid for mechanical novelties, was in favour of the armoured division ideas put forward by Guderian, and in 1934 an 'Armoured Troops Command' was formed, headed by General Lutz (who had been Guderian's commanding officer in Munich in 1922 and

his commander in the Inspectorate of Motorised Troops in 1931). Lutz virtually gave Guderian his head, though some of his theories were stamped on by Beck, and in 1935 came the first of three Panzer Divisions.

In fact, they were not quite so revolutionary as might have been expected, insofar as they were more or less the same sort of mixture as found in other countries at that time. Each division was based on a tank brigade, together with a brigade of motorised infantry and with artillery support. This was practically the same as the French Army's 'Light Mechanised Division' (Division Légère Mechanique, or DLM) adopted in 1934, and similar to the British Tank Division which had been put together for the 1934 manoeuvres.

Below: A French Char FCM36 built in 1936. It had a crew of two and a 37-mm gun

Left: General Heinz Guderian mastermind of the German panzer divisions
Below left: American officers examine a Somua H35 captured in North Africa

Associated Press

But at least there were three of them, and they had the tanks: the tank brigade mustered 561 vehicles, including command tanks; the infantry component was a motorised regiment in trucks and a motor-cycle battalion; and the artillery was a motorised regiment of 24 10-mm howitzers and an anti-tank battalion of 37-mm guns. There was also a motorised engineer company and a reconnaissance battalion provided with armoured cars and motor-cycles. And it was this additional component, over and above the tanks, which made the Panzer Divisions what they were – balanced forces of all arms, capable of manoeuvre at high speed and capable of integrating the various capabilities of the components. The tanks provided the thrust, the artillery the support, and the infantry the basic fighting power. The engineers could deal with obstacles, while the reconnaissance element acted as the old-time cavalry screen and scouted for opposition, tested routes, by-passed problem areas and generally acted as the eyes and ears of the force. It was this degree of self-sufficiency which marked the Panzers apart from any other tank force then in being.

Since the French DLM was similarly composed, it might be argued that it was the fore-runner of the Panzer Division; this could be true as far as the date of formation goes, but no further. The DLM was the lineal descendent of the cavalry division, and its functions were defined as being solely concerned with reconnaissance and with screening the rest of the army from discovery. Its tank strength was well below that of the Panzer Division, with only 180 fighting tanks, plus 60 light tanks dispersed among the infantry companies, and it did not have the capability of fighting as a self-contained unit as did the German division.

The other country with a respectable tank strength at this time was, of course, the USSR. The tank, being forward-looking and technological, had caught the Soviet imagination; moreover, the Red Army were fairly certain that the tank, together with aviation and poison gas, was the key to future warfare. One line of reasoning was that since these weapons had come into their estate during the First World War, then there was no background of traditional development and long research, and the newly-born Soviet state could compete on equal grounds with every-

one else, since they were all at more or less the same level of competence and knowledge where these new weapons were concerned.

There was some degree of truth in this assumption, but the condition in which Soviet Russia found itself after the revolution and civil war was not the sort of industrial ambience in which to think about building tanks. Moreover, the employment of armour, which we have seen to be a bone of contention in better armies than was the Soviet at that time, was ill-suited to be a subject of discussion when the principal problem was defined as 'evolving a theory of proletarian revolutionary warfare', as if the principles of war were capable of manipulation to suit political dogma.

Due to the need to reconstruct the Soviet Army and get the country on to a reasonably sound footing first, it was not until the late 1920s that the Soviets began to make progress with armour. During the 1920s they had, as will be outlined in the next chapter, done some small amount of study into tank design, but it was of little consequence. But in 1928 the First Five Year Plan was announced, the main accent being on the modernisation of the heavy industries needed to produce armaments, and the

mechanisation of the army. The target of this Five Year Plan was that by 1934 the Army would have three mechanised brigades, 30 mixed tank battalions, four reserve heavy tank battalions, 13 mechanised cavalry regiments with tanks and armoured cars, and an armoured car company in each infantry division, a total of roughly 3500 combat vehicles.

In 1928, when the plan was announced, the Army's tank strength was about 100 machines, almost all of which were either wartime left-overs, foreign-bought machines, or Russian copies of foreign designs built simply as prestige exercises to show that the Soviets were capable of making tanks. Now the designers began to take a closer look at what was currently happening in the tank world and began to draw up designs of their own.

By 1930 the Soviets began to suspect that they were not getting full value from the German-Russian set-up at Kazan – and they were right, since the Germans carefully avoided sending their best ideas there. Acting on these suspicions, the Russians set up another test facility of their own, without telling the Germans, at Voronezh, and it was here that their development

Above: A civilian car with canvas and wood 'armour' – one of the dummy tanks used by the *Reichswehr*. Though these tanks were the object of ridicule by the infantry with whom they were cooperating in joint exercises, their use laid the ground for the successful tank/infantry campaigns of 1939 to 1942

Left: A French AMR-33 (Renault VM) light tank which first appeared in 1938. This two man tank had steel die stamped tracks of the Carden Loyd system

work was carried out, just sufficient low-grade work being sent to Kazan to keep the occupants busy and convince the Germans that they knew what was going on in Russian tank circles. But Kazan was finally closed down in 1934 after Hitler came into power; he wanted no part of any deals with the Soviets, and in spite of the army's protests he ordered the whole affair to be wound up as soon as possible and the German instructors brought back.

This gave the Russians a clear run to go ahead and develop their own ideas without the feeling that their shoulders were being looked over. In the matter of tank distribution and the type of formations to be adopted there were two schools of thought. The first adhered more or less to the French and American idea of tying the tank to the infantry, while the other was more in favour of adopting some of Fuller's 'all-tank army' ideas and using tanks as independent forces. Other armies had to settle for one idea or the other, or, at best, achieve some sort of compromise. But the Soviets, thanks to their Five Year Plan, were to be provided with sufficient tanks to allow both systems to be tried side by side. The infantry supporters were placated by allocating a tank battalion to each infantry division, with additional tank brigades under the direct hand of each army headquarters, solely for infantry support; while the all-tank promoters were given independent tank brigades to which a small proportion of mechanised infantry were grafted.

Once these independent brigades had been formed and trained, the next move was to increase their strength and build up larger formations, mechanised corps consisting of two or three brigades, a motorised infantry brigade and a motorised artillery group. By 1933 the Soviet Army had almost 7000 tanks, ranging from two-man 'Tankettes' to 50-tonners.

The next stage in the Army's development was the Second Five-Year Plan of 1933–38; the first Plan had prepared the heavy industry foundation and had begun to mechanise the army. The next stage would be to complete the mechanisation and bring in the next generation of armour.

Automobile and truck factories were expanded, and by the end of the five-year period there were over 30 factories producing trucks, tanks and self-propelled guns.

One minor difficulty was the provision of drivers for all these vehicles; trained drivers were scarce among the annual intake of conscripts, and a massive instructional programme had to be launched. It was aided by the activities of OSOAVIAKHIM ('The Association of Societies for the Promotion of Defence and Aero-Chemical Development'), a para-military training and youth organisation which gave basic pre-military training to the young before their induction into military service. By 1936

OSOAVIAKHIM had trained over a million drivers for the army, thus helping to remove what could have been a serious bottleneck in the expansion of mechanisation.

In 1936 the Spanish Civil War broke out, and the clash of ideologies was assisted by military aid from the totalitarian states, Germany, Italy and Soviet Russia. This was not entirely a matter of altruistic support: it also offered a supreme opportunity to test the latest weapons in actual combat and to provide, by means of 'volunteers', some

Above: A Soviet T26 light tank. This was a copy of the Vickers-Armstrong six ton tank. It had a crew of three and one 37-mm gun.
Below: A PzKpfw I Ausf A in Catalonia in 1938 during the Spanish Civil War. The Ausf A was armed with two 7.92-mm machine-guns and had a crew of two

MOI

live training for their troops. The German and Italian contingents supported Franco's Nationalist cause, while the Russians joined in on the Republican side. The exact numbers of tanks sent by the various factions are not precisely known but it seems likely that the Soviet contribution might have been as many as 700 tanks and armoured cars, together with the crews to man them and some generals to control them. The Germans sent a number of their Panzer I (Panzerkampfwagen I, or armoured fighting vehicle mark I) tanks, while the Italians sent light tanks and machine-gun carriers, all of which were to be graced with the name 'tank' in the newspaper reports.

Equally, it is difficult to assess the degree of effect that the armour had upon the actual conflict, largely because most of the writing about the Civil War is more concerned with political argument than with precise military assessment. The Republican tank force was commanded by General Pavlov of the Soviet Army, ostensibly an 'adviser', while the Nationalist force was under the hand of General Ritter von Thoma of the German Army, and the first force to indulge in a major action was that of Pavlov's when some 50 tanks went into a headlong confrontation with a force of Nationalist cavalry in October 1936. The horsemen were, of course, cut down fairly rapidly, but the tanks, in their enthusiasm, rushed ahead of the infantry they were supposed to be supporting and left them to be cut up in their turn.

In January 1937 the German tanks had their first major outing and broke through the opposing lines in fine style, similarly outstripping their infantry. More difficult to swallow was the appearance of anti-tank guns on the Republican side, and these played havoc with the relatively thin armour of the Panzers. Moreover, what the Republican tank force lacked in tactical ability was soon made up for by the speed of the riposte which Pavlov organised, an armoured counter-attack which stopped the Panzers in their tracks.

In March came the chance for the Italian armour to show its paces, in the Guadalajara sector. Some 300 light tanks, carriers and armoured cars breached the Republican lines but were then put off their stroke by

Right: A US Combat Car T5, one of a range of light tanks developed in the United States between the wars

Top: A Soviet BT 5V commander's tank with its distinctive frame radio antenna around the turret
Above: A Soviet T 28B rumbles through Red Square during a pre-war May Day parade

Right: A PzKpfw I. This light tank was used in the campaigns in Poland and France though its armour and armament were obsolescent by 1940

Below: A US T3 light tank with its efficient Christie suspension

two days of heavy rain which bogged them down and denied them air support. The Republicans countered by pulling in reinforcements from other sectors of the front and, aided by a tank counter-attack by Pavlov's force, the Italians were routed. The rout might have been even worse had not the Soviet tanks again left their infantry far behind and then compounded the mischief by outrunning their fuel supplies and thus bringing their pursuit of the Italians to a halt somewhere short of complete victory.

The Spanish Civil War was the graveyard of a good many military theories – notably those tied to political theses – but to balance this it was the birthplace of a good many more, most of which, as time went by, were exposed as worthless. In Britain, in later years, membership of an International Brigade carried a cachet out of all proportion to its worth and several individuals made a minor industry out of peddling Civil War tactics to the British Army and Home Guard in 1940–41. This, though, was relatively harmless when compared to the false lessons taken home by the 'advisers' from Russia, Italy and Germany in 1938–9.

General Pavlov returned to Russia convinced that tanks could only achieve anything when they were working in close co-operation with infantry, basing this assumption on the poor showing of his own force once they had outrun their infantry groups. This idea, in its turn, led to a wholesale reorganisation of the Soviet armoured force and, eventually, to Pavlov being put against a wall when his theories were proved wrong.

The German advisers pushed the same argument, but they were resisted furiously by Guderian who argued that false lessons were being read into the Spanish experiences and that the scale of tanks involved there could not begin to prove his points about Panzer Divisions. Von Thoma was less dogmatic, though he gave Guderian some anxious moments when, for example,

he argued against the widespread use of radio for controlling armour.

The Italians at least learned that light tanks were useless, though this seems to have escaped the Germans and Russians who both continued to produce lightweight vehicles. The British and Americans, who kept well clear of the war, appear to have learned very little from it, so that at least they had the benefit of not being affected by the wrong lessons.

Indeed, it seemed that the Americans had spent the 1920s and most of the 1930s in a sort of vacuum, learning very little from anybody or anything. Their Secretary of War, Dwight Davis, had attended the 1927 manoeuvres in England and had seen the Experimental Armoured Force in action, and he had then returned to the USA fired with enthusiasm and had directed the formation of a similar force in the US Army. A force was assembled in July 1928 at Camp Meade, Maryland, consisting of elements from all arms supported by infantry tanks, but a shortage of money soon put an end to the experiment, and in less than three months from its inception the force was disbanded. However, the Chief of Staff of the Army was sufficiently impressed by the reports of the War Department Mechanization Board, who had witnessed the experiment, that in 1930 he directed the formation of a permanent mechanised force

at Fort Eustis, Virginia.

Unfortunately, his successor, General Douglas MacArthur, was not of the same opinion. He felt that mechanisation should be pursued throughout the army and not confined to a corps d'elite, and the 'permanent' force was dispersed in 1931, with a parting shot by MacArthur to the effect that no separate tank corps would be formed in the foreseeable future. However, MacArthur's policy of dispersal had the effect of forcing mechanisation on to the cavalry at a rather faster speed than the old guard liked, and in 1933 the 1st US Cavalry Division arrived in Fort Knox, Kentucky, to hand over its horses and become a completely mechanised force. Due to the phrasing of the old National Defense Act the cavalry could not possibly own tanks, since, by the Act, tanks were reserved to infantry. So the cavalry had 'combat cars'. They may have looked like tanks, sounded like tanks and worked like tanks, but the nomenclature lists of the Army described them as 'combat cars', so the cavalry could safely own them. And so with the cavalry performing cavalry manoeuvres in their combat cars, and the infantry walking alongside their tanks as if 1918 were only yesterday, the US Army had arrived in the middle 1930s with some sort of an armoured force; and it stayed like that for the rest of the decade.

BETWEEN THE WARS 11

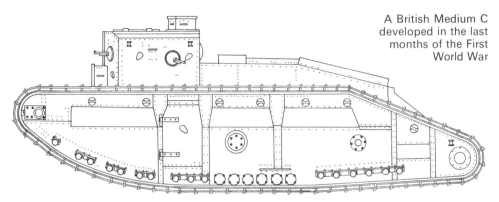

A British Medium C developed in the last months of the First World War

After the Armistice of 1918, with the transition from war to peace, one of the first things to suffer was the tank construction programme; contracts were pared to the bone and vast quantities of material sent to the scrap pile.

At the end of the war the British Army were developing two new models, the Medium C and the Medium D. The Medium C was to be the ideal medium tank, 19½ tons in weight, 25 ft 10 in long and with the familiar rhomboidal unsprung track layout. The principal change was that it mounted a single 6-pdr in a turret which was fixed on top of the hull. Known as the 'Hornet', no less than 6000 were ordered shortly before the Armistice, but the order was cancelled in December 1918 and only 36 were ever made.

The Medium D had been conceived, in accordance with the requirements for 'Plan 1919', as a fast tank which could manoeuvre around the flanks of a position and rapidly move along the lines of communication, and the principal requirement was simply that it should be able to reach a speed of 20 mph; if it could do that, little else mattered. The design of the Medium D was by a Lt Col P Johnson, who was on the engineering staff of the Tank Corps. In 1919 he was given the task of organising an official Tank Design Department, and it was in this department that he completed the work on the Medium D.

The Medium D broke new ground in many ways. The track supports were low, not the overall track of the wartime tanks, and the outline was peculiarly wedge-shaped, higher at the back than at the front, The tracks were of an unusual pattern which Johnson called the 'snake', separate plate shoes held on a wire-rope support, so that the plates were articulated laterally. Suspension was sprung by a system employing a steel cable around the track rollers anchored to a heavy coil-spring at one end. A fixed turret at the front of the hull was intended to carry either a 6-pdr or three machine-guns (the idea of 'male' and 'female' tanks still lingered) but, in fact, no armament was ever fitted. Power was delivered by an Armstrong-Siddeley 'Puma' engine of 250 hp, driving via a planetary transmission, and on test it attained a speed of 28 mph, which was quite remarkable for that time.

At this period Colonel J F C Fuller was responsible for initiating design policy in the Tank Corps, and he now asked Johnson to turn the Medium D into an amphibious vehicle. This became the 'Medium D Modi-fied'. It was slightly larger and heavier than the original, but of the same general form, and according to some reports sank on its maiden voyage in the Thames. It was rescued, however, and whatever defect had caused the sinking must have been cured, since it later took part in a number of trials and demonstrations.

At the same time as the Medium D was being perfected, work began on a second design, the 'Light Infantry Tank'. This was much the same shape as the Medium D but weighed only 17½ tons and was powered by a 100-hp Hall & Scott aeroplane engine to give it a top speed of over 30 mph.

Development also progressed on a 'Light Tropical Tank' intended for use overseas. This was a much smaller vehicle with a box-like superstructure and two small turrets, side-by-side, each mounting a machine-gun. Powered by a 45-hp engine it could reach 15 mph.

In pre-war years the weapons of the British Army were produced under a system of competitive tendering. If a new gun was required, a specification would be drawn up and sent to all the commercial gun-makers and to the Government facilities. Each then produced their own design, which was forwarded to the War Office for examination, and the best design was selected for production. In one or two cases individual design features from different factories were combined. Once the design was settled on, all the gunmakers, including the Government arsenals, were contracted for manufacture. In this way the War Office got the best available talent working for it, the commercial companies competed, and a healthy engineering industry was maintained, a policy which paid off with the start of the First World War.

The same policy was now applied to tanks; admittedly, only Government establishments had so far produced a tank, but it was an infant weapon and there would be room for ideas. Consequently, when the Tank Design Department was given the specification for the Light Infantry Tank, the same specification went to Vickers, a company well known in the gunmaking field and one which expressed interest in this new type of weapon.

Vickers produced their answer in 1921, the 'Vickers No 1' which had a rhomboidal track outline resembling the early tanks

A Vickers Light Infantry Tank, or No. 1 Tank developed in 1921

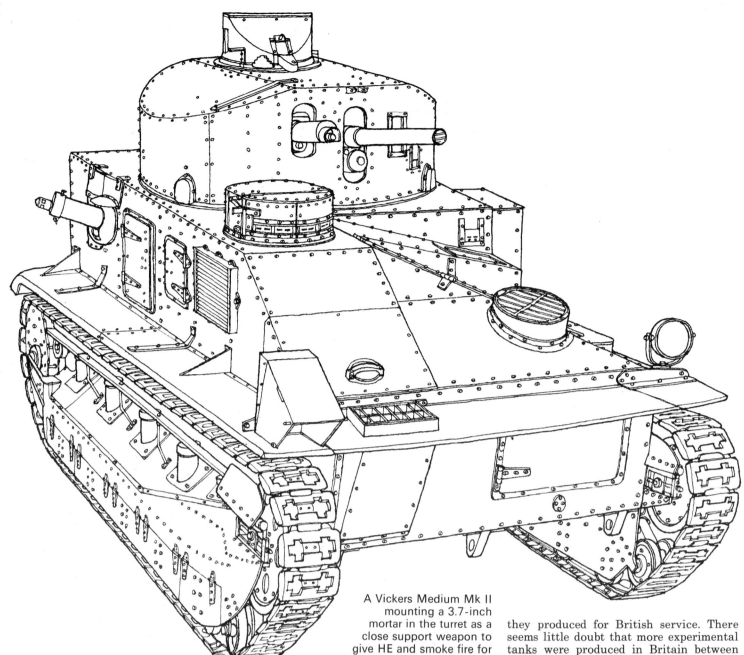

A Vickers Medium Mk II mounting a 3.7-inch mortar in the turret as a close support weapon to give HE and smoke fire for attacking infantry

but carried a revolving turret on top, a turret with a hemispherical outline and a small commander's cupola on top. Armament was either three Hotchkiss machine-guns or one 3-pdr gun and three Hotchkiss, plus an anti-aircraft machine-gun in the cupola. Powered by an 86-hp engine it could make 15 mph and carried a five-man crew.

Trials of the Light Infantry Tank and the Vickers design showed that they both suffered from mechanical troubles. The Tank Design Department was still designing tanks to the wartime standard; working on the principle that provided it would go into action and stay functioning for about 100 combat miles, that was sufficient and it could fall to pieces thereafter. This attitude was, of course, precisely the opposite of the Treasury Department's views on military equipment, which was that it should last for ever, cost nothing for maintenance, and run on fresh air. But the TDD had gone a little too far and the Light Infantry Tank persisted in breaking down during its trials. The Vickers model also gave trouble, due largely to being fitted with an unreliable pattern of hydraulic transmission. Nevertheless, Vickers were

given a development contract. And in 1923, as an economy measure, the Tank Design Department was closed down, killing any further development of the Medium D or the Light Infantry Tank.

In 1924 the result of the Vickers contract appeared as the 'Light Tank Mk 1', an 11½-ton vehicle with a crew of five, powered by a 90-hp Armstrong-Siddeley air-cooled engine to give a speed of 15 mph. It had low-set tracks, a fully revolving turret carrying a 3-pdr gun, spring suspension, four machine-guns in the turret and two more in the hull. Its layout was, in fact, not as good as the first Vickers design, and the problems of trying to operate all the armament must have been trying, but it had the virtue of being reliable and fast and inexpensive enough to equip all the remaining four battalions of the Royal Tank Corps. And so the Vickers became the backbone of Britain's tank force for the next two decades.

This is not to say that, with the Vickers in service, everybody switched off; far from it. Vickers themselves, in order to keep their design and construction force in being, went into the export business and designed a number of tanks quite apart from those

they produced for British service. There seems little doubt that more experimental tanks were produced in Britain between the wars than were produced anywhere else in the world, and although few of them ever got past the prototype stage, they proved to be invaluable as test beds for new ideas on suspension, motive power, transmission, communication and every other possible aspect of tank design.

One of the most famous of these experimental vehicles, and probably the one with the greatest influence outside Britain, was the Vickers Independent Tank of 1925. This was actually designed around a specification laid down by the British Army, but too much should not be read into that fact. The Army frequently put up specifications not because they thought that they would ever have the money to equip with them, but simply to keep abreast of new ideas, keep designers on their toes and keep the craft of tank building alive. It was to the credit of the various commercial firms involved that they were willing to spend time and effort on these specifications, in the knowledge that nothing beyond a pilot model was ever likely to be ordered.

The 'Independent' took its name not, as is often thought, because Vickers concocted it themselves, but from the role in which it was cast – that of operating independently of the infantry. To do this the Independent required firepower, speed and protection in good measure, and, by 20's standards, it was equipped with them. Weighing 31½ tons and 25½ feet long, it had a long track base, with the hull slung between and built up above the tracks and no less than five revolving turrets. At the front were two machine-gun turrets, with the driver's vision cupola between. The main turret, mounted a 3-pdr gun and had an offset commander's cupola. There were also two more machine-gun turrets covering the rear quarters of the tank. It required an eight-man crew to operate, and the commander was in voice communication with all his men by an intercommunication system known as the 'Laryngophone', since the microphones were clipped over the wearer's throat instead of being in front of his mouth, a system which cut out the background noise. Another innovation was a complex fire-control system whereby the commander could signal the position of targets to each turret. In truth, the Independent was a hangover from the 'land battleship' days, and the task of trying to control it in battle would have been a difficult one – as several nations, who tried such tanks, found out. Perhaps the financial stringency of the times was, for once, working in the army's favour when it prevented the manufacture of more Independents.

Although the Vickers military design was called a 'light tank', it was really a medium, and something lighter and more nimble was still required. Finance was the stumbling block, and eventually a British officer, Major G le Q Martel undertook to build a prototype at his own expense. This he did, in his own garage, using trade components, the engine coming from an elderly Maxwell car and the rear axle from a Ford truck. It had a short track assembly and a trailing wheeled axle for steering, similar to those used by the Mark I tanks in 1916. The body of the prototype was of wood and was no larger than was needed to contain the engine, controls and one man. Martel demonstrated his machine to the War Office in 1925 and, as a result, a contract was given to Morris Motors to make four pilot models, one of which was adapted to take a two-man crew, These were delivered in 1926 and tested, one result of which was to drop the whole idea of one-man tanks, since it was out of the question for one man to drive the tank and fire the machine-gun.

Eight two-man tanks were ordered and were used as scouting vehicles in the Experimental Mechanised Force.

The publicity surrounding the Martel design led other people to try their hand, and two men named Carden and Loyd designed a small tracked 'One Man Tankette'. This was little more than an open-topped steel box with tracks, the occupant being exposed from his shoulders upwards, but the War Office was sufficiently interested to order a number of prototypes of varying design as Carden and Loyd developed their ideas. They eventually moved to a two-man design, lower and wider, and a number of these were bought and used in the Mechanised Force tests in 1928–29.

By this time, opinion had crystallised into two distinct views on light armoured vehicles. One was that there should be a light turreted tank for the Tank Corps, and the other that there should be a light, tracked, 'carrier' for the infantry to allow them to keep up with the tanks. Both ideas had merit, and as a result development of light armour in Britain was to follow two paths, one for tanks and the other for machine-gun carriers. The result of the latter was, of course, the ubiquitous 'Bren Gun Carrier', introduced in 1938.

In 1928 the Carden-Loyd Tractor Company was bought out by Vickers and the design staff amalgamated. The development of the Carden-Loyd carriers continued, but at the same time Vickers began to develop a turreted light tank on the Carden-Loyd chassis and suspension. A number of light tanks were built and sold throughout the world, and in 1930 the 'Light Tank Mark 1' was accepted by the British Army. (One consequence of this was that the existing Vickers Light Tanks had to be rapidly renamed the 'Medium Mark 1' to avoid confusion.) These weighed just under five tons, had a two-man crew, were armed with a single machine-gun in the revolving turret, and could reach 30 mph.

Four Mark 1s were built, all differing slightly since they were still only pilots, and the design was then changed to the

Mark 1A, with better sloped armour and other smaller changes. Again, these models exhibited differences as various ideas were tried out; one, for example, mounted two machine-guns in the turret, one .50 Vickers with a .303 Vickers above it, a peculiar arrangement never duplicated elsewhere.

Eventually the design seemed to settle, and production of a quantity sufficient to begin issues to the service battalions was authorised. In 1931, 50 tanks, to be called the Mark 2, were authorised, 29 to be built by the Royal Arsenal at Woolwich, and 21 by Vickers. There were small differences between the two, so the Vickers models became the Mark 2B and the Woolwich design the Mark 2A. Subsequent improvements were made to the basic design, such as the adoption of a two-man turret with two machine-guns, and the Mark number was gradually advanced until, at the outbreak of war, the Mark 6 was in service.

The only defect was that they were being asked to do too much. Their principal attraction was that they were cheap and reasonably reliable, but adding radio, heavier machine-guns, more armour, extra fuel tanks and all sorts of other impedimenta gradually over-burdened them. In the search for economy, the Vickers Carden-Loyd virtually became the prime tank of the Tank Corps, a role for which it was not suited.

In France the production of tanks was also brought to a sudden end at the Armistice and the French Army found itself in possession of some 3000 Renault two-man tanks and very little else, the earlier designs by St Chamond and Schneider having almost all succumbed to combat or old age. However the construction programme for the Char C2, the projected heavy tank, was allowed to be completed and eventually ten were built.

The programme had run very slowly on this design, one hold-up being the development of a suitable engine. The end of the war, however, enabled the French to obtain a number of German Mercedes airship engines as reparations, and two of these

A Vickers experiment with track and wheel mobility. Over roads and easy going the wheels could be lowered to give greater speed and endurance, but in action or on rough going the tank would travel on its tracks

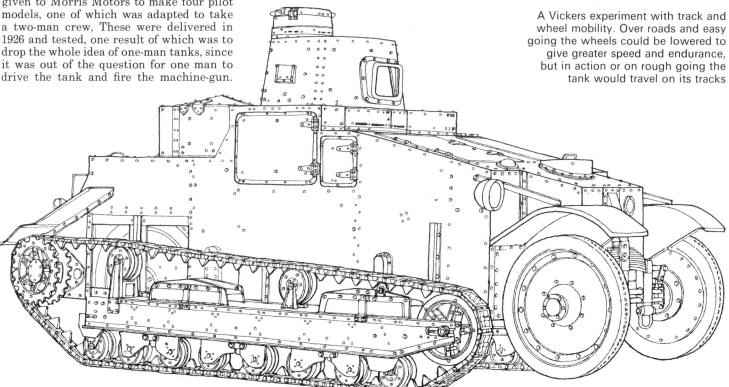

Above: A Carden-Loyd Mark VI .303 Vickers machine-gun carrier, with enclosed head-covers, designed for export. The gun could be fired from the carrier or inshipped and mounted on its tripod

Below: Universal Carriers career across a training area in Britain. The vehicle in the foreground mounts a Bren LMG, while the one in the background has a Boys Mk I anti-tank rifle

were fitted to the first tanks to be completed. These were only 180 hp each, which were not ideal for moving 68 tons, and later models were equipped with two Mercedes 250-hp engines which improved the performance.

In some respects the Char 2C resembled the 'Independent'. The track line was low and it carried two separate turrets, one at the front mounting a 75-mm gun, and one at the rear with an 8-mm machine-gun. In spite of its size the armour was only 45-mm thick and it could move at no more than 9 mph. The precise number made was kept secret for many years, and by skilled use of photographs the French gave the impression that they had a great many more than did in fact exist. One was converted in the late 1920s by fitting a 155-mm howitzer in the front turret. Again, astute propa-

ganda gave the impression that the French had a whole stable full of these 'Char 2C-bis' models and foreign observers credited the French Army with being much stronger in armour than it ever was.

Towards the end of the 1920s, though, the French Army decided it needed something to replace the ageing Renaults, and contracts were let for small numbers of light tanks. Renault had maintained their interest in this area by making improved models of their two-man tank for export, and they now produced their 'Type 33', which entered service as the 'Automitrailleuse de Reconnaissance Renault' (AMR). A 5-tonner capable of 40 mph, it carried a single machine-gun and a two-man crew and became standard equipment in cavalry regiments. It was followed by the AMR35, an improved design of which 200 were made.

While the AMRs were satisfactory for reconnaissance, something better was needed as a fighting tank, and Renault produced the AMC34 for this role. It was little more than a heavier version of the AMR series, with slightly thicker armour, less speed, and a 25-mm gun in the turret. It was not very good and was superseded in 1935 by the AMC35, which improved several details, such as suspension and tracks, and fitted a 47-mm gun into the turret.

The other French commercial maker to take an interest in tanks was the Hotchkiss Company who produced the 'Char Léger H-35' for use by French cavalry units. This used a cast turret and partly-cast hull, mounted a 37-mm gun and could achieve 17 mph. However, like every other French tank of the period it had a one-man turret, which placed a considerable strain on the

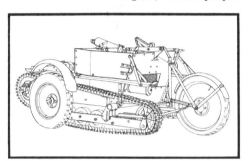
Wheel-cum-track Carden-Loyd Mk V Tankette of 1927

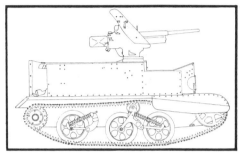
3.7-cm PAK mounted by the Germans on Bren Gun carriers captured at Dunkirk

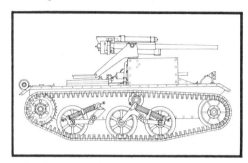
A 2-pdr mounted on a Carden-Loyd chassis an experimental design of 1935

occupant who had to command the tank, plan his tactics, operate the radio and fire the gun.

It will be remembered that the French had, like the Americans, drawn a sharp line between tanks for use by infantry and those for use by cavalry. The cavalry were now well attended to with their light tanks and it was then the turn of the infantry to be re-equipped. In 1929–30, in answer to a specification for a heavy infantry accompanying tank, three pilot models of the 'Char B' appeared. In some respects this was a throwback to 1917, with tracks which went around the hull profile, a 75-mm gun mounted in the front plate, alongside the driver, and a small command turret on top. Weighing 25 tons it carried a four-man crew and could move at 12½ mph with the wind behind it.

These three pilots were extensively tested and modified during the next few years and eventually a perfected design was approved. This went into production in 1935 as the 'Char B1'. It now weighed 30 tons, had 40-mm armour, a 47-mm turret gun and a 75-mm hull gun, and could manage a speed of 17 mph. Technically, it was one of the most advanced tanks of its day; the steering system was capable of fine control in order to aim the hull-mounted gun, while the transmission was extremely reliable. Maintenance was simplified by centralised lubrication and the track tension could be adjusted from inside the tank. But the turret still held only one man, while the rest of the crew were spread around in isolation and had to be highly trained.

After a few B1s had been made the design was modified to provide greater armour protection and a more powerful engine; this became the Char B1-bis, and the weight went up to 32 tons without any improvement in performance.

The last French tank of any importance to appear in these years was the SOMUA S35 medium tank, also destined for the cavalry. This was probably the best design of fighting tank of its period, with cast armour, a speed of 25 mph and a good 47-mm gun, but it was hampered by having only a three-man crew.

One of the reasons for the French being slow to produce tanks was that most of the available finance was being poured into the Maginot Line. On the far side of that barrier the German Army was also working on tank design.

Although the Versailles Treaty prevented any overt work being done on German armoured vehicles, there had been much activity under the surface. Design studies went on, and with the formation of the joint German-Soviet facilities, some chassis were put together clandestinely and shipped to Russia for testing. Krupp, Daimler-Benz and Rheinmetall were all given contracts to design new tanks of two basic types, a 20-ton medium and a 9-ton light. Altogether about ten of these were constructed and tested at Kazan in Russia, and as a result of this programme further specifications were drawn up and passed back to the manufacturers.

The outcome of these experiments was a new medium tank, the *Neubaufahrzeug* or 'New Model Vehicle', a 23-tonner with three turrets which appeared to have been influenced by the Vickers 'Independent'. A main turret carried a 75-mm gun, while two smaller turrets, one at the front and one at the rear, carried a machine-gun each. A 37-mm gun was also fitted co-axially with the 75-mm weapon in the main turret, giving a remarkable ability to choose either high-velocity anti-tank fire or low-velocity supporting fire. A modified model had 105-mm and 37-mm guns in the turret, mounted one above the other.

Five of these NbFz tanks were built and tested. They were kept well concealed from prying eyes and were first revealed during the war, when a carefully posed picture of one of these tanks in Norway led to a great deal of excitement among Allied intelligence staffs who had suddenly discovered a new German super-tank. In fact, they were scrapped the following year, being more or less worn out by that time.

The development of these medium tanks was taking more time than had been anticipated, and in order to have some tanks – any tanks – for training purposes, the German High Command decided to

equip with light tanks similar to the Carden-Loyd designs adopted in Britain. In 1933 orders were given for a 5-ton, two-man vehicle under the cover name of *Landwirtschaft Schlepper* or 'agricultural tractor'.

Various makers produced prototypes but the Krupp model was selected for production, becoming the *Panzer Kampfwagen I* (PzKpfw I). Weighing 5.4 tons, and with a crew of two, it had two machine-guns in its revolving turret and could travel at 25 mph. Primarily it was intended as a cheap and cheerful training vehicle, but in the event many of them were in service during the

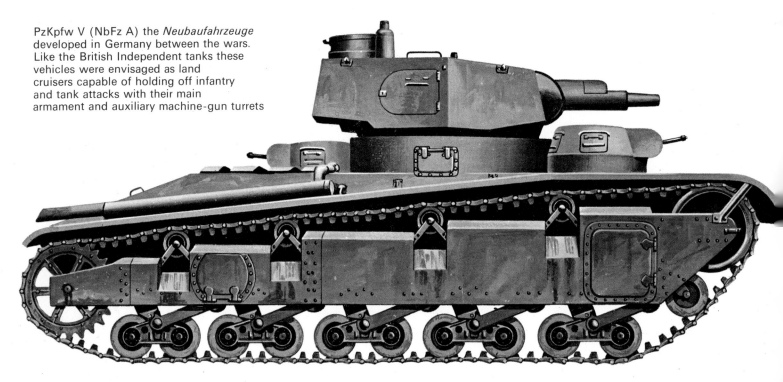

PzKpfw V (NbFz A) the *Neubaufahrzeuge* developed in Germany between the wars. Like the British Independent tanks these vehicles were envisaged as land cruisers capable of holding off infantry and tank attacks with their main armament and auxiliary machine-gun turrets

early part of the Second World War.

Having got the light tank under way, the High Command now issued a specification for a 10-tonner to carry a 20-mm gun in its turret. The Krupp company produced a scaled-up version of the PzKpfw I which was refused, and the contract went to the Maschinenfabrik Augsburg-Nürnberg (MAN), the result entering service as the PzKpfw II. This was to go through several minor changes before the design settled down. The first models had a suspension composed of three pairs of small wheels linked with an external balance beam, and about a hundred were built. Then in 1937

came the 'Ausfuhrung C' version (roughly translatable as 'Modification C') which changed the suspension to five large-diameter road wheels held by quarter-elliptic leaf springs. Two thousand of these were built and became the primary equipment of the newly-formed Panzer divisions.

Next in the programme was a 15-ton medium tank, for which a Daimler-Benz design was selected and which went into production as the PzKpfw III. Ten of the first production model were built in 1937, and it featured a 37-mm gun in the turret, a five-man crew, and a suspension very similar to that of the PzKpfw II, with five

Above: PzKpfw VI (NbFz B) mounting a 10.5-cm gun as its main armament it had a co-axial 3.7-cm and two auxiliary turrets with 7.92-mm machine-guns. Only two tanks were built and they were scrapped along with the model V in 1941

Below: The NbFz heavy tanks arrive in Oslo during the German invasion in April 1940. The Germans deployed all their NbFz tanks as a propaganda exercise and show of strength

PzKpfw II Ausf F, this was basically an Ausf C with spaced armour added against hollow charge anti-tank weapons

large road wheels. After trials, the design was changed to a form of suspension using eight small wheels with semi-elliptic springs above them and this became the standard for mass production, just over 400 being built in 1938–39. In later models the 37-mm gun was replaced by a short-barrelled 5-cm weapon.

The last of the series of tanks demanded by the High Command was a 20-tonner, cover-named the 'Batallion Leader's Vehicle'. Krupp, MAN and Rheinmetall-Borsig all made prototypes. The final production vehicle, which entered service in 1937 as the PzKpfw IV, was an amalgam of the best features of all three designs. It was destined to become the backbone of the Panzers, more of these (as improved versions) being produced than of any other tank in Germany. In spite of being designed to a 20-ton specification, it actually weighed only $17\frac{1}{2}$ tons in its original form, carried a short-barrelled 75-mm gun in the turret, had a five-man crew, and its 250-hp engine could move it along at just under 20 mph.

With production of these four basic vehicles under way, tank design in Germany more or less came to a standstill, a piece of complacency which they were to regret later.

If the British had the most experimental tanks and the Germans had the most ruthlessly logical and orderly production programme, there is no doubt that the Russians had more tanks in the hands of their troops in the 1930s than the rest of the world put together. The production of an armoured force was given high priority in Soviet Russia and in 1928 the First Five-Year Plan set, as its target, the provision of three mechanised brigades, 30 mixed tank battalions, four heavy reserve tank battalions, 13 mechanised cavalry regiments with tanks and armoured cars, and an armoured car

company in each infantry division. A grand total of about 3500 combat vehicles which were to be in service by the end of 1934.

When this grandiose plan was drawn up the Red Army had about 100 tanks and 50 armoured cars, most of which were left-overs from the war or which had been purchased from abroad. Initially more tanks were bought in, in small numbers, to enable the designers to see what other people were doing, though a number of Vickers tanks were also bought, in order to equip two battalions.

For the first two years the accent was on factory construction and equipping, but once this was done, in 1931, a 'Tank Programme Schedule' was drawn up, demanding the following:
1. Reconnaissance tanks. Light, fast, lightly armoured and armed, difficult to detect, and, if possible, amphibious.
2. Pursuit tanks. Weighing 12 to 15 tons,

PzKpfw II Ausf D. Armed with a 2.0-cm gun, this tank was similar to the E except the suspension was changed to four large suspension wheels sprung on torsion bars

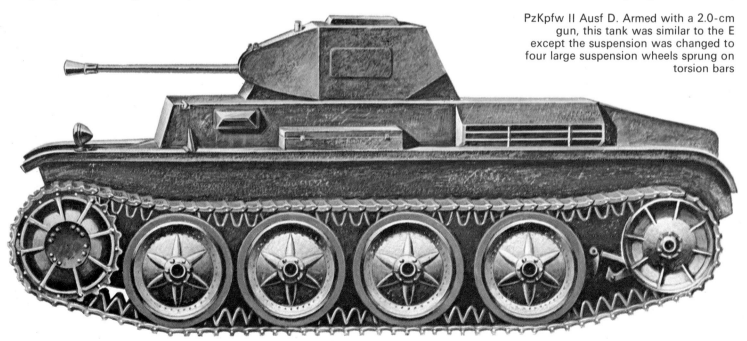

these were to be the battle tanks, capable of dealing with enemy armour, machine-guns and battlefield strongpoints. They were to be heavily armoured and carry powerful guns.

3. Breakthrough tanks. Heavy, powerfully armoured and armed, for dealing with fortifications and prepared defences.

4. Special-purpose tanks. Flame-throwers, bridge-carriers, smoke-screen layers, gas dispensers, minelayers, self-propelled guns, communication and command vehicles.

5. Armoured cars.

There were two lines of approach in Soviet tank design at this time; the first was to develop purely native ideas, while the second was to take what was best from foreign designs. The result of the first approach was uniformly disappointing. This line had begun by basing its ideas on the general layout of the Renault two-man FT design, of which numbers were in Russian service, and the first model was the MS-1, which took the Renault turret but rebuilt the hull to mount the engine transversely and give more room inside.

Over 900 of these were built, but they were, like the German PzKpfw I, principally for use as training vehicles and could hardly be called combat machines. This total includes later variations, the MS-2 and MS-3, which showed gradual improvement over the original design. The whole design was then given a thorough shaking to produce a larger version called the TS-12, a

Above: PzKpfw III Ausf B or C, only 15 of these tanks were built in 1937. They featured a new leaf spring suspension and a third machine-gun fired by the radio operator

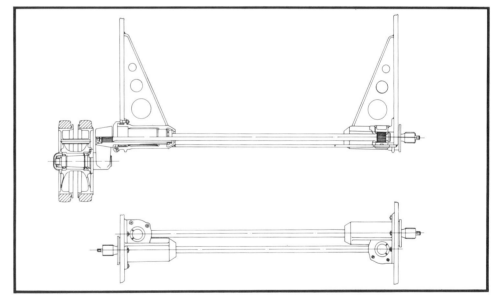

Above right: PzKpfw III Torsion Bar Suspension as fitted in Panzer IIs from the Ausf E onwards. It used the tensile strength of an anchored metal bar to float the vehicle's weight.
Right: The PzKpfw III Ausf E, the first mass-produced version of the Panzer III

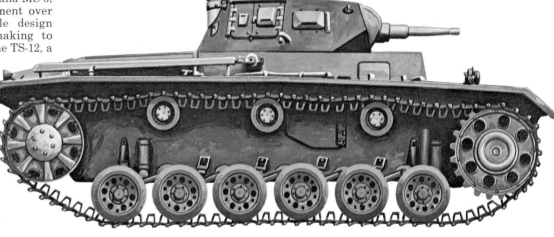

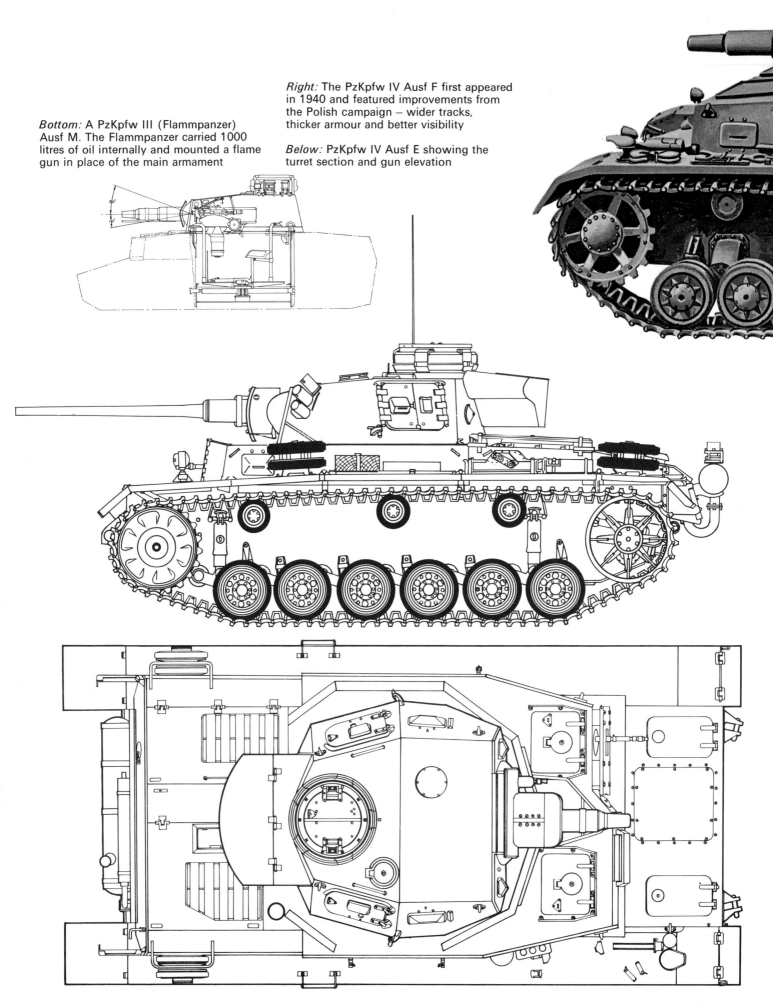

Bottom: A PzKpfw III (Flammpanzer) Ausf M. The Flammpanzer carried 1000 litres of oil internally and mounted a flame gun in place of the main armament

Right: The PzKpfw IV Ausf F first appeared in 1940 and featured improvements from the Polish campaign — wider tracks, thicker armour and better visibility

Below: PzKpfw IV Ausf E showing the turret section and gun elevation

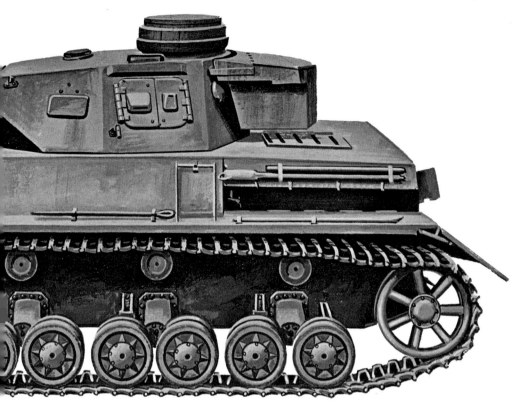

Below Far Left: PzKpfw IV Ausf E in a top plan view

Below: Front and rear views of the Ausf E. Though well designed by Western standards the mainstay of the *Panzerwaffe* lacked the sloped armour and fire power of the T-34. The Germans were forced to make up for this technical inferiority by the excellent quality of their tank crews

Bottom: The men of the *Panzerwaffe*, a crew of a PzKpfw IV Ausf E during operations in Russia

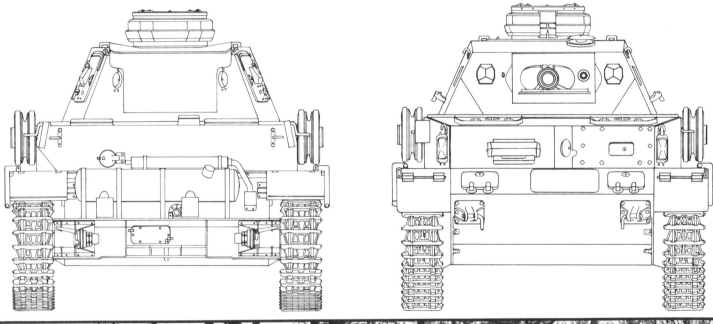

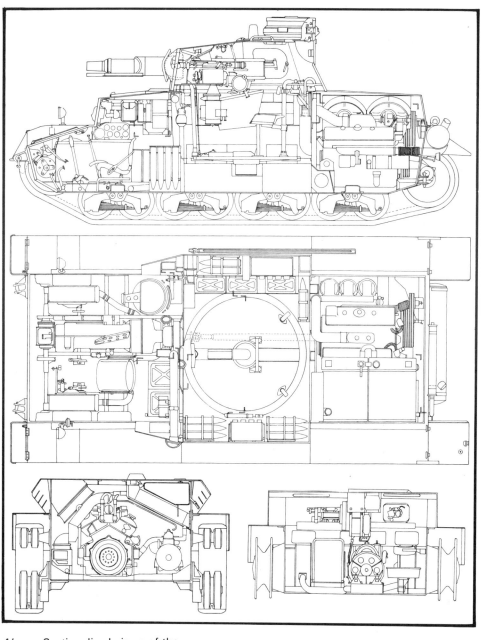

20-tonner armed with a 45-mm gun. One prototype was made, which was mechanically unreliable, and the designers moved on to make the T-24. This was a great improvement as far as armour and layout went, but it still suffered from mechanical troubles and no more than 25 were ever made. With the T-24 the 'native' line of development came to a halt for a while.

The principal foreign tanks purchased were the Vickers Medium, as used by the British Army, the Vickers 'Six Ton', a commercial design, the Vickers-Carden-Loyd tankette and also an amphibious model developed by Vickers, and a high-speed track-or-wheeled vehicle designed in the USA by Walter Christie. These formed the basis of the second line of approach to Soviet tank design.

The Vickers Medium was placed straight into Soviet service as the 'English Workman' and the Six-Ton became the T-26. No further work was done on the Medium, but the T-26 was subsequently built under license in Russia, with numerous modifications. The original Vickers product was the T-26A1; the T-26A2 was Russian-built, and identical but for the substitution of a Degtyaryov machine-gun for the Vickers gun in the turret. The T-26A3 changed the armament again, using a 12.7-mm Degtyaryov DK machine-gun in one of the two turrets; the T-26A4 replaced the 12.7-mm with a 27-mm quick-firer, and the T-26A5 changed that to a 37-mm gun.

The Carden-Loyd tankette was built under licence as the T-27 and over 4000 of these were eventually built before production ended in 1941. Although found to be of little use as combat tanks, they were extensively employed as reconnaissance vehicles and as towing vehicles for anti-tank and light artillery.

One of the most interesting developments was that based on the Carden-Loyd amphibious tankette. This had been developed by Vickers in the hope of interesting the British Army, and the handful which were taken by Britain were given the designation A4E11. But there was no money in Britain for such luxuries, and Vickers turned to the export market.

Above: Sectionalised views of the PzKpfw IV Ausf D including views through the engine and driving compartment

Below: PzKpfw IV Ausf D was first produced in 1938 and was similar to the A, B and C models, though it had an improved commander's cupola and bow machine-gun position

The Russians could see plenty of scope
for such a vehicle in Eastern Europe, where
rivers were more common than roads, and
took to the idea with alacrity. With heavier
suspension it became the T-37, the original
balsa-wood-filled side floats being abandoned. Weighing 3.5 tons, with a two-man
crew and armed with a single machine-gun
it was lightly armoured but fast, it was
steered by a moveable rear propeller in
water and could reach a speed of 27 mph
on land and 3.5 mph in water.

Finally came the American Christie tank,
purchased from the USA in 1931. This was
designed to be fast, a lightly-armoured 10-
tonner which could have its tracks quickly
removed to run at 60 mph on its rubber-
tyred road wheels or, with tracks on, could
speed across country at 40 mph. To achieve
this performance it was driven by a 350-hp
Liberty aero-engine. This design was copied
more or less as it stood, the only Soviet
change being a new turret with a 37-mm
gun and a machine-gun. This became the
BT-2, BT standing for *Bystrochodny
Tankovii* or 'Fast Tank', and it was certainly that.

Development continued, and the BT-3
was armed with a 45-mm gun, while the
BT-4 had two turrets side by side; neither
of these went into mass-production however,
and a major overhaul of the design resulted
in the BT-5. This, which became the major
production model, had an enlarged turret
with a 45-mm gun, a new 350-hp engine of
Russian design, and the suspension was
considerably modified and strengthened.

All the BT series had retained the Christie
form of track-or-wheel suspension, but the
Soviets now began to query the worth of

this complication. The original idea was
that when on wheels the vehicle could make
high speeds as an armoured car and could
also do the long approach marches to battle
which often wore out the tracks before
combat was joined. But improved designs
of track and suspension were now allowing
long distances to be covered on tracks and
at higher speeds, and there seemed little
point in removing the tracks before battle
and refitting them afterwards. The BT-7,
therefore, had the tracks permanently in
place. It also had the surfaces of the armour
on hull and turret sloped in order to deflect
shot, a notable innovation.

The next requirement was for a medium
tank in the 'Breakthrough' class, and here
the Vickers Medium was taken as the
starting point for the suspension, with
overtones from the 'Independent'. A cent-
rally-mounted main turret carried a 45-mm
gun in the prototype, changed to a 76-mm
gun in production. Two smaller turrets on
the front corners of the hull carried machine-
guns, though some of the production tanks
mounted a 45-mm gun in the right-hand
turret. Weighing 29 tons and with a crew
of six, this went into volume production as
the T-28.

The T-28 stressed firepower at the expense
of protection; its maximum armour was no
more than 30 mm. For the breakthrough
role, however, something more resistant to
enemy fire was needed, and the heavy T-32
tank was the last of the designs to come
from the First Five-Year Plan. This was
quite definitely inspired by the 'Independent', carrying five turrets. The main turret
mounted a 76-mm gun, the right front and
left rear turrets mounted 37-mm high-

velocity guns, and the left front and right
rear turrets carried machine-guns.

Weighing 45 tons and with a crew of ten
men, the T-32 fell short of its planned
specification in armour thickness, since
adding armour would have taken it over
weight and completely ruined the performance. It was subsequently re-designed as
the T-35, having thicker armour and a more
powerful engine, but the greatest fault
which these vehicles displayed was that
the commander could not control the fire
of all five turrets, direct the driver, read
the map, think about tactics and answer
the radio all at once. Unfortunately this
defect did not make itself felt to any great
degree during training, and numbers of
these tanks survived to meet the Panzers
in 1941, when their shortcomings were
ruthlessly exposed.

The first post-Armistice tank to appear
in the USA was a private venture by J Walter
Christie, an automobile engineer who had
come into the armoured vehicle field by
way of an involvement with a wartime
design of self-propelled gun. Inspired by
this, he set about designing tracked vehicles
to his own specifications and was to become
the *enfant terrible* of tank design for the
next ten years or so.

His first tank was the M1919, built to his
specification by the Front Drive motor
company, and it was quite an advance on
anything that had been seen before. The
low hull was surmounted by a turret carrying a 57-mm gun, with a .30 machine-gun in
a rotating cupola on top. Suspension consisted of front and rear wheels and a two-
wheeled bogie in the middle of the track
run. For running on roads the tracks could

be removed and the central suspension unit raised from contact with the ground. Weight was 13.5 tons, it was driven by a 120-hp engine of Christie's own design, and with the tracks on it could move at 7 mph.

The army made some experiments with Christie's tank, and then sent it back to the makers to be rebuilt in accordance with the army's requirements. The 57-mm gun was moved to the front hull plate, the turret removed, and the driver and commander located in a fixed cupola in the centre of the chassis. The suspension was changed, two large wheels replacing the small ones of the original side units. The weight went up to 14 tons, but the speed also improved, to 15 mph, though the power unit was the same Christie engine. But like most of Christie's designs it seemed to spend more time in the workshop than it did out on the road, and the army lost interest in it.

Shortly after the Armistice the US War Department produced a policy document which proposed the development of two types of tank: a 23-ton tank capable of high speed, and a 15-tonner, this size being dictated by the capacity of the standard Divisional Engineer bridge of the time. It should perhaps be pointed out that this recommendation did not come, as has often been claimed, from the report of the Westerveldt Board; that board was solely concerned with artillery development and made no recommendation whatsoever about tanks. From the War Department's suggestion, the Chief of Tank Corps drew up specifications and passed them to Rock Island Arsenal, which had been designated as the future tank design establishment.

The first to appear was the Medium Tank M1921, a 23-tonner which, in general layout, resembled the British Medium D, having a low track line and a prominent turret set well forward and carrying a 57-mm gun. Armour was up to 1-in thick, and it was powered by a 250-hp marine engine to give it a speed of 10 mph. It was followed by the M1922, which was even more like the Medium D, the track being distinctly higher at the rear and of the same 'floating shoe' flexible type pioneered by Col Johnson in Britain.

At about this time the War Department had a change of heart and decided that the 23-tonner was unnecessary, that the 15-tonner should be pursued more actively, and a small tank, about five tons in weight and capable of being carried to battle in a truck, should be developed. Rock Island obtained permission to continue working on the improvement of the M1922 and in 1925 they produced the Medium Tank T1, a reversion to the M1921 in general shape. In 1928 it was recommended for standardisation as the M1 but approval was rescinded and it remained in Rock Island as a test vehicle.

For reasons which are not entirely clear, the Ordnance Department now went outside Rock Island Arsenal and invited a commercial firm to develop the light tank. In 1927 J Cunningham Sons & Company produced their idea, the Light Tank T1. They had gone well over the weight limit, the vehicle weighing 7.5 US tons, but apart from that it was serviceable enough within the limitations laid down. The engine was in front, and a revolving turret high at the rear mounted a 37-mm gun and a machine-gun. Two men were carried, and driven by a V-8 Cunningham engine it could move at 20 mph. It was followed by a number of minor variants until 1931, when Rock Island took the reins again and drastically improved the whole design. The engine was shifted to the rear of the tank, the turret moved forward to a central position, the suspension completely altered and a more powerful engine installed. This became known as the Light Tank T1E4 and it was the starting point for the family of US light tanks which were to enter service.

Cunninghams were also given a development contract for the medium tank, the 15-tonner, and in 1930 they produced the T2. It appeared to have done some good to go outside the establishment, since Cunninghams produced a far better vehicle than the Ordnance Department's T1 and did it within the 15-ton weight limit. The T2 resembled Vickers practice, particularly in its tracks and suspension, and carried a 47-mm gun in the turret with an auxiliary 37-mm gun in the hull front plate. Armour was up to 1-in thickness, and with a 312-hp V-12 Liberty engine it could travel at 25 mph.

Following the development of the Cunningham T2 Walter Christie bounced back into the limelight with his M1928 tank. (He had spent the intervening years on amphibious tank designs.) This introduced what was to become known as the 'Christie Suspension', which consisted of large road wheels, which touched the tracks at top and bottom, carried on a suspension arm controlled by a long coil spring mounted vertically in the hull sides and allowing extremely large deflections of the wheels to conform with rough ground. As before, it could run on either tracks or wheels, and it was powered by a 338-hp V-12 Liberty engine to give it the

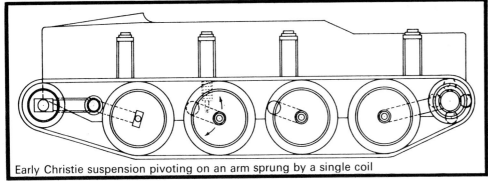
Early Christie suspension pivoting on an arm sprung by a single coil

phenomenal speed of 70 mph on wheels or 40 mph on tracks. Weighing 8½ tons, it was unarmed, though provided with a dummy gun in the front plate, and the armour was only ½-in thick.

Nevertheless the astonishing performance captivated all who saw it, and five were ordered by the Ordnance Department. Two were also ordered by the Russian Government and two by the Polish Army, and for Christie and his 'United States Wheel and Tracklayer Corporation' it looked as if things were going well. The machines ordered were produced in 1931; the Polish Government cancelled its order, and the US Army agreed to buy them instead, so the US Cavalry had four of them under the designation 'Combat Car T1' and the infantry had three as the 'Medium Tank T3'. The Russians, as we have seen, adopted their two as the BT-1 and used them as the basis of a whole new family of armour.

The delivered models were fitted with turrets and 37-mm guns (as tanks) or .50 Browning guns (as combat cars), and after some testing the Infantry Board asked for

another five, but with modifications. Unfortunately by this time Christie, who was a very prickly gentleman to deal with, had fallen out with the Ordnance Department over a matter of contractual terms, and so the Department by-passed him and gave the order for manufacture to the American La France company, more noted for making fire engines. It has been suggested that part of the Ordnance Department's disenchantment with Christie was due to their having paid him about $800 000 over 12 years and never received a machine that worked properly.

The La France Company produced the five tanks required, called the T3E2. Rock Island produced two more designs using Christie suspension, the T4 and T4E1, but in 1936 they dropped the idea completely and never picked it up again. While the Christie suspension was the best of its kind, it was also the most expensive, and in the financial climate of the Depression years, money counted more than cross-country performance.

While work had been going on with the

Christie designs, Rock Island had also been busy with the light tank series and for these they had developed a totally new type of suspension, the 'volute spring' type. The volute spring can be best likened to a coil of flat sheet steel which has had the centre pushed out so as to show a conical shape. The base of the coil is anchored against the tank's hull, while suspension arms attached to the bogie wheels press up against the conical end of the volute spring, so that the tension is placed across the width of the spring and it acts, effectively, as an extremely stiff coil spring. The advantage lies in that the length of a volute spring is considerably less than that of the equivalent power of coil spring and thus it can be fitted neatly into the bogie unit. It is undoubtedly one of the great, if unsung, inventions of the tank's history and Rock Island brought it to a pitch of perfection; so much so that, during the Second World War when money was relatively free, they preferred to stay with the volute spring than to start developing the Christie system again.

The tank which introduced this system was the Light T2E1; the T2 had been a re-hash of the old T1, with a suspension based on a Vickers design, but it introduced one notable innovation – the use of an air-cooled aeroplane engine. Rock Island had been searching for a powerful conventional water-cooled engine but could not find one suitable for their purpose; those that were powerful enough were too big, while those that were small enough hadn't the power. At last, somebody suggested using a Continental radial aeroplane engine; it could produce 260 hp, was air-cooled and so required no radiators or plumbing, was only 32-in long and weighed just over 1000 lb. The only problem was that it was 43-in high, which led to the rear deck of the tank having to be raised, but this was a minor drawback. Installed in the 9-ton T2 it drove it at 27 mph, which was just what was wanted.

Since the cavalry were not allowed to have tanks, the combat car had to be developed for their use, and this had been done in step with the light tank development. The only difference between the two was that in the early stages the combat car variants had fixed superstructures instead of turrets and carried a heavy machine-gun as main armament.

When the Light tank T2E1, which combined the radial engine idea with the volute

Far Left: A Soviet T-35 knocked out during fighting in 1941

Below and left: A captured T-35 showing the layout of the turrets and the armour thickness which have been painted on the hull and turret sides. The tank mounted a 76.2-mm gun and two 50-mm guns as main armament

RAC Tank Museum

RAC Tank Museum

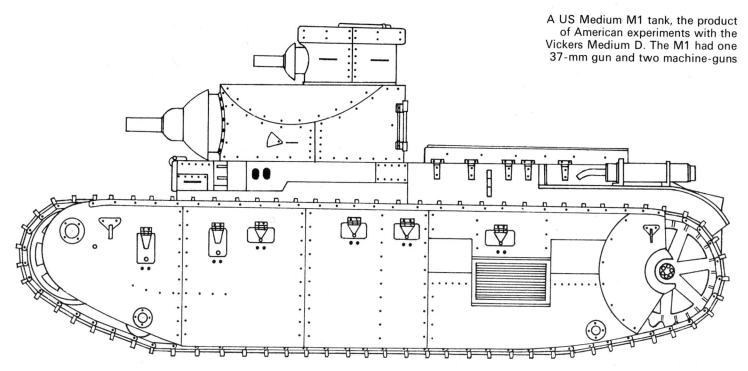

A US Medium M1 tank, the product of American experiments with the Vickers Medium D. The M1 had one 37-mm gun and two machine-guns

spring suspension, was produced, the Combat Car T5 came with it, using many of the same component parts. The principal difference was that it had two small side-by-side turrets mounting machine-guns. A variant of this, the T5E3, was fitted with a Guiberson diesel engine, in an endeavour to find out if diesel power held any advantages. At that time it didn't appear to, but the pioneer work done by Rock Island on diesels at that time was to come in useful during the Second World War.

During the 1930s one American commercial firm, the Marmon-Herrington company, went into the tank export business, producing a variety of two- and three-man tanks which were sold to China, the Dutch East Indies, Persia, Mexico and other countries. They were all light vehicles, using many commercial vehicle components. They were not fitted with turrets, all having fixed barbette-type superstructures, and were armed with nothing heavier than the .50 Browning machine-gun. Engines were usually six-cylinder Ford truck types, and the tanks weighed around five to seven tons. In 1937 the US Marine Corps, who were somewhat of a law unto themselves when it came to equipment procurement, bought some of these tanks, their object being to find a suitable vehicle for amphibious landings from ships.

J Walter Christie also continued to design tanks, even though he failed to raise any interest by the US Ordnance Department. In 1932 he produced a new model, very much like the M1931, which used a great deal of duralumin in its construction, weighed five tons and was propelled by a 750-hp Hispano-Suiza V-12 aero engine. Christie claimed a top speed of 60 mph on tracks and 120 mph on wheels.

In the following year he went even further out by adding wings and a tail unit to the tank; the theory was that with the tracks off it could reach a high enough speed to become airborne for short distances, hopping and gliding across the battlefield. Or, if that idea didn't appeal, it could be slung beneath an aircraft and then dropped, to glide to the ground, the drive being engaged just before touch-down. He failed to interest anybody in America, other

than the more sensational newspapers, with this idea, though the M1932 was bought by the Soviet Government.

Christie produced some more designs and in 1936 one was sold to Britain where it became the basis for the cruiser series of fast tanks. He then returned, during the war years, with a self-propelled gun and more ideas for airborne tanks, but none of them was ever taken seriously. While Christie produced some brilliant ideas, particularly on suspension and power-to-weight ratio, he was a grossly impractical man who never stopped to think of how his machines would function in combat. His designs never gave a moment's thought to the commander or the gunner. Moreover once an idea was built he wanted to move on; the practical aspect of getting his design into production form never interested him.

The only other country involved in major tank development in the 1920s and 1930s was Japan. They had obtained a small number of British Mark 5s and Renault two-man tanks after the Armistice, and after trying these out for a few years, in 1925 they decided to try their hands at designing a tank of their own. Osaka Arsenal was given the task of producing a medium tank, weighing about 22 tons and with a 70-mm gun as the main armament. Like so many others of the day it was heavily influenced by the Vickers 'Independent' and was to have a main turret and two subsidiary machine-gun turrets. The suspension was a highly complicated design which had no fewer than 19 bogie wheels on each side.

While Osaka were at their labours, the army decided to buy a few tanks from abroad in order to examine the state of the art. They purchased a number of Renault models, a Vickers Medium C which was specially designed for the Japanese, some Carden-Loyd tankettes and a Carden-Loyd amphibious tank. The Vickers became the origin for a fresh design effort, since the Osaka Arsenal had run into problems with their design. After several re-workings it finally emerged in 1932 as the Heavy Tank Type 92, weighing 18 tons and armed with a 37-mm gun in the main turret and

machine-guns in the front and rear subsidiary turrets. With a five-man crew it could attain a speed of 14 mph and had armour 15 mm thick

The Type 92, however, was not a success, and Osaka went back to try again, eventually coming up with the Type 95, which was much the same but weighed 24 tons, had a 70-mm gun as the main armament, a 37-mm gun in the front sub-turret, and a vastly simplified suspension system. Even though it was an improvement on what had gone before, it was never put into production.

With the Vickers to guide them, the Model 89A tank was now produced by the Mitsubishi Heavy Industries Company. It entered service in 1931, weighed 12.7 tons, carried a four-man crew, and was driven by a petrol engine at about 15 mph.

In 1931 the 'Manchurian Incident' began and the Japanese Army went to war, taking its few tanks with it. Experience in

The US Combat Car T-2 was essentially a reconnaissance vehicle with a top speed of 30 mph on wheels and 20 mph on tracks. Its comparatively low weight of eight tons was achieved by the use of aluminium in part of the design

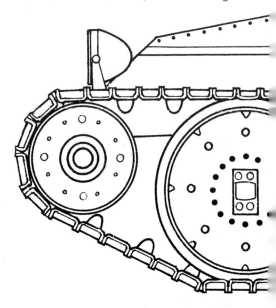

Manchuria seemed to show that tanks were most useful as individual supporters of infantry and, since their opponents had nothing which could stop even the poorest tank, the Japanese became very enthusiastic about light tanks and tankettes, their few Carden-Loyds having proved to be very useful. As a result the Osaka Arsenal now went over to producing a modified version of the Carden-Loyd, calling it the 'Type 92 Tankette', a three-man four-tonner which carried a machine-gun in a small turret and another machine-gun in the hull alongside the driver. After building a few of these the design was further simplified to a 2½-ton two-man model with a single machine-gun, the 'Type 94'.

One problem that the Manchurian campaign brought to light was that of operating motor vehicles in sub-zero temperatures, and in 1932 the Mitsubishi Company produced an air-cooled diesel engine suitable for tank use, a technical step far in advance of anyone else at that time. The engine was a six-cylinder model producing 114 hp, and it was fitted into the light tank 'Type 95' which went into quantity production in 1936.

The Type 95 was an advanced design and one of the best to come from Japan. Weighing 7½ tons, it had a three-man crew, a 37-mm gun in the turret, a machine-gun in the hull, and could travel at 25 mph. Its only defect was in the thickness of armour, a maximum of ½ in, and this was probably due to a combination of desire to keep the weight down and absence of any form of anti-tank weapon in the Chinese Army of the time. As a result the Japanese tank designers were prone to underestimate their opponents, which led to some painful

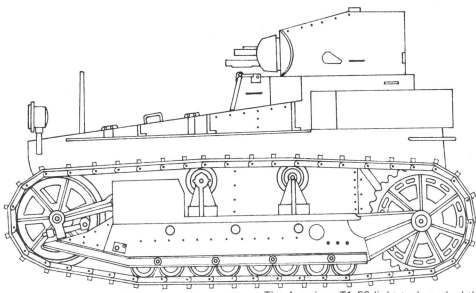

The American T1 E2 light tank marked the swing away from heavy vehicles to 'cavalry tanks' and an attempt to combine speed with a saving in the cost of each vehicle

encounters when, in later years, Japanese tanks met British or American ones, and to virtual annihilation when, in 1945, they were confronted with Soviet armour.

The diesel engine was now applied to the Type 89 tank to produce the 89B, and by the middle of 1936 tank production was running at about 400 vehicles a year. Finally, in 1937, came the 'Medium Type 97', probably the best Japanese design. This had better armour, of 25 mm thickness, and a two-man turret mounting a 57-mm gun. The engine was a 170-hp air-cooled diesel

which could move the 15-tonner at just over 25 mph. The worst feature was the gun which, though of respectable calibre, was in fact an obsolescent model of low velocity, and this fact was well appreciated by the Japanese Army who pressed on with a design of 47-mm high-velocity gun, though this modification was not completed until 1942.

It would be as well to explain the Japanese system of nomenclature; it will have been seen that the type number can be duplicated, and that there is, for example, a Type 92 Heavy Tank and a Type 92 Tankette. The Type number refers to the year, in the Japanese calendar, that the design was approved for service. Thus all Type 92 equipment appeared in 1932. In view of this it is not sufficient to refer to a Japanese tank as the 'Type 92' or 'Type 97', it must be qualified by saying whether it is a medium or heavy tank.

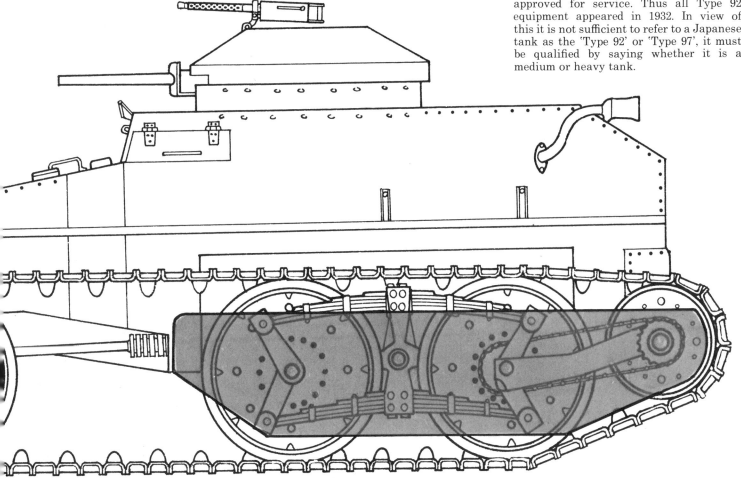

BLITZKRIEG
the Panzers strike

Of all the nations concerned with tank development, there was none which saw more activity in the latter half of the 1930s than Britain. This was largely due to the fact that in 1935 Britain did not really have a worth-while tank or even a design on the drawing boards, and the war clouds were beginning to gather.

In 1934 General Elles, who had been commander of the Tank Corps during the First World War, was appointed Master-General of the Ordnance, making him responsible for all the Army's equipment. After looking at the tank situation he set forth a demand for a new infantry tank which was, in many respects, a throw-back to 1917. Speed was of little importance, armour protection was to be all, and, in keeping with the spirit of the times, it was to be built down to a price and not up to a standard.

The result appeared in 1936, the Infantry Tank Mark 1, heavily armoured, with a maximum speed of 8 mph, a crew of two and a single machine-gun as armament. It weighed 11 tons and the suspension had a peculiar, spindly appearance which led Elles, when he saw it, to liken it to a contemporary cartoon character, 'Matilda the

Left: A PzKpfw III in the perfect tank country of northern France in the summer of 1940.
Below: Matilda II from the 7th Battalion of the British Royal Tank Regiment

Comical Duck'. The name stuck, and it became the Matilda tank.

In spite of its shortcomings, 139 were acquired and, if nothing else, it was a useful training tank. But as soon as trials had been conducted with it, it was obvious that it was not capable of serious action and a successor was required. Fortunately, at this time the threat of German rearmament had begun to make itself felt and the Treasury was prepared to disgorge money.

The Tank Design group at Woolwich Arsenal had prepared a design of infantry tank, leaning heavily on a design they had produced three or four years before. As time was pressing, the usual development process was abbreviated, and, like so many weapons in those years of 'Paper Rearmament' it was ordered into production straight from the drawings. Even so a result was not reached as quickly as had been hoped, since the 78-mm armoured hull was a casting, as was the turret, and castings of this magnitude were not a common manufacturing process at that time. So it was some time before production facilities could be set up and the war had begun before Matilda II got into service.

The Vickers Medium tanks were by now feeling their age, and in 1934 a new specification was set up for a replacement medium tank. This became known as the A9 and was designed by Vickers, entering service in 1938 as the 'Cruiser Tank Mark I'. It was

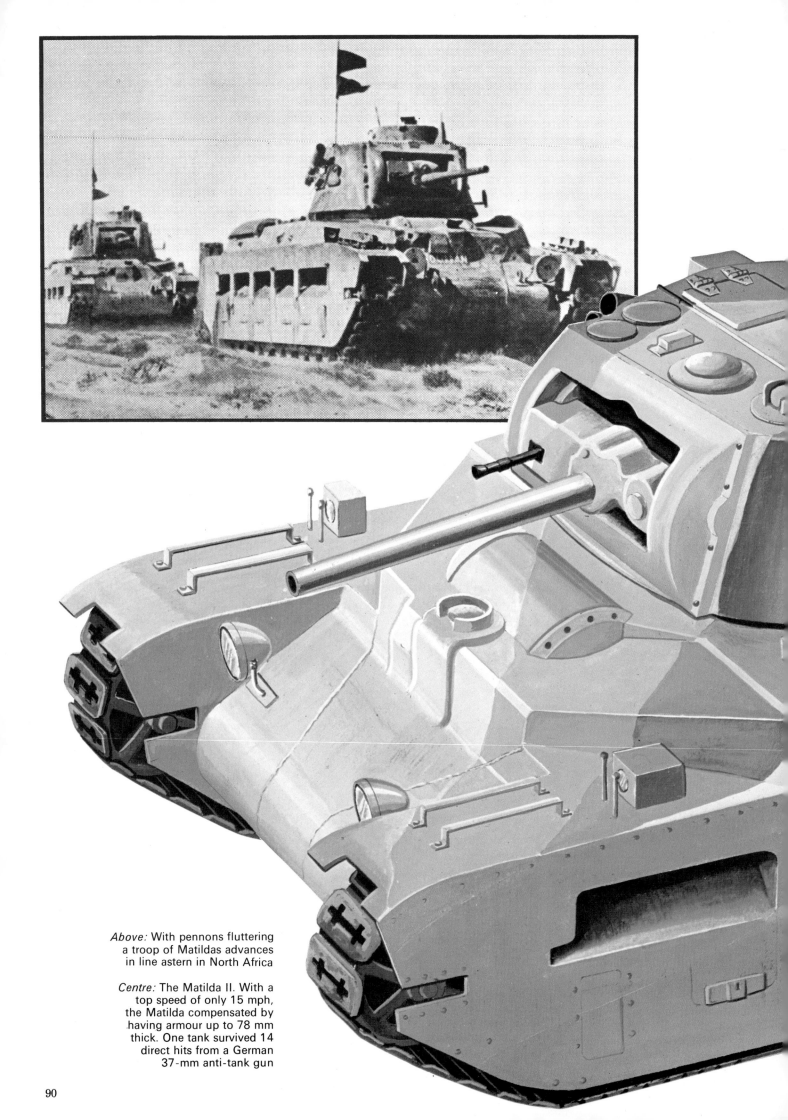

Above: With pennons fluttering a troop of Matildas advances in line astern in North Africa

Centre: The Matilda II. With a top speed of only 15 mph, the Matilda compensated by having armour up to 78 mm thick. One tank survived 14 direct hits from a German 37-mm anti-tank gun

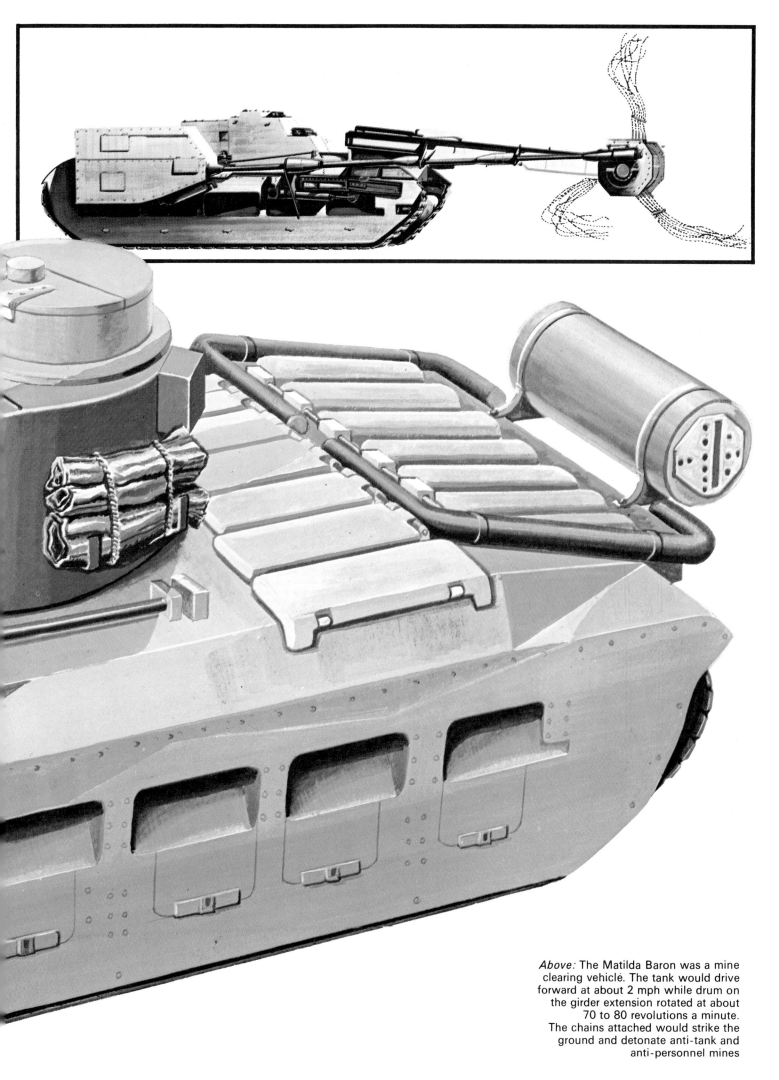

Above: The Matilda Baron was a mine clearing vehicle. The tank would drive forward at about 2 mph while drum on the girder extension rotated at about 70 to 80 revolutions a minute. The chains attached would strike the ground and detonate anti-tank and anti-personnel mines

Matilda II, its 2 pounder gun was too small a calibre for HE shells

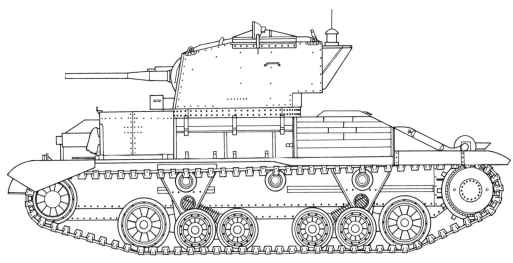

The A-9 contained many innovations in British tank design including a fan for the fighting compartment and hydraulic turret traverse

The A-10 shown here mounts a 94-mm howitzer for close support

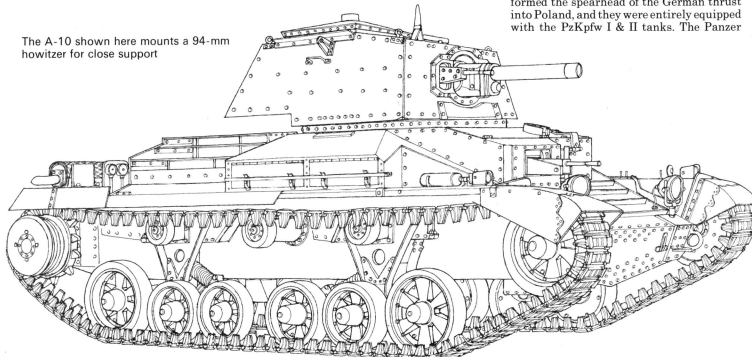

one of the last tanks with auxiliary turrets to be designed in Britain, having one central turret mounting a 2-pdr gun and two secondary turrets at each front corner armed with machine-guns. It weighed 12 tons and had a six-man crew.

The armour was relatively thin, and Vickers were asked to produce a stronger version for use as an infantry tank. In this modified version the auxiliary turrets were removed, the armour increased from 14 mm to 30 mm, bringing the weight up to 14 tons, and it became the A10, or Cruiser Tank Mark II, which entered service in 1939. Although intended as an infantry tank, the Matilda had assumed that role, and the Cruiser II became a 'heavy cruiser' tank for use by the Tank Corps, no longer tied to the foot soldiers.

In 1936 a party of War Office observers was invited to attend the Soviet Army Manoeuvres and the one thing there that impressed them was the armoured force. Most particularly, they were impressed with the high speed and manoeuvrability of the BT tanks, and upon reporting back to Britain it was decided to begin work on something similar.

The Nuffield Organisation was given the contract, and they bought Christie's M1936 tank in order to study the suspension. Within two years of setting to work the tank was in production as the Cruiser Mark III. It used a 340-hp Liberty engine, Christie suspension, and mounted a 2-pdr gun in its turret. Weighing 14 tons with a crew of four, it could reach 30 mph and had a cross-country performance far in advance of anything else at the time.

Once the Mark III had been put into production a variant model with more armour was developed, one feature of which was the addition of wedge-shaped plates to the turret to give a peculiar 'squashed' appearance; the object being to deflect shot from the turret sides. This became the Cruiser Mark IV, and with the Matildas and Cruisers beginning to come from the production lines, the British Army breathed sighs of relief. They now had an effective armoured force to combat any German developments in that field.

Six Panzer and four Light Divisions formed the spearhead of the German thrust into Poland, and they were entirely equipped with the PzKpfw I & II tanks. The Panzer

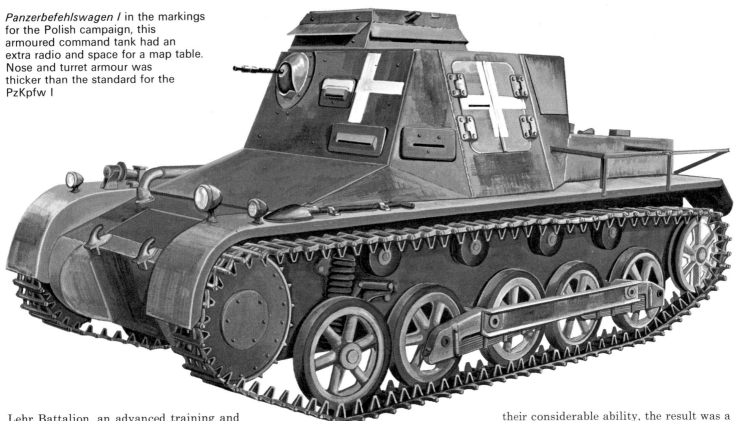

Panzerbefehlswagen I in the markings for the Polish campaign, this armoured command tank had an extra radio and space for a map table. Nose and turret armour was thicker than the standard for the PzKpfw I

Lehr Battalion, an advanced training and instructional formation at that time, had been specially incorporated into the Order of Battle and was equipped with PzKpfw III and IV tanks, largely in order to evaluate their performance in action. Their presence had been insisted upon by Guderian, who was anxious to prove that the PzKpfw I and II were already obsolescent and that manufacture should be concentrated on the III and IV.

The Polish opposition was, effectively, 13 tank battalions which mustered between them 169 TP7 tanks (a ten-tonner derived from a Vickers original design with a three-man crew and 37-mm gun as main armament), 50 Vickers six-tonners, 53 Renault R-35 purchased from France less than a year before, 693 Tankettes derived from Carden-Loyd designs and armed with machine-guns and about a hundred armoured cars. The German line-up was 1445 PzKpfw I, 1226 PzKpfw II, 98 PzKpfw III, 211 PzKpfw IV and 215 command tanks of various sorts. In total, 3195 well designed and reliable tanks operated by one of the best-trained and highly motivated armies in history, against 1065 machines of doubtful efficiency, the best of which had not been on issue long enough for the owners to be familiar with them.

Although the Poles fought to the best of their considerable ability, the result was a foregone conclusion to anyone who appreciated the armoured doctrines of the German Army. But at that time few people did. They had been conditioned to thinking about war in terms of trenches and mud, and the speed of the German advance, the surgical precision with which the armoured spearheads carved their way into the victim and dissected it bit by bit, was a terrible shock. Tactical air support in the shape of the Stuka dive-bomber, together with the irresistible advance of the Panzer Divisions brought a new dimension to war, the 'Blitzkrieg', and as Poland was rapidly swallowed up the soldiers of the rest of the world wondered what the answer might be.

Map in hand an officer observes from the turret of a PzBefWg III Ausf K. The tank had extra radio equipment and a 5.0-cm gun

Above: A PzKpfw 35(t) in Swedish camouflage. The 35(t) had a crew of 4 and with power steering and gear change was a very easy vehicle to drive

Right: The 38(t) had a crew of 4 and a 3.7-cm gun. Its 125 hp engine gave a top speed of 20 mph

Below: The Czech PzKpfw 38(t) a tank which served in France and Russia and its chassis was used subsequently for a series of successful tank destroyers

For six months they pondered, while the war in the west turned from 'Blitzkrieg' to 'Sitzkrieg' and the French sat inside the Maginot Line while the British, who had a shrewd idea how things would go, were prevented from doing much about it by political touchiness. Then in May 1940 the Panzers rolled again, through the impassable Ardennes and neutral Belgium to roll-back the Allied armies, drive the British into the sea and conquer France and the Low Countries.

The Polish campaign had taught the Germans some useful lessons. The PzKpfw I and II had been shown to be of little use as fighting tanks, while the value of the III and IV had been well demonstrated. The tank balance was therefore altered by thinning out the I and II models and increasing the numbers of III and IV. In addition large numbers of Czechoslovakian tanks, the excellent Models 35 and 38, were acquired and issued. The Light Divisions had been shown to be badly balanced in their equipment, having but one tank battalion, and this was rectified by turning them into full Panzer Divisions, using the Czech tanks to flesh them out. As a result, the German Army, when it crossed the French and Belgian borders, had much the same tank strength as it had had in Poland – 3379. But the number of PzKpfw III and IV had increased, and of the total number there was actually 2574 in the combat divisions.

In terms of pure numbers this was, in fact, a good deal less than the number of tanks which the British and French could jointly muster. Where the Germans had the advantage was that all their armour was concentrated into a massive thrust, while the Allied strength was scattered through the length and breadth of France, and the speed of the German movement prevented the Allies from bringing their tanks together in time to provide an effective defence.

The fighting in France demonstrated that the combat was not so much between machines as between systems of armoured warfare. The Panzers were self-sufficient integrated units, capable of independent movement and carrying with them all they needed in the way of support – artillery, engineers and reconnaissance units. To confront them the French had their two-tier system of 'cavalry tanks' and 'infantry tanks', as did the British.

The first French armour to confront the Panzers was a two-division force from the Cavalry Corps which spread out in front of

Left: A self-propelled gun version of the Valentine mounting a 57-mm gun with a restricted traverse. It was an unsatisfactory vehicle since the same gun could be mounted in a tank with a fully rotating turret. *Below:* A line up of Valentine tanks during an inspection in England

the Panzer thrust and was immediately punched through by superior tactics. Thereafter, in the eyes of the French command, the 'cavalry phase' was over and the 'infantry phase' had begun, and so the remaining tanks were removed from their divisions and split up one by one to act as semi-mobile pillboxes with the front-line troops.

The French had formed four armoured divisions in 1938–39, and these were now mobilised. One ran out of petrol before it got to the battle area; one was busy removing its tanks from the railway train which had brought them when it was overrun by Panzers; the third was presented with a golden opportunity to take a Panzer division in flank, but wasted so much time organising and arguing that the opportunity passed by, and they were eventually split up and spread about like the cavalry's tanks had been; the fourth, under de Gaulle, short of tanks, artillery and supporting infantry, charged headlong against Guderian's own division and was shrugged off as being of no importance or danger.

The British were receiving similar treatment in Belgium. Indecision there led to futile orders, and tanks being chased from one end of the country to the other on will-o'-the-wisp missions, so that by the time

Imperial War Museum

they found the battle they were mechanically unfit for action. The greatest lesson learned by the British from all this was that mechanical reliability is worth more than mechanical innovation. It is useless to have a highly sophisticated tank if it spends over half its time being mended or fastidiously maintained.

On occasions, though, the Panzers were given a nasty reminder that they were not entirely perfect. Near Arras a mixed force of British Matilda I and French Somua 35 tanks, making a reconnaissance in force, fell upon the tail of a Panzer column; the German tanks had moved on ahead, and the soft part of the column, infantry and artillery, received a heavy hammering from the Allied tanks. German anti-tank guns made little impression, for these were the best-armoured tanks of the day, and recourse was had to the 88-mm anti-aircraft gun, the only weapon capable of stopping the Matilda at that time. The German Panzers came racing back to assist their infantry and lost over 20 tanks to carefully-sited British 2-pdr anti-tank guns which had been deployed on the flanks to protect the Matildas and Somuas.

It was a salutary lesson to the Germans, and one which should also have taught a few things to the Allies, but it was lost in the general confusion, and it was not until a long time afterwards that the significance of the Arras affair was appreciated by either side.

After the fall of France there was another pause in the war, during which the combatants – and others on the side-lines – took stock. A lot had happened in the past twelve months and the whole business of armoured warfare had become one of prime importance, demanding some serious thinking by both tacticians and technicians.

The Germans were convinced that they had got it right. Their initial success against Poland had been considered, by some of the High Command, to be inconclusive because, after all, the Poles were a second-class army. But the overwhelming success of the same tactics against the French and British, both first-class powers, now proved that Guderian's theories were correct and that the Panzer Division was the dominant

arm of the land forces. As a result the number of Panzer Divisions was increased. There was, however, no great incentive to step up tank production, since the existing tanks seemed to be quite satisfactory, and as a result, although the number of Panzer units was doubled, the number of tanks was not, and the tank strength had to be diluted, gaps being filled with captured French vehicles in many cases.

The British Army was in a difficult position. The results of the campaign of 1940 had shown that armoured divisions were necessary, and the army was quite ready to organise them, but the tanks in production had been specified in the days when there was still the rigid split between 'cruiser' and 'infantry' tanks, and neither of these was the right sort of vehicle for an armoured division. The cruisers were deficient in fire-power, while the infantry tanks were deficient in both fire-power and speed. There was also the imminent possibility of a German invasion to be considered, and the tactics developed to deal with this demanded a high proportion of infantry-type tanks.

Two new designs of infantry tank were now on the way into production. The first was the Valentine, a re-design of the A10 Cruiser with 60 mm armour and a two-man turret carrying a 2-pdr gun, and the other was the Churchill, a slow-moving 38-tonner with 100-mm armour, a 3-in howitzer in the hull front plate and a 2-pdr in its turret. Although both of these were obsolescent before they appeared, production was geared to them and the army had to do what it could with them.

A new cruiser tank, the Covenanter, was also beginning to come into service. This used Christie suspension with a powerful V-12 engine of 300 hp to give it a speed of over 30 mph, but it was plagued by mechanical troubles throughout its life and was never sufficiently reliable to go into action as a combat tank, being relegated to training roles. This failure was redeemed by a re-design, using the well-tried Liberty engine, which became the Crusader. It was still not entirely free of mechanical problems but it was a better tank than the Covenanter and over 5000 were built.

The first production Valentine which saw action in North Africa. It has a Bren gun on an AA mounting on the turret

Imperial War Museum

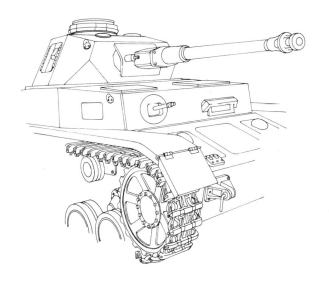

Right: A PzKpfw IV Ausf H showing the increased use of spaced armour and the coating of anti-magnetic mine cement on all the vulnerable areas

Left: A detailed view of the turret and hull front of a PzKpfw IV Ausf F2. The tank mounts the long barrelled 7.5-cm KwK L/43 gun

Below: The interior detail of a PzKpfw IV showing the turret and fighting compartment with the driver's and machine-gunner/radio operator's hull positions

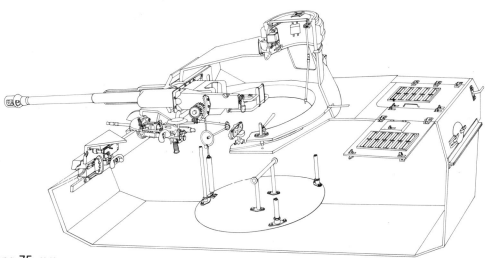

Fitting the long 75-mm gun to the PzKpfw IV Ausf Fz was an attempt to match the firepower of new Allied vehicles

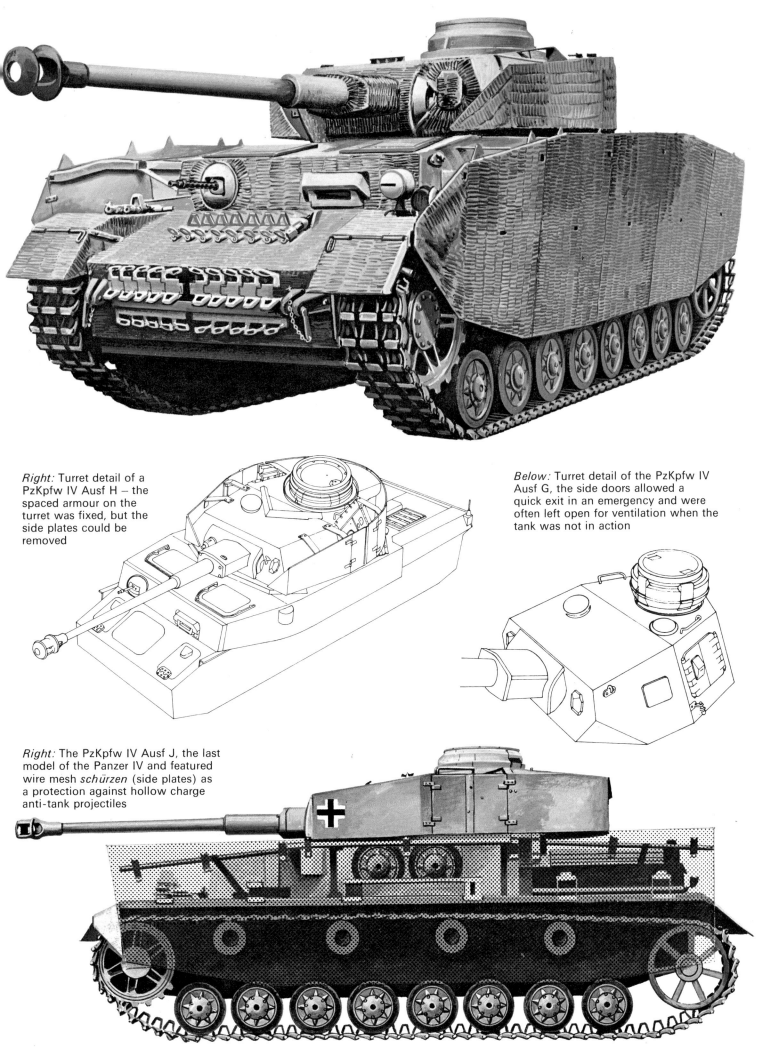

Right: Turret detail of a PzKpfw IV Ausf H – the spaced armour on the turret was fixed, but the side plates could be removed

Below: Turret detail of the PzKpfw IV Ausf G, the side doors allowed a quick exit in an emergency and were often left open for ventilation when the tank was not in action

Right: The PzKpfw IV Ausf J, the last model of the Panzer IV and featured wire mesh *schürzen* (side plates) as a protection against hollow charge anti-tank projectiles

A troop of T-34/76s advance across an autumn landscape. Wide tracks allowed the T-34 to move through snow and soft ground where German tanks bogged down

The T-34/85 which featured a bigger cast turret and an 85-mm gun. It was to soldier on in Eastern Bloc armies long after the end of the war

The Russians were also having an active time in tank-building. In 1939–40 their Winter War against Finland had given them the opportunity to find out how their tanks performed in action, and the results were salutary. As we have seen, the Spanish Civil War had caused the Soviets to have second thoughts about large armoured formations; moreover Stalin's purge of the army in 1938 had removed most of the armour experts. As a result, the emphasis was placed on decentralisation, and tank units were split up and dispersed among infantry battalions. The performance of the German Panzers in Poland, however, led to another change of heart, and tank brigades and mechanised corps were formed, just in time to be used in Finland.

By 1939 the various experimental designs of the previous ten years had all yielded what information they could, and the Soviet tank designers then had to try and bring together all the various lessons learned so as to be able to put down on paper the specification for a new generation of vehicles.

The first priority was a high-powered diesel engine. This had been under development by the Kharkov Locomotive Works since 1934 and was now perfected as a 3.8-litre liquid-cooled V-12 producing 500 hp at 1800 revolutions per minute.

Next came the question of armour. It was to be thick, sloped so as to deflect shot, and cast or welded instead of riveted, since experience in Spain and on the Manchurian border (in minor clashes with the Japanese) had shown that rivets were often sprung free by shot which otherwise did not damage the tank, and these flying rivets were lethal missiles for the tank crew.

Armament was to be a high-velocity 3-in gun, and work was to progress on devising a stabiliser which would allow the gun to be fired accurately while on the move. Tracks were to be wide, so as to give good flotation on mud and snow, and the whole thing was to be designed so that it could be cheaply made and simply maintained in the field. All in all, an ideal specification made by men who appreciated the vital parameters of speed, protection and firepower.

Faced with this demand, the designers produced their ideas by December 1939, and the Kharkov Factory immediately built two prototypes. These were designated Medium Tank T-34, and after a long travelling trial they were sent up to the Finland front to be tried in battle. Unfortunately the war was over by the time they got there, but since it was obvious that the design was a good one, production began in May 1940 at the Kirov Tank Factory in Leningrad, the first production model coming off the line in June.

The same production programme was responsible for producing a design of heavy tank. During 1938 a specification had been drawn up and two prototypes had been built. The T-100 began with three turrets, but had the rear one removed to save weight and allow for more armour. The end result was one of the most peculiar tanks ever seen, a 30-ft long, low-set hull with a 45-mm gun turret at the front; behind this, on top of a barbette, so as to raise the turret above the level of the front one, sat the main turret carrying a 76-mm gun. The whole thing weighed 56 tons, had up to 60 mm of armour, a six-man crew, and could move at less than 20 mph. The second prototype, known as the SMK, was exactly the same in general outline but had some changes in design detail and was lighter.

Both were sent to Finland in 1939 where they were soon demonstrated to be quite impractical. In the first place the commander was overburdened by the responsibility of trying to control everything that was going on, and secondly these enormous vehicles presented such silhouettes that they were a gift to anti-tank gunners. So both these were abandoned, though they deserve a place in history for being the last of the multi-turret designs to actually see combat.

Taking the basic hull of the T-100 as a starting point, the designers now went to work on a new heavy tank. The hull was shortened to 23 ft, the same torsion bar suspension was used, and a large single turret with a 76-mm gun was fitted. Total weight was now 46 tons and a 550-hp diesel engine moved it along at 22 mph. This was

Equipped with an experimental snorkel fitting a T-34 wades a river. With no special equipment it could wade up to 4½ foot water gaps

101

Klimenti Voroshilov I. Though this tank mounted similar armament to the early T-34 it had thicker armour – between 30 and 100 mm as against 20 and 75 mm

a much more practical machine and, after a brief test against the Finns in the closing days of the war, went into production as the KV (Klimenti Voroshilov) 1.

With two sound designs in production the Soviets could now feel more secure on the material side, and now went to work to re-organise the tactical side by reinstituting armoured divisions. Progress was slow, however, and the new formations were nowhere near completed when the storm broke upon them in 1941.

When Hitler invaded Poland, the United States were completing their trials of the M2A4 light tank, 11½ tons, with a 37-mm gun, a radial engine giving it a speed of 35 mph, and 10 mm of armour. The events in Europe hastened its standardisation and instead of being yet another development stage it became the first mass-production tank and the principal training vehicle for the US Army in 1940.

In the area of medium tanks, however, there was nothing immediately available. In 1938 Rock Island Arsenal began developing a totally new medium tank using the same volute spring suspension as the light tank series, with the intention also of using as many light tank components as they could for the sake of standardisation and economy.

The resultant design, the T5, was a peculiar affair which had a high hull superstructure with six machine-guns poking from it in all directions, surmounted by a turret carrying a 37-mm gun. The first model was powered by the same Continental radial aeroplane engine as the light tank. Subsequent pilot models tried using different engines, such as the Wright Cyclone radial and the Guiberson diesel radial.

Among these experimental variations was one which took over part of the machine-gun barbette and mounted a 75-mm pack howitzer on the right front of the hull, and removed the gun turret to replace it with a small cupola carrying an optical rangefinder and a machine-gun. Eventually, in August 1939, the multiple machine-gun and 37-mm turret version was standardised as the Medium Tank M2. Production was authorised and Rock Island Arsenal in-

structed to build 15 of them; they were the only ones ever to be made.

With the invasion of France, tension mounted in the US, and there was a good deal of public disquiet about the state of the armed forces, particularly about tanks. Senator Henry Cabot Lodge, after witnessing the Louisiana Manoeuvres of 1940, said in a Senate speech 'I have just seen all the tanks in the United States – about 400 in number . . . about the number destroyed in one day's fighting in the current European War . . .'

Arguments like this led to the passing of the National Munitions Program on June 3, 1941 which, while dealing with all arms of the services, specified the manufacture of 1741 medium tanks in the following 18

months. Shortly after this the legal restrictions of the 1922 Defense Act were swept away by the formation of a new Armored Force, under the command of General Adna R Chaffee, with the responsibility for all tank functions, taking over the tanks of the infantry and cavalry.

The problem now was how to translate the Munitions program's call for 1741 tanks into reality. Rock Island Arsenal were the only people with the know-how, and they were primarily an artillery arsenal with limited facilities for tank construction. Their task had simply been to produce prototypes and small production runs. Mass-production was therefore out of the question. The Ordnance Department thought of

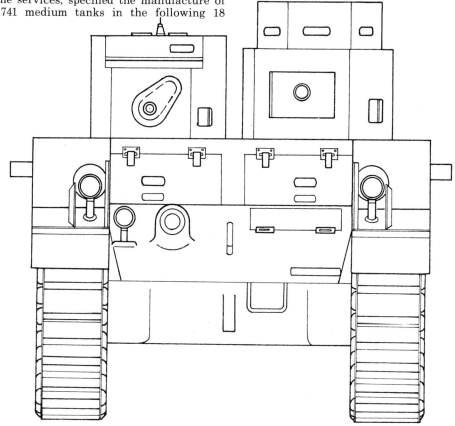

Marshal Klimenti Voroshilov, the Soviet People's Commissar for Defence: though he was no tank expert his name was used for the KV I and II heavy tanks

calling upon the heavy engineering plants, such as the American Locomotive Company, the Baldwin Locomotive Company and similar concerns, judging them to have the facilities for handling the massive structures of tanks, but it was pointed out that locomotive building was hardly a mass-production operation either.

Eventually it was decided to go to the automobile industry, and with the assistance of the Chrysler company plans were drawn up for the construction of a complete new factory, the Detroit Tank Arsenal. This was to cost $21 million and would eventually have a capacity of ten tanks a day. In August 1940 a contract along these lines was given to the Chrysler Company,

Below and Left: The US combat car M-2 A1, the last tank to reflect the demands by the Infantry for a weapons carrier. It had two turrets like the British Vickers tanks and mounted three machine-guns. Top speed was 45 mph and it weighed 9.7 tons

on the understanding that the plant would be completed inside a year and would be by then turning out 100 M2A1 tanks a month.

While all this was going on the Chief of Infantry – who was still responsible for tanks, since this was shortly before the Armored Force was formed – sent a report to the Ordnance Department, based on his assessment of the battles in Poland and France. In this he noted that German tanks were using 75-mm guns, and urged that any future medium tank produced for the US Army should have at least a 75-mm gun as the main armament. At that time both the light and medium tanks were armed with 37-mm guns.

Shortly afterwards, when the new Armored force was in being, General Chaffee conferred with the Ordnance Department about this 75-mm proposal. The only fly in the ointment was that the current turrets could not physically accept a gun bigger than the 37-mm, and it would take some time to design a new, larger turret. At this juncture one of the Ordnance officers recalled the T5 pilot model with the 75-mm pack howitzer in the hull.

Taking this as a starting point, it would be possible to modify the M2A1 design by moving the turret to one side and installing a 75-mm gun in the side hull mounting. This would mean that most of the existing components and designs for the M2A1 could be used, the only changes being in the hull structure and relatively simple to accommodate. The idea was accepted and the Chrysler contract was immediately cancelled, to be replaced by the new design, now known as the Medium Tank M3.

This was a fine and bold decision to take, but firstly the M3 had to be designed – and the Ordnance Department reckoned it would take two months to produce the ten thousand detail drawings necessary to guide

manufacture, and secondly the construction at Detroit had to go ahead even though the new design of tank might mean some considerable changes in the production line layout. Nevertheless, work on the new arsenal began in September 1940 and the actual building was largely completed by March 1941.

Meanwhile the Chrysler engineers were working on the design of machinery and production lines bit by bit as the drawings came from the Ordnance Corps. The final drawings appeared in March 1941 and the first tanks came off the line less than three weeks later, a staggering performance by any standards. True, the first off the line were almost hand built, they lacked guns, and had to be sent back later for modification, but in spite of that it was a notable piece of engineering.

The original plan to bring in the locomotive companies had also been revived and contracts were passed to Alco and Baldwin in October 1940. In fact they managed to turn out their pilot models a few days before Chrysler, largely because they were using existing machinery and were not trying to design the factory as they went along.

An amusing tale is told of the first pilot models. Apparently when the Alco tank was ready, in the first week of April 1941, only one complete transmission and final drive unit had been made by the sub-contractor responsible. This unit was rushed to the Alco factory and installed in the M3 tank so that it could perform a ceremonial drive past the Secretary of War. As soon as the tank drove back into the factory the transmission was stripped out, thrown on a truck, and rushed to the Baldwin factory to be installed in *their* first tank for *their* ceremonial drive-past.

At the same time as the Chief of Infantry had made his request for a 75-mm gun tank, he had requested a design of heavy tank as well. It was to weigh not more than 80 tons, be armed with a gun bigger than 75-mm in the hull, a 37-mm to 50-mm gun in a rotating turret, and eight machine-guns. In other words, the complete infantry-accompanying firepower tank. No heavy tanks had been designed since the First World War, but the

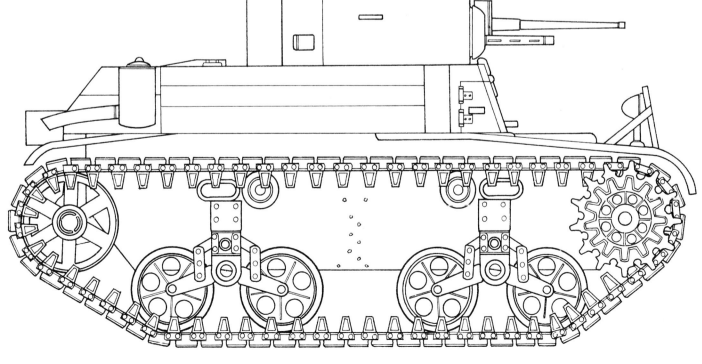

Ordnance Department set to work to produce a 50-tonner, which they considered to be as heavy as was necessary. Starting with a clean sheet of paper, they were able to produce something completely different.

The hull and turret were to be cast, main armament was to be a 3-in gun borrowed from the anti-aircraft department, and power was to come from a Wright Whirlwind radial aeroplane engine of 925 hp. A number of pilots were planned, using different transmissions and different forms of hull construction, and the first pilot was completed in December 1941.

Initial tests of the new tank, tentatively called the T1E2 Heavy, showed that the great weight and power led to problems with the brakes and problems with cooling the massive engine. Modifications were made and in May 1942 it was standardised as the Heavy Tank M6. With up to 82-mm of armour, a 3-in turret gun capable of killing any tank in the world at that time, weighing 56 tons and capable of 22 mph, it was undoubtedly the most powerful and best-armed tank in existence, not excluding the then-unknown Soviet T-34 and KV models.

However, at this point, something went wrong, and although production of 5500 was planned, no more than 40, including the pilots models, were ever built. The Armored Board objected to the design on the grounds that it was overweight, too complicated, unreliable, and they didn't want it. Ordnance offered to attend to the defects which the Board put up, but they were ignored. The Army Ground Forces Board concurred with the Armored Board, adding the clincher that the M6 took up too much shipping space and that for every M6 shipped overseas two medium tanks could go. It was the end of the M6.

But to turn back to 1940; after the fiasco at Dunkirk, the British were desperately short of tanks (and practically everything else) and sent a purchasing mission to the US to try and persuade American manufacturers to make British tanks. The US Government, aware of the problems they were having in finding enough manufacturing capacity to build tanks of their own design were, understandably, against the idea of parting with some of their factory facilities on these terms and more or less told the British mission that they could either have American tanks or none at all.

Since the two tanks then scheduled for production were the M3 Medium and the M3 Light, these were accepted, though the British mission insisted on having the turrets modified to take radio sets. It was British practice to carry the set in the turret, while American practice was to carry it in the hull. This was agreed and early in 1942 the first British M3 Medium tanks, named by them the 'General Grant', were delivered and shipped straight to North Africa. They were accompanied by first shipments of the M3 Light tanks, called by the British the 'General Stuart'.

The reason for sending the tanks straight to the Western Desert was simply because, for the British, this was where there was most activity at that time, and a reliable tank with a 75-mm gun looked like being their salvation. The desert campaign had begun in 1941 with the virtual annihilation of the Italian Army, using the sort of tank tactics that had been preached by Fuller and others in the 1920s; sweeping flank moves by fast cruiser tanks while heavily armoured infantry Matildas engaged the frontline troops.

The recipe worked perfectly, and in a series of audacious moves the British Army gained control of Cyrenaica and imprisoned Italians by the tens of thousands. It was not completely one-sided; although the Italian armour was mostly obsolete and badly handled, Italian artillery performed well, but in terrain where concealment was almost impossible and the vast expanse of desert gave tank units a degree of mobility unattained in any other sort of terrain, it was the movements of armour which dictated results.

It also brought home a few lessons to the British, lessons about reliability, maintainance, repair facilities and supply. By the time the campaign against the Italians was ended the Matilda Is were completely worn out, and the rate of attrition in cruiser tanks was horrifying. Vehicles designed to work in the clean conditions of England's green fields were at a disadvantage when thrown into the dust of the desert, and engines were worked to death, wearing out in half the forecast time and thus placing an enormous demand on the supply lines for spare parts. Fortunately the same problem was confronting the other side, and when the German Panzers under General Rommel made their appearance, they had precisely the same trouble.

The war in the desert became primarily a gun duel, and here the British were at a disadvantage, since an adequate measure of armament had never been part of British tank designer's philosophy. As long as some sort of gun went into the tank, that was supposed to be sufficient. Performance and protection were thought of first, and gunpower came a long way behind. As a

Right: The production line for the Grant Mk I. It mounted a 37-mm gun with a co-axial machine-gun in the turret and a 75-mm gun in the hull. The first four marks had a 9-cylinder radial air-cooled 340 BHP engine

Below: An M3 General Lee attached to a Canadian Armoured Division lurches through a frozen stream during training in Canada

International News Photos

Below: A Lee Mk I on an exercise in England in 1942. The subsequent marks abandoned the riveted hull in favour of casting or welding

Fox Photos

Fox Photos

International News Photos

William Knudson of General Motors member of the National Defence Commission

Above: American crews scramble aboard their M3 Grant tanks during manoeuvres in southern England. The turrets have the early insignia used in England

result, the standard British gun was the 2-pdr of 40-mm calibre, which had been a perfectly adequate gun when it was first invented in the early 1930s but was, by the 1940s, hopelessly outdated. In the eyes of the British tank men, its gravest defect – apart from its lack of penetration – was that the ammunition provided was nothing but solid piercing shot. There was no high explosive shell, and in that calibre it would have hardly been much good if there had been.

Better guns were available – on paper. The army's tank and anti-tank guns were always tied together, and a 6-pdr 57-mm anti-tank gun had been tested in 1938 and then put to one side. In 1940 the design was taken out again, but to put it into production would have meant taking away a factory from the production of 2-pdr anti-tank guns; and since the Army had lost almost all its anti-tank guns at Dunkirk, interference with production was unthinkable. It was better to have an uninterrupted flow of known guns than a hiatus followed by a slow pre-production run of a new and untried weapon. So the 6-pdr had to wait. However, even if it had been available, it would still have done the tank men no good, for the simple reason that it was too big to fit inside the existing tank turrets. New turrets would have had to be designed and built before the 6-pdr could have been used.

So the tank men – and the anti-tank gunners – in the desert had to make do with

Above: A factory fresh Grant passes a railway gun at a factory in the USA

Below: Grant crews board their vehicles. The tank in the foreground has a muzzle brake fitted to the 75-mm gun

the 2-pdr, although the anti-tank balance was helped by siting the 25-pdr field gun in positions where it could double as an anti-tank protector; its 20-lb steel shot could wreak havoc with anything on tracks and at a long range too.

The Germans, on the other hand, were provided with high-velocity 50-mm guns which fired both piercing shell and high-explosive anti-personnel shells. They also

107

Below: The last of the Stuarts — the M5A1-Stuart Mk 6. It had twin Cadillac V8 engines of 220 BHP and hydromatic transmission — armament was similar to earlier marks, a 37-mm gun and MGs

Right: The Stuart in the deserts of North Africa and the snow of the Aleutian Islands

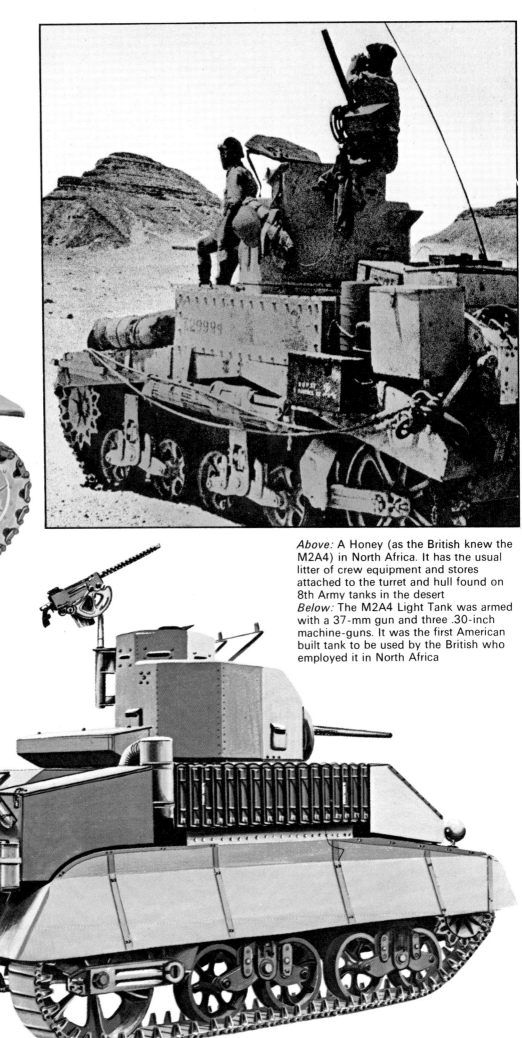

Above: A Honey (as the British knew the M2A4) in North Africa. It has the usual litter of crew equipment and stores attached to the turret and hull found on 8th Army tanks in the desert
Below: The M2A4 Light Tank was armed with a 37-mm gun and three .30-inch machine-guns. It was the first American built tank to be used by the British who employed it in North Africa

had 75-mm guns with a similar range of ammunition. Their anti-tank guns were of 50-mm and 75-mm calibre, and there was always the threat of the 88-mm anti-aircraft gun which could, when called on, double as a potent anti-tank weapon.

Thus the German tanks could stand well off from the British and shell them with high explosive or punish them with solid shot while the British were too far away for their 2-pdr to have any effect. And when that didn't work the Germans would withdraw and let the British run into their screen of anti-tank guns, all of which could pierce the relatively thin British armour with no trouble. The gun disparity was responsible for the tactics; the only way the British could fight was to charge the enemy and hope to get in close before they were knocked out.

While the M3 was greeted with enthusiasm, and used to good effect, there was no gainsaying that it was a bad design from the tactical point of view. It stood so high that much of the tank had to be exposed before the hull-mounted gun could be fired, and the lack of turret armament was undesirable. On the credit side, however, the US tanks opened British eyes to the meaning of the word 'reliability'. The hard work done by Rock Island Arsenal in the dark days of the 1920s and 1930s had paid off in a design which, mechanically, was above reproach. The General Grant went on and on, with minimum maintenance, proof that simplicity and well-tried mechanics were better than novelty and sophisticated design when it came to combat.

In the USA the short-comings of the M3 were well appreciated and in March 1941 the Ordnance Department had begun work on its successor, the T6. This, for simplicity,

construction was authorised. The welded hull pattern became the M4 while the cast hull type became the M4A1.

No less than 11 different major plants, as well as scores of sub-contractors, became involved in production of the M4, or, as it became known in British service, the 'General Sherman'. It was eventually built in greater numbers than any other American or Allied tank, over 48 000 being made before production stopped in 1945. There were numerous variant models with different engines, different hull construction, some with 105-mm howitzers in place of the 75-mm gun, some with 76-mm guns, some with British 17-pdrs.

It was far from being the best tank of the war – the Germans nicknamed them 'Ronsons' because of their tendency to burst into flames. when hit – and except when armed with the 76-mm or 17-pdr guns they stood little chance against the German tanks of 1944–45 except at close range. But

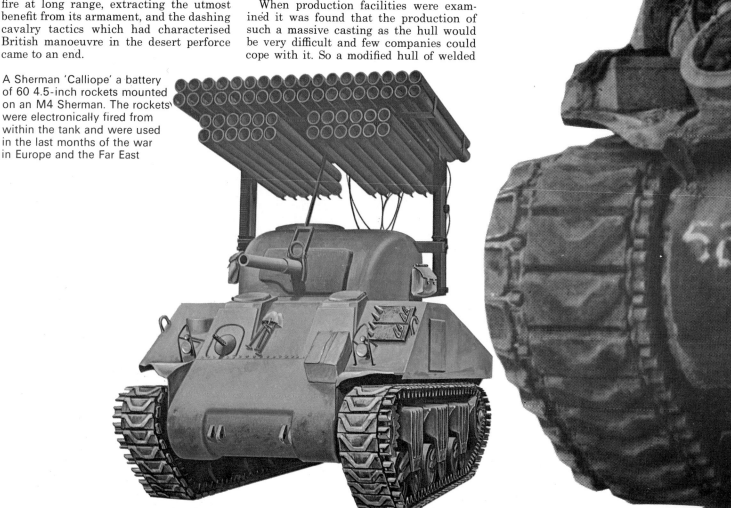

It was into this imbalance that the American-built M3 tanks were thrust, carrying a sound and effective 75-mm gun which was as good as those on the German tanks. And at much the same time the 2-pdr anti-tank gun was finally replaced by the new 6-pdr, which also helped to balance the affair.

The arrival of the M3 tank also brought about a change in tactics. Due to the gun being barbette-mounted in the hull, it could not fire to all points of the compass as could a turret gun, and charging into the fray was a waste of time. The tank had to take up a position from which it could fire at long range, extracting the utmost benefit from its armament, and the dashing cavalry tactics which had characterised British manoeuvre in the desert perforce came to an end.

was to have the same chassis and mechanical features as the M3 but would have a cast, turtle-shaped hull and a central turret mounting the 75-mm gun. A co-axial machine-gun would go into the turret, a 'flexible' machine-gun in a ball-mounting in the hull front alongside the driver, and two fixed machine-guns would be centrally placed in the hull front. The first prototype model was completed in September 1941, and at the conclusion of its trials, in October, it was standardised as the Medium Tank M4.

When production facilities were examined it was found that the production of such a massive casting as the hull would be very difficult and few companies could cope with it. So a modified hull of welded

there were always plenty of them, they were reliable, they were easy to operate and maintain, and after some of the tanks that had gone before them, that was good enough.

A Sherman 'Calliope' a battery of 60 4.5-inch rockets mounted on an M4 Sherman. The rockets were electronically fired from within the tank and were used in the last months of the war in Europe and the Far East

Below: An M4A4, Sherman Mk5C, or Firefly with a 17-pdr gun. The greater penetrating power of the 17-pdr compared to the standard 75-mm gun made the Firefly a welcome addition to the Allied tank forces

WORLD-WIDE WAR
Barbarossa and after

In June 1941, when the German Army swept across the Russian borders, the Panzer divisions comprised about 3350 tanks. Confronting them, the Soviet Army had something in the region of 24 000 tanks, though only a small proportion of these were in the combat zone. In spite of this disparity of numbers, the German armour soundly defeated its opposition, captured or destroyed about 17 000 tanks in the first months of the invasion for the loss of 2700 of their own, and came within a short distance of making the invasion a success. Only after five months of battle did the effects of over-stretched supply lines, wear and tear on the tanks and the Russian winter bring the onward rush to a halt.

The reasons for the initial German success were many. In the first place Hitler was astute enough to attack early on Sunday morning, when he was certain that a high proportion of the Russians would be lost in a vodka-induced sleep. The attacker, of course, having the choice of time and place is always at an advantage, but another factor was that the re-organisation of the Soviet armoured forces had not yet been completed. Some units had not received all their equipment, there were no spares and many of the men posted to the new formations had no practical experience.

Even the Soviet Official History admits that only a quarter of the tanks available were in running order and that many of the drivers had had less than two hours actual driving experience. With the opposition labouring under this sort of handicap, the success of Hitler's army, which at that time was probably the most confident army the world has ever seen, was unremarkable.

Although the German Army did not know the precise number of the Soviet tank force, they knew that it ran to several thousand and thus to numerical superiority. This did not worry them, however, since they also knew full well that their Panzers were more than a match for the Soviet T-28, T-35 or BT tanks. Moreover the Germans had undeniable superiority in training and tactics, and it took no great skill to evade the headlong rush of a Soviet tank and deal with it. Another factor was the speed of the German advance, which frequently

caught Russian units long before they expected an attack, often, indeed, before they had realised there was a war on. But within a couple of weeks of the invasion some disquieting reports were reaching the German commanders.

One was from von Manstein's 56th Corps. They had charged deep into Russian territory and had stretched their supply line to its limit, a stretching which snapped when an enormous and apparently impervious Russian tank of a totally new type suddenly appeared on the supply road and, for 48 hours, stood off every German attempt to shift it. Attempts to bring an 88-mm gun into action were prevented by the fire of the tank's powerful gun, and eventually it required a major diversion to draw off the monster and pull it into an ambush where

an '88' could finish it off. That was the German Army's introduction to the KV-1.

At about the same time the 17th Panzer Division discovered a 'strange low-slung tank of formidable appearance', which emerged from the brush near the Dniepr River. With German shot and shell bouncing off its armour, it forged forward, crushed a 37-mm anti-tank gun beneath its tracks, shot up two PzKpfw IIIs and tore through the German front. It left a nine-mile trail of destruction behind it before being stopped by blasting at short range by a 105-mm field howitzer which it had carelessly ignored. That was the T-34. It was beginning to look as if the Russians had something up their sleeves.

They had, but there wasn't much of it. Estimates vary, but it is unlikely that the Russians had as many as a thousand of both types in total, and most of these were scattered across Russia. However, it was soon appreciated that the T-34 and the KV were the only two Soviet designs which could hope to be effective against the Panzers, and with admirable single-mindedness the Russians abandoned every other design for the time being and concentrated on obtaining maximum production of these two.

That in itself was going to be a struggle,

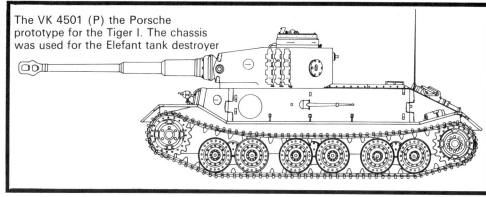

The VK 4501 (P) the Porsche prototype for the Tiger I. The chassis was used for the Elefant tank destroyer

for the initial German advance had overrun the tank factories of Kharkov, Zhdanov and Kirov, while the factory at Leningrad was soon within range of German heavy artillery. What could be saved from the overrun plants in the face of the Germans was pulled out and shipped east to Chelyabinsk, while the Leningrad factory was totally dismantled and also sent east. These evacuees were then integrated to form a new combine called 'Tankograd' and within two months of its establishment the first KVs were rolling from its doors, the first of 18 000 tanks and 48 000 engines it was to produce before the war ended.

A similar combination of evacuated factories went to form 'Uralmashzavod' at Nizhni Tagil, which became one of the principal sources of T-34 tanks. By 1943 there were 42 factories across Russia doing nothing but turn out T-34s and KV tanks. The Soviets could make tanks faster than the Germans could destroy them.

A PzKpfw II Ausf B passes a BT-7A during the opening moves of Barbarossa

Once the seriousness of the situation was realised, the German army turned first to the gunmakers for more powerful anti-tank guns to stop these new monsters and then to the tank builders to produce some better tanks to give them an equal chance. The first response was to provide the PzKpfw IV with a better gun, a long-barrelled 75-mm with high velocity, capable of piercing the T-34 armour at 1000 metres range – providing it got a fair hit and the shot didn't bounce off the well-sloped armour. But that was only a stop-gap, and a new tank was needed.

In fact a successor to the PzKpfw IV had been begun as far back as 1937, but it had a low priority, and every time the designers were getting near to a solution a new set of requirements would come down from the High Command and the drawing began all over again. It had started as a 30-ton model, then gone to a 65-tonner, then back to a 32-tonner. Then came orders for a 36-tonner and then this changed to a 45-ton version.

Then came the T-34 scare and Henschel, who were doing all this development, were told to bring their latest design to finality and have it ready to demonstrate on Hitler's

Associated Press

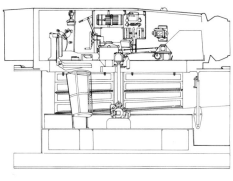

Above and right: The turret side and rear views of a Tiger 1, driver and bow machine-gunner's positions and overall side view of the engine and fighting compartments. Of interest is the stowage of the 8.8-cm ammunition in the turret, the gas respirators in the crew positions and the water bottles strapped within easy reach of the driver and machine-gunner. The 7.92-mm machine-gun ammunition is in flexible containers in the bow position and around the inside of the turret. *Left:* A Tiger on the production line at the Henschel works. Total production at the end of the war stood at 1348

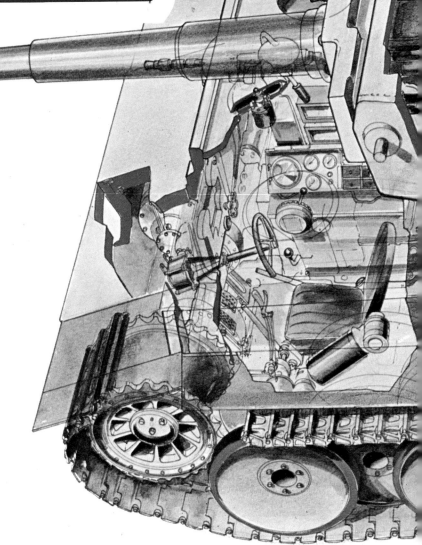

birthday, April 20, 1942. The Porsche company had also been given contracts and they were now given the same instructions, so that two competing models would be on display and a decision taken as to which would go into production. The demonstration took place on the appointed day and the Henschel design was judged the better of the two. Instructions were given for it to go into production, and it was officially christened the PzKpfw VI 'Tiger'.

The Henschel Tiger was an outstanding design and a formidable tank. Its principal assets were 100 mm of armour on the front and a powerful 88-mm gun in the turret. The suspension was triple overlapped, full-size road wheels on torsion bars which gave a surprisingly soft ride, and the track was 28 in wide, giving excellent flotation on soft ground. In order to make construction easier and quicker the hull was of flat plates welded together; there was no subtlety of slope to deflect shot, and for this reason the armour was made as thick as could be supported. Largely because of this the planned 45-ton weight was well exceeded and the production models weighed 56 tons.

There was, in fact, only one defect of design, and that was in the turret traversing mechanism. Due to the enormous weight of

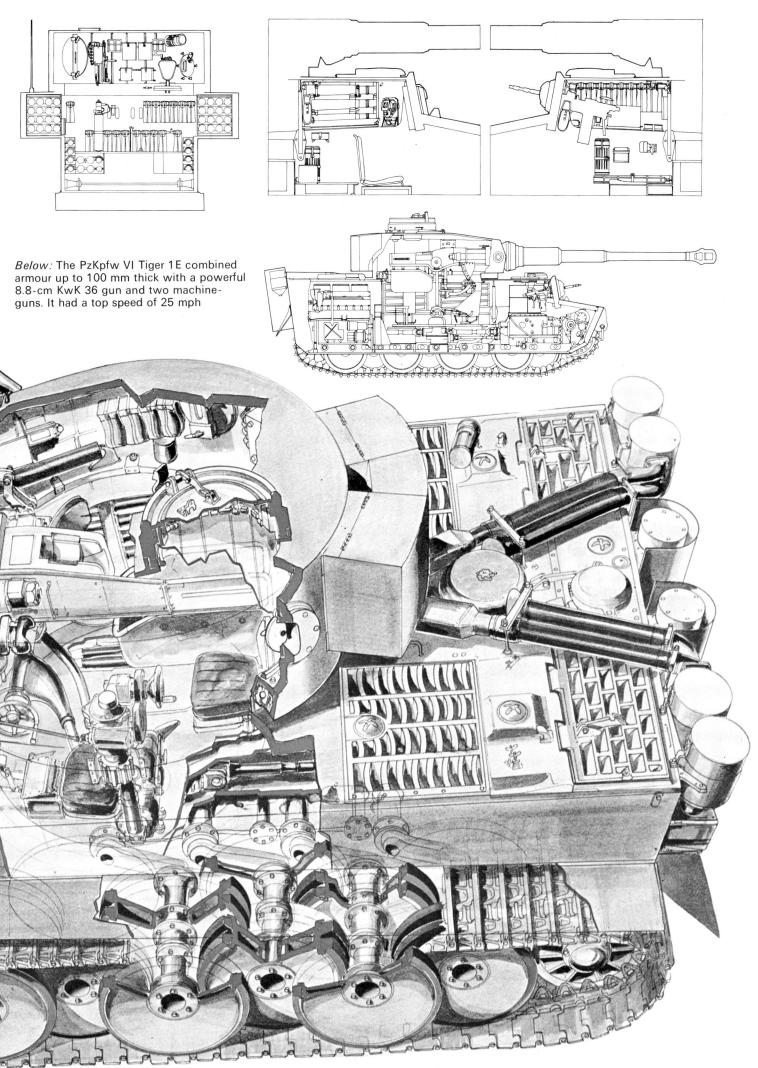

Below: The PzKpfw VI Tiger 1E combined armour up to 100 mm thick with a powerful 8.8-cm KwK 36 gun and two machine-guns. It had a top speed of 25 mph

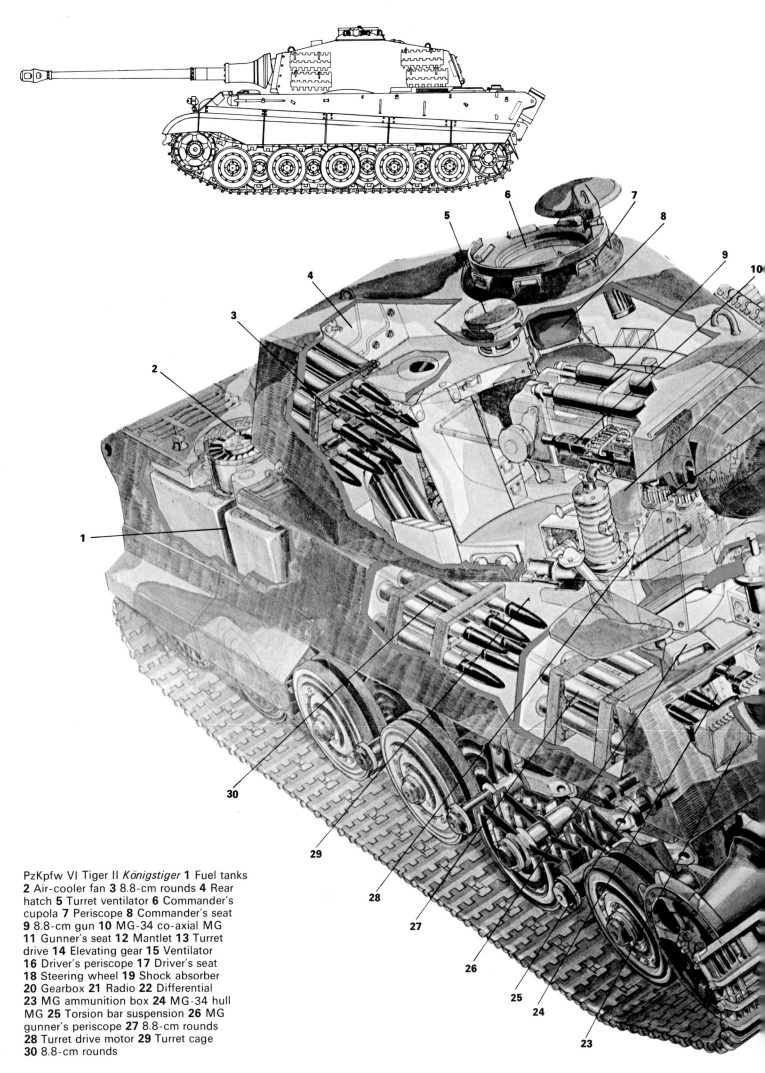

PzKpfw VI Tiger II *Königstiger* **1** Fuel tanks
2 Air-cooler fan **3** 8.8-cm rounds **4** Rear
hatch **5** Turret ventilator **6** Commander's
cupola **7** Periscope **8** Commander's seat
9 8.8-cm gun **10** MG-34 co-axial MG
11 Gunner's seat **12** Mantlet **13** Turret
drive **14** Elevating gear **15** Ventilator
16 Driver's periscope **17** Driver's seat
18 Steering wheel **19** Shock absorber
20 Gearbox **21** Radio **22** Differential
23 MG ammunition box **24** MG-34 hull
MG **25** Torsion bar suspension **26** MG
gunner's periscope **27** 8.8-cm rounds
28 Turret drive motor **29** Turret cage
30 8.8-cm rounds

the turret the traversing gear had to be low-ratio, and the turret gunner had to make 720 turns of his handwheel to swing the turret completely round. Some optimists in the British Army calculated that an unarmed man could defeat a Tiger by simply trotting steadily round and round at a range of 50 yards or so, keeping in front of the turning gun barrel, until the crew inside dropped dead from exhaustion!

Production of the Tiger was begun in August 1942 and continued until August 1944, by which time 1350 had been built. It was unfortunate that in its first actions against both the Russians and the British it was roughly handled; in Russia it was sent in over unsuitable, boggy country where it was forced to move along narrow forest tracks, rendering it a sitting target for anti-tank gunners who had sufficient nerve to let it get close. In similar fashion its first outing in Tunisia, at Pont-du-Fahs, was stopped by British 6-pdrs at a range of 500 yards. In spite of this poor start, and in

spite, too, of early mechanical troubles, the Tiger went on to become a tank of considerable renown.

The Porsche design, which had been passed over, was, like many of Porsches designs, a somewhat unconventional vehicle. Its principal novelty lay in the transmission which used petrol-electric drive. This system had been experimented with by almost every country and manufacturer at some time or another, but the Porsche appears to have been the only one to see action in any numbers. The main petrol engine drove an electric generator which fed an electric motor driving each track. Thus steering could be effected by altering the speed of the electric motors. This led to some complications, and since the design was not thoroughly tested before production began, it was dogged with mechanical trouble for the rest of its life.

Although the Henschel design had been selected, Porsche had actually begun making the tanks in advance, and, as a result,

there were 90 chassis available. A very small number were turned into Tiger (P) tanks, but the remainder were re-worked, having the superstructure built up to carry a long 88-mm gun in the front plate. With limited traverse it thus became an anti-tank self-propelled gun rather than a tank, and it had increased armour added to bring the frontal thickness up to 200 mm.

Christened the 'Ferdinand' (after Dr Porsche) these models were issued to Panzer Regiment 654 on the Russian Front and went into action for the first time at Kursk in July 1943. The result was disastrous. Due to their limited forward arc of fire and restricted vision in other directions, they were an easy target for infantry tank-hunting parties or KV tanks which came on them from the flank. There was no doubt that nothing could survive once the Ferdinand saw it, for the gun, derived from the Flak 41 anti-aircraft gun, was extremely powerful and accurate. But flank attacks were its Achilles heel, and the majority of

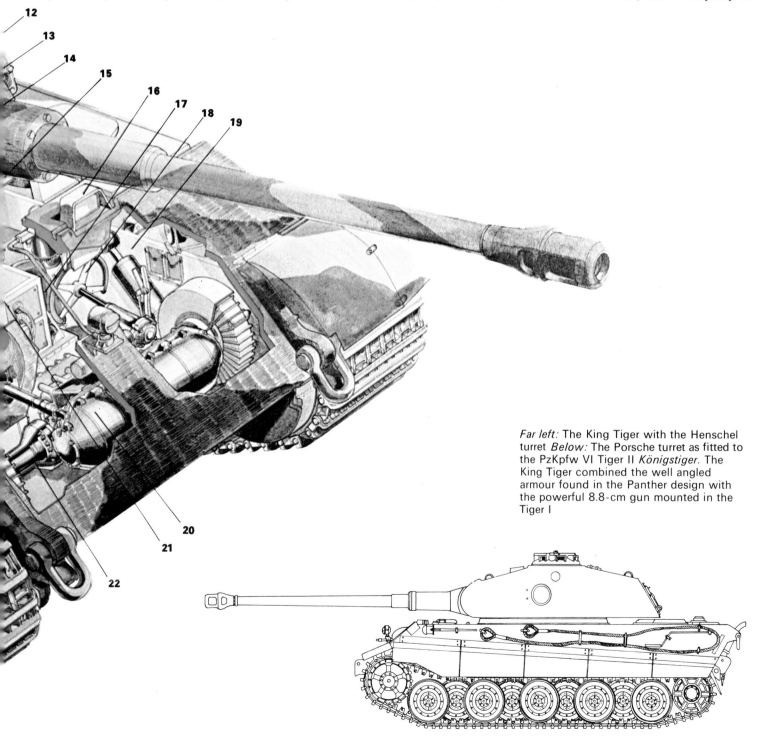

Far left: The King Tiger with the Henschel turret *Below:* The Porsche turret as fitted to the PzKpfw VI Tiger II *Königstiger.* The King Tiger combined the well angled armour found in the Panther design with the powerful 8.8-cm gun mounted in the Tiger I

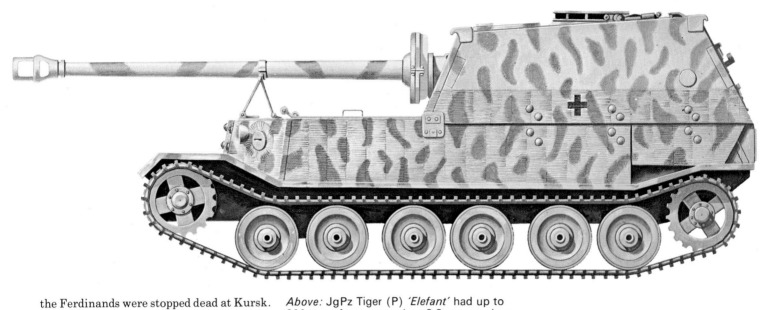

the Ferdinands were stopped dead at Kursk.

The task of removing them from the battlefield was formidable for they weighed 68 tons, and the usual 18-ton recovery vehicle couldn't move them. But many were recovered and reconditioned and some were sent to Italy, where they were found to be too heavy for the roads and bridges. By this time the disillusioned soldiers had christened them the 'Elephants' and most of them were either abandoned, captured, or blown up by their own crews long before the war ended.

While the Tiger had been accepted for service it was appreciated that it was not the best of designs, and something of less weight and better agility was wanted. The first suggestion was simply to copy the T-34 as it stood, but this was recognised as being impossible since it would have demanded engineering techniques not readily available in Germany. Common sense prevailed and development contracts were given to Daimler-Benz and MAN, asking for a 30–35 ton tank with 60 mm of sloped armour, a 75-mm gun and a speed of 55 km/h (34 mph).

The Daimler-Benz design was practically a copy of the T-34 in essentials; sloped armour, large road wheels (though not a Christie suspension) and the turret set well to the front. Forethought was shown in providing a fighting compartment big enough to take a larger gun in time to come, by fitting a diesel engine, and by using leaf springs and steel wheels to save rubber and avoid the costly torsion bars. All things considered it was an excellent design with much potential.

The MAN design, on the other hand, was more complicated; it was higher, had the turret set well back, used a petrol engine, had torsion bar suspension with interleaved rubber-tyred wheels and, in standard German fashion, drove the tracks from the front sprocket, the drive from the engine passing down the spine of the tank. Hitler was much taken with the Daimler design and authorised production, but the Army Weapons Office preferred the MAN design since it had a familiar feel to it, so for once the Fuhrer's orders were quietly cancelled and MAN got the contract.

The new vehicle was to be called the PzKpfw V 'Panther'. Production began in November 1942 and by the end of the war 4814 had been built. In spite of the fact that the MAN design was not as good as that of Daimler-Benz, the fact remains that the

Panther was one of the best tanks of the war.

Production of just over 6000 of their best tanks in three years doesn't sound like a very great effort on behalf of the German manufacturers, especially when one considers that Britain, with a comparable industrial base, built 8600 in 1942 alone. There were two reasons for this; firstly that Hitler refused to cancel production of the out-dated PzKpfw III and IV and allow capacity to be turned over to Panthers; and secondly because a large amount of the available factory space was devoted to turning out a wide variety of self-propelled guns.

After the shaky start made by self-propelled guns in 1918, development proceeded slowly for many years. This was not because the artillerymen of the world failed to perceive the potential, rather that they knew they were unlikely to be given the money to develop them, and what money they did get was better spent on other things. The Americans, on the recommendation of the Westerfeldt Board, produced a handful of prototypes in the early 1920s before the end of the financial boom. One of these was an interesting 120-mm anti-aircraft gun on a Christie chassis.

The next step came in Britain with the development of the 'Birch Gun', named after General Birch, then Master-General of the Ordnance. This was a standard 18-pdr field gun mounted into a chassis derived from the Vickers Medium tank. The first model, tested in 1925, had the gun protected by a conical turret, but this made the equipment too heavy and restricted the gun's elevation. The next version mounted the gun on a pedestal, protecting it by a small shield. The mounting allowed the gun to

Left: PzKpfw V Panther Ausf D, the first production model had a top speed of 25 mph, weighed 43 tons, a maximum armour thickness of 120 mm and mounted a 7.5-cm KwK 42 L/70 gun

be elevated to 80° so that it could function as an anti-aircraft gun as well as a field piece, a dual-purpose role which was much in vogue in those days.

Eight Birch Guns were built and issued in 1926, and later became part of the Experimental Mechanised Force. The gun's role was officially described as that of a 'close support tank battery', an unfortunate piece of terminology which revived partisan feeling between tank men and gunners. The stated purpose was for the gun to be used either as an assault gun, firing direct at obstacles or enemy tanks, or as a close support artillery piece, sited close behind the front line in the normal artillery indirect-fire position. In addition, of course, it had the anti-aircraft capability in case the need arose.

Unfortunately, although the Birch Gun was a sound design, the collapse of the Experimental Mechanised Force, and the financial climate of the time, sealed the fate of the weapon. In the rush to discard the armoured concept, the baby got thrown out with the bathwater, and there was no more talk of self-propelled guns for several years in Britain.

The next move came from Germany. The artillery which formed the integral support of the Panzer divisions was wheeled, and the complaint arose that it could not keep up with the armour once the roads were left behind. The obvious answer was to put it on tracks, but although the idea was agreed, putting it into practice was deferred because all the available capacity in pre-war years was devoted to tanks. Then the infantry began agitating; in the First World War they had been provided with their own light artillery, and this practise continued, a range of 'infantry guns' being produced, but they now began asking for some of this support to go on tracks so that it, again, could keep up with the motorized elements of the Panzer divisions.

The campaign in Poland demonstrated this need, and in 1940 the 'Sturmgeschütz' or 'assault gun' made its appearance, a PzKpfw III chassis with a fixed superstructure carrying a short-barrelled 75-mm gun firing to the front. Before this, in late 1939, their standard 15-cm heavy infantry gun had been mounted on a primitive carrier, based on the chassis and running gear of the PzKpfw I. On top of the chassis the entire SIG 33 gun, wheels, shield and all, was bolted down and then surrounded on three sides by an armoured cabin. What resulted was an awkward and top-heavy contraption, but it did give the gun extra

Above: A StuG Ausf G in white wash winter camouflage. It had a 10.5-cm StuK 42 and one machine-gun, armour up to 90 mm thick and a top speed of 25 mph with a range of 105 miles

Right: A *Jagdpanzer* IV mounted a 7.5-cm StuK 40 on a PzKpfw IV chassis and was the first true 'hunting tank', previous track mounted anti-tank guns offered poor crew protection

Below: JgPz V *Jagdpanther*, the best of all the 'hunting tanks' had a top speed of 29 mph and a range of 130 miles. The àrmour was well sloped and maximum thickness was 80 mm. The gun was an 8.8-cm Pak 43/3

mobility and allowed it to get closer to the front and assist in assault.

The next catalyst was the Eastern Front, as the Russian tank strength began to build up. Anti-tank guns were required in large numbers or, failing that, anti-tank guns with good mobility, and the solution was found by taking innumerable different types of foreign and captured chassis and mounting upon them an equally diverse collection of captured and spare anti-tank guns. This led to such peculiar arrangements as ex-Czech 47-mm guns on top of ex-British Carden-Loyd carriers; 37-mm German anti-tank guns bolted to the top of ex-Soviet artillery tractors; and 47-mm French anti-tank guns on top of de-turreted, captured Matilda tanks.

In slightly more sensible vein, there were numbers of standard German half-track personnel carriers provided with German anti-tank guns and ex-Soviet 76-mm guns mounted neatly onto the ex-Czech Model 38 tank chassis.

From all this improvisation some firm ideas about what was desirable in a self-propelled anti-tank equipment came to the surface, and resulted in the 'Jagdpanzer' or 'tank hunters', specialised armoured vehicles with limited-traverse guns in the front plate, whose task was, as their name implied, to search out and destroy tanks.

To ensure success, the Jagdpanzer were invariably provided with much more powerful guns than the equivalent turreted vehicles, largely because the restrictions on size and recoil thrust laid down by the size of the turret no longer applied. Armament was therefore the long-barrelled 75-mm gun or the 88-mm. The search for more performance culminated in the Jagdtiger, a 'King Tiger' chassis with a fixed superstructure,

Right: The JgPz 38(t) *'Hetzer'* used the chassis of the PzKpfw 38(t) to mount a 7.5-cm Pak 39. Maximum armour was 60 mm. The vehicle had a top speed of 26 mph and maximum range of 110 miles

Below: The armour distribution on the Hetzer. Thickest around the glacis and the base of the gun it was well angled around the flanks and rear. The first models appeared in 1944 and by the end of the war over 1500 had been built. A number were fitted out as flame throwers and a remotely controlled MG 42 was fitted to the roof for close in defence

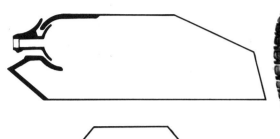

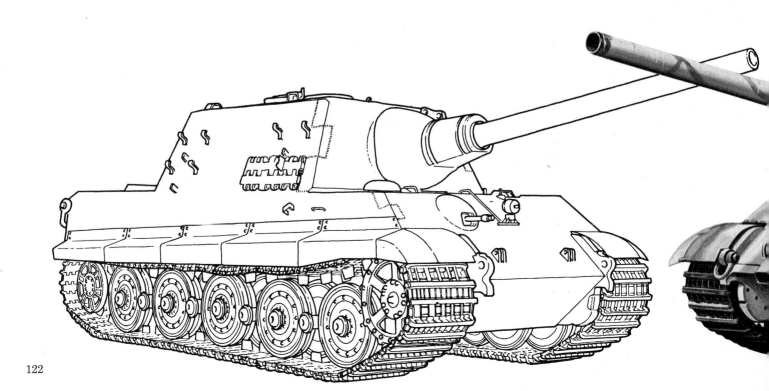

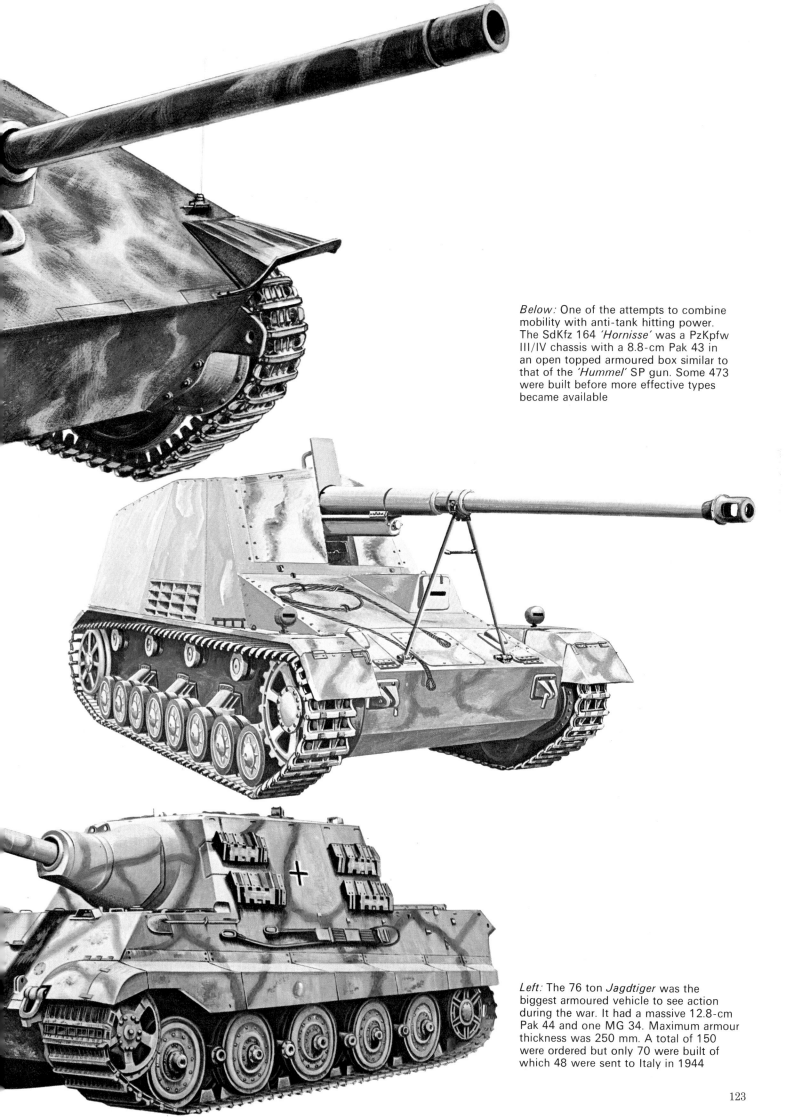

Below: One of the attempts to combine mobility with anti-tank hitting power. The SdKfz 164 *'Hornisse'* was a PzKpfw III/IV chassis with a 8.8-cm Pak 43 in an open topped armoured box similar to that of the *'Hummel'* SP gun. Some 473 were built before more effective types became available

Left: The 76 ton *Jagdtiger* was the biggest armoured vehicle to see action during the war. It had a massive 12.8-cm Pak 44 and one MG 34. Maximum armour thickness was 250 mm. A total of 150 were ordered but only 70 were built of which 48 were sent to Italy in 1944

The SdKfz 138 *'Marder'* III was the late model Marder with the fighting compartment extended to the back of the hull. It mounted a 7.5-cm Pak 40/3

carrying a massive 128-mm anti-tank gun. This fired a 28-lb piercing shell which would go through 7 in of best armour plate at two miles range.

As a result of all this enthusiasm, by the latter part of 1944 there were more self-propelled gun mountings coming from the German factories than there were tanks, and by January 1945 the army had more assault guns than it had tanks. As a corollary to this the assault gun tended to be used instead of a tank if a tank was not available.

The Soviet Army, after exposure to this type of vehicle in German hands, recognised its worth and began to produce similar types of assault and anti-tank gun. The first was the SU-76, a translation of the 76-mm field gun to the chassis of the redundant T-70 light tank. Its performance was quite reasonable, but the maximum of 25-mm of armour was insufficient for the role of tank destroyer and it was soon relegated to the position of infantry support assault gun, in which it performed well.

The Soviets have always adhered to the policy, in artillery, that a good big 'un will always beat a good little 'un, and they rapidly produced the SU-85, a T-34 chassis mounting an 85-mm gun derived from a high-velocity anti-aircraft gun. They followed this with the SU-122 which mounted a 122-mm howitzer on the same chassis. These vehicles were of the simplest form; a massively armoured box on top of the basic chassis, though the front plate was generally well sloped to give frontal protection.

In Britain the move to self-propulsion came with the invasion scare of 1940, when a mobile reserve of artillery was a desirable feature. As with the early German attempts, guns of various sorts were placed on top of equally assorted tracked and wheeled chassis, but few of these were ever produced in large numbers.

The first serious British attempt to see service was the 'Bishop', or Valentine

Carriage 25-pdr. As the name implies, it used the chassis of the Valentine tank surmounted by a large steel box, from the front of which a standard field artillery 25-pdr protruded. Due to the construction the gun could only elevate to 15°, which cut the gun's maximum range to 6400 yards, less than half that attained on the normal field carriage.

One hundred Bishops were built, commencing in October 1941, and were used in the North African campaign. At the end of this campaign an investigative commission went out to Tunisia to analyse weapon performance in action and, in their report, they observed, 'Nothing good can be said of the Valentine SP, although the detachments were efficient.' The range limitation was the principal drawback, and as soon as something better was developed, Bishop was discarded.

The next British self-propelled gun to be produced was known as 'Sexton' (in keeping with the clerical tradition for British SP names) and was a 25-pdr fitted into an open-topped superstructure on the chassis of the Canadian 'Ram' tank. The 'Ram' had begun life as a Canadian attempt to produce a variant of the American Medium M3, using the M3s suspension and mechanical layout but with a new hull and turret, which, in the event, almost turned it into an M4.

The Ram turret had originally been designed to be big enough to take a 75-mm gun with room for future improvement, but in spite of this the British Tank Design hierarchy ruled that, like every other British tank of the day, it had to take the ridiculous 2-pdr. The Canadians were astute enough to design the turret with a removeable front plate so that when the British eventually saw sense and decided on a better gun, it could be fitted with the minimum of effort. When the better gun came, it proved to be the 6-pdr, which, by the time production got under way was also obsolescent.

So, one way and another, the Ram never

had a showing as a British combat tank, and the numerous chassis which had been built were converted into the 'Sexton' SP gun by simply opening out the top of the hull. This combination gave the gun its maximum elevation and performance, and the hull was roomy enough for all the gun detachment and some ammunition besides. It became an excellent equipment, well-liked by its operators (except for a tendency to burst into flames when started) and it remained in British service for many years after the war.

The Bishop and Sexton were both normal artillery weapons, handled in the normal way. The only difference between them and the standard 25-pdr was that they went into action on tracks instead of being towed. They did not, therefore, function as assault guns or tank destroyers; this side of armoured combat had been practically ignored by the British.

The only self-propelled anti-tank gun to see service was known as 'Archer' and was a 17-pdr gun mounted in a Valentine chassis. The turret was removed and the hull built up into an armoured box, the gun being mounted so as to fire to the back of the vehicle. This had its drawbacks; getting the gun into position meant some delicate handling by the driver as he inched backwards into cover, and as soon as the vehicle stopped he had to be out of his seat, otherwise the recoiling gun would take his head off. But for all that it was a nimble and easily-concealed weapon which did great execution in 1944-45.

Not surprisingly the Americans, with their great tradition of motor-mindedness, embraced the idea of self-propelled guns with great enthusiasm. Merely to list,

Right: The Soviet SU-85 used the well tried T-34 chassis to mount an 85 mm gun. The gun fired a 20 lb shell at a muzzle velocity of 2625 ft/sec a performance only slightly inferior to the German 8.8-cm Flak/Pak

without describing, the vast number of projects in this field would take several pages, so it is only possible to cover the most important of the developments and those which actually reached the status of service weapons.

Much of the early American work was spurred on by the 'tank destroyer' concept. Most nations regarded anti-tank work as a purely defensive affair, a case of siting the gun and waiting for the tank to come up to it. The US Army, however, formed Tank Destroyer Battalions and encouraged an aggressive attitude towards hunting out tanks and dealing with them. They considered that the best way to do this was to put the gun on wheels or tracks. This led to some lightweight and unprotected devices such as the 37-mm gun on a jeep, the 3-in gun on a commercial tractor chassis, even a 75-mm gun on a 'Swamp Buggy'.

The first of this class of weapon to be accepted for service was the ubiquitous 75-mm field gun (actually the old French 75-mm M1897 in modern guise) mounted on a half-track personnel carrier and firing forward, over the driver's head. It was followed by a similarly mounted 105-mm howitzer, again the standard field piece. Both these were used in small numbers in the Tunisian campaign, and while they gave worthwhile training for handling self-propelled guns in action, they were far from being serviceable machines.

The first major step came in mid-1941 when the Armored Force Board suggested mounting a 105-mm howitzer on a medium tank chassis. An artillery officer and an ordnance officer drew up a specification and eventually, in November 1941, the Ordnance Committee agreed to the production of two pilot models. By March 1942

they were ready and were then tested for three days by the Armored Force Board. At the end of the trials one pilot, marked off in chalk to indicate modifications required, was shipped off to the American Locomotive company to act as a pattern for the production engineers. It was standardised as the 'Howitzer Motor Carriage M7' in April 1942.

The M7 was based on the chassis of the M3 medium tank; the hull was left open-topped and the howitzer mounted on the front plate. To the right side, above the position of the 75-mm gun in the tank version, was a high round, anti-aircraft machine-gun mount ring, and the appearance of this, particularly when occupied, gave rise to the nickname 'Priest' in British service. The first production models were sent off to the British 8th Army in the Western Desert and were issued to Royal Horse Artillery regiments accompanying armoured formations. They played a vital part in the subsequent battles, from Alamein onward, but were replaced in British service by the 25-pdr Sexton, as that gun became available, simply on the grounds of ammunition commonality.

The M3 was also used as the basis for the second US field artillery SP gun, the 155-mm Gun Motor Carriage M12. This broke new ground in that it was no more than a convenient method of carrying and emplacing a heavy gun. There was no pretence at protection for the crew, and what armour there was was there simply by virtue of its being part of the converted hull. This gun was to be used in the normal indirect-fire role and was not intended to go rushing into combat and mixing with the enemy.

The guns used in the M12 were the 155-mm M1917 or M1918. These were the original 'GPF' guns of the French Army, which had been adopted by the Americans in 1917. The M1917 was of original French make, the M1918 of American make. By 1942 they were being replaced in field service by the much better 155-mm Gun M1, a modern design, but there was still life in the old guns and there was still plenty of

ammunition available for them. An SP mounting was suggested as being a useful way to use them up, but there was objection on the grounds that the heavy firing shock would probably be too much for the suspension.

Rock Island Arsenal decided to look into this problem and they devised a system which has remained in use ever since, as well as being widely adopted in other countries. A steel blade, similar to that of a bulldozer, was hung at the rear of the chassis; when the gun went into action this could be dropped to the ground and the vehicle reversed a few inches so that the blade dug in. This then acted as a rigid strut and took the firing shock off the suspension. To go out of action all that was necessary was to start up and drive forward; the blade was pulled free and hoisted clear by a rope and pulley, and the gun was out of action and ready for the road. This was a considerable improvement on the twenty minutes or so of hard work needed to displace the towed version of the gun.

While the M12 was a good technical solution, the fact remained that it was perpetuating an obsolete gun, and relatively few were made, though 26 went to Europe with the US 1st Army and served throughout the campaign. But when it was proposed to take the same gun and mount it on a later type of chassis, the idea was turned down. Instead of the old M1917 gun, the new M1 was to be used for future development, and this weapon, allied to a chassis derived from the M4 medium tank, entered service as the 155-mm Gun M40.

In artillery service the 155-mm Gun M1 used the same split-trail carriage as the 8-in howitzer M1, so it was logical to make a similar partnership on tracks, and a small modification to the M40 to suit the balance of the 8-in howitzer produced the M43.

Alongside the development of field artillery the Americans were devoting much attention to tank destroyers. This role had initially been filled by the development of the 3-in Gun Motor Carriage M10, an M4 diesel-engined chassis with a flat-topped hull and an open-topped turret carrying a

3-in gun M7. This was derived from the anti-aircraft 3-in M3 and had been originally modified for use in the abortive M6 heavy tank. It could pierce 100-mm of plate at 1000 yards which, at the time of its standardisation in mid-1942, was acceptable.

In December 1943, however, after about 8000 had been made and more information about German tanks was to hand, it was realised that a more powerful gun would be needed in order to ensure success against Tigers and Panthers. The 3-in AA gun had given way to a 90-mm model of much greater power, so the obvious answer was to re-gun the M10 with this 90-mm weapon. This upped the performance so that the new equipment, known as the M36, could take on any German tank with a good chance of defeating it. Large numbers of M10s were taken into British service and as soon as there were sufficient guns to spare, the 3-in were removed and replaced by British 17-pdrs, which had a performance even better than the American 90-mm.

By the time the M36 went into service the designers were beginning to look beyond the M4 as a suitable chassis, because the tank designers had been improving the army's tanks. The Light M2 and Medium M3 had formed the start of mass production; they had been supplanted by the Light M3 and M5 and the Medium M4, and once these were in production the designers had, while maintaining a stream of improvements and modifications to these, been busy designing something better as their replacements.

Although the light tank had been discredited in every other army, it stayed in service until the end of the war with the Americans, largely because they possessed the best light tank ever developed. The Light M2 had subsequently become the M3, by virtue of minor improvements, and then became the M5 when given a change of engines, but by middle 1942 it was struggling on the battlefield and there was also a movement afoot to develop a tank which could be carried in an airplane for use by airborne troops. All this pointed to a new light tank design, the principal requirements of which were more armour and a lower silhouette.

One team of designers produced the T7 which looked very much like the M2 but for a welded turret and a cast hull, however, the weight then exceeded 22 tons, so it was no longer a light tank. Meanwhile another team had developed the T9 for airborne use; this weighed only 7½ tons, had a three-man crew and was armed with a 37-mm gun. As a combat light tank it had gone the other way and was too light, but as an airborne tank it was suitable and was standardised as the M22. It later went into British service as the 'Tetrarch'.

Those responsible for the light tank had been forced to the conclusion that the degree of protection and armament demanded meant no return to pre-war weights, and their next offering, the T24, turned the scales at 18 tons, had 2.5-in armour and carried a 75-mm gun. Ultimately standardised as the M24, it was known in British service as the 'General Chaffee', in tribute to the first commander of the US Armored Force who had died of overwork shortly before the US had entered the war and was thus denied seeing the fulfilment of all he had worked for.

Next for replacement was the medium tank; this turned out to be a long job. Several prototypes were built but none was found satisfactory, although several individual features were grafted on to the current production of the M4, leading to all sorts of variants.

Eventually the designers got it right, with the T26E1 prototype. This used an entirely new torsion bar suspension with large road wheels, a heavy cast turret with a powerful 90-mm gun, and a 470-hp Ford engine with Torquematic drive. Unfortunately it weighed 38.6 tons, and as a result it was re-classified and standardised

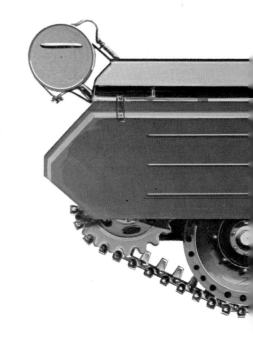

as the Heavy Tank M26 or 'General Pershing'. This was in March 1945, and in one blow the designers had solved two problems; they had built the last medium tank in US service and also produced a serviceable heavy tank. Indeed, it was probably the success of the M26 which began the move away from trying to classify tanks into particular groups.

On June 6, 1944 the British, Canadian and American armies crossed the English Channel and landed in Normandy to commence the liberation of Europe and the eventual invasion of Germany. In preparation for this event, the tank designers had been hard at work in Britain, firstly to try and evolve some sound and combat-worthy tanks to make up for the rather less than perfect examples they had produced previously, and secondly to develop some variations on the tank theme to provide solutions to some of the problems associated with the amphibious landing and the penetration of Hitler's Atlantic Wall.

The Christie-suspended cruiser-tank line had been brought up to date by a fresh design using a respectably sized turret which could take the 6-pdr gun with room for future improvement. The first of these to appear was the Cavalier, which was

Left: A US M7 105 mm SP gun — known by the British as 'The Priest' because of the pulpit style AA position

Right Top: A US M12 SP Howitzer which mounted the 155 mm Gun M1917 which was derived from the French 155 mm GPF taken over in the First World War

Right: The US M10 tank destroyer mounted a powerful 3 in M5 anti-tank gun

Below: The British Cavalier developed in 1941 was based on battle experience with the Crusader

succeeded by the Centaur and Cromwell. The difference between these three was largely a matter of the engine. The Cavalier took a Liberty engine and was almost immediately relegated to training roles. The Centaur showed some detail improvements and also mounted the Liberty engine; most of these had 6-pdr guns but a number were fitted with 95-mm howitzers as close support tanks for the invasion, being manned by Royal Marines. Finally, the Cromwell had a Rolls-Royce Meteor engine; early models had the 6-pdr but this was soon replaced by a 75-mm gun, the same weapon as was then being fitted into American tanks. The Cromwell was to become the most important British tank in the last year of the war.

Below: A British built A27 Cromwell Mk IV. Powered by a Rolls Royce V-12cyl and armed with a 75-mm gun, this tank had a top speed of 40 mph and a laden weight of 27½ tons

In the hope of providing a knock-out punch, the Cromwell chassis was given an enlarged turret and fitted with a 17-pdr gun, the result being called the Challenger. However relatively few of these were made, since it was found possible to shoe-horn the 17-pdr into the turret of an M4 tank, to produce the combination which the British called the 'Firefly'. This was a most effective tank hunter, but, being easily recognised by its extra-long gun barrel, it became the prime target of the Tigers and Panthers in France and Germany.

With the Firefly holding the ring, the designers went back and had another look at the Challenger idea. In order to do the job properly a vast amount of re-design would have to be done, though the gun-makers stepped in providentially with a shortened version of the 17-pdr called the 77-mm gun. It fired the same shells but with a slightly shorter cartridge case, and although the result was a little less powerful than the 17-pdr it was still a very potent armament for a tank. A new turret was designed, the Christie suspension was altered, some changes made to the construction of the hull, and the result was the Comet, which, unfortunately, appeared just too late to join the war in any number.

The 'infantry tank' idea still lingered on, and much effort was wasted on pursuing the idea of a slow-heavily-armoured vehicle. Eventually, by taking the Churchill as a starting point and enlarging it, the Black

Right: The M24 Chaffee had specially designed 75-mm gun and three .30-inch Browning machine-guns, Introduced in 1943 it subsequently saw action in Korea. It was powered by two Cadillac V8s, rated at 110 bhp, 4F (twin Hydramatic) plus 2F1R transfer case. Loaded weight was 40,500 lbs

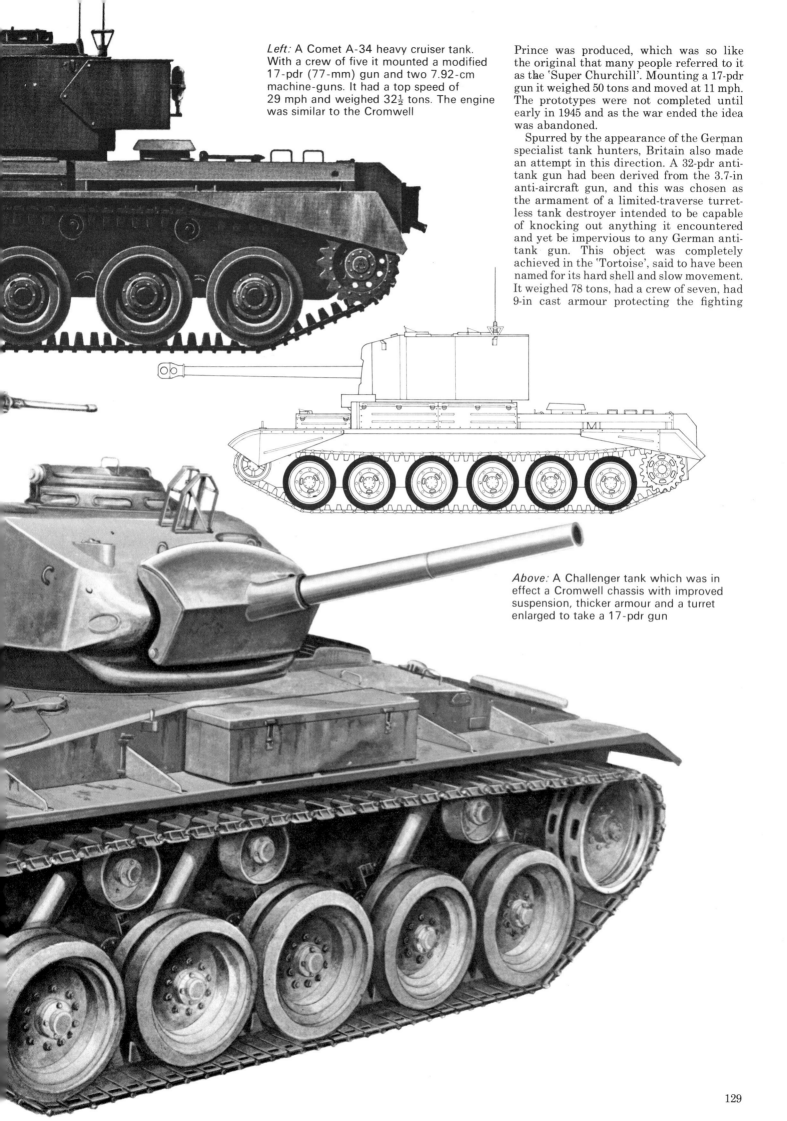

Left: A Comet A-34 heavy cruiser tank. With a crew of five it mounted a modified 17-pdr (77-mm) gun and two 7.92-cm machine-guns. It had a top speed of 29 mph and weighed 32½ tons. The engine was similar to the Cromwell

Prince was produced, which was so like the original that many people referred to it as the 'Super Churchill'. Mounting a 17-pdr gun it weighed 50 tons and moved at 11 mph. The prototypes were not completed until early in 1945 and as the war ended the idea was abandoned.

Spurred by the appearance of the German specialist tank hunters, Britain also made an attempt in this direction. A 32-pdr anti-tank gun had been derived from the 3.7-in anti-aircraft gun, and this was chosen as the armament of a limited-traverse turret-less tank destroyer intended to be capable of knocking out anything it encountered and yet be impervious to any German anti-tank gun. This object was completely achieved in the 'Tortoise', said to have been named for its hard shell and slow movement. It weighed 78 tons, had a crew of seven, had 9-in cast armour protecting the fighting

Above: A Challenger tank which was in effect a Cromwell chassis with improved suspension, thicker armour and a turret enlarged to take a 17-pdr gun

compartment, and moved at 12 mph driven by a 600-hp engine. Work began in 1944 but it was 1947 before the six pilots were completed. After their trials four were scrapped and the other two were sent to museums as a reminder of how not to build tanks.

The provision of specialist tanks for the invasion was a totally different design problem. The question here was not so much a matter of armour and armament as the addition of devices to perform special tasks. In August 1942 a Commando raid on Dieppe had included some Churchill tanks, the intention being to land them on the beach and then use them as armoured support in the subsequent action. After landing, however, they were confronted with various obstacles which they could neither climb over nor blast a way through, and they remained on the beach throughout the entire operation, rendering very little help. This lesson was not lost on those beginning to plan for the final invasion, and in late 1942 a special formation, the 79th Armoured Division, was activated.

The problems facing a landing force were, briefly, mines on the beaches, ditches, vertical walls, and, most basic of all, actually getting on to the beach in the first place. These problems were solved by a variety of specialised vehicles.

Firstly, to get ashore, swimming tanks were developed. These were Sherman M4s with screens running around the hull, attached to the hull just above the track and extending above the turret roof. The space thus enclosed added to the buoyancy of the tank and allowed it to float. A propeller at the stern was driven by a power take-off from the gearbox, leading to the official nomenclature of 'Duplex Drive' or 'DD' tanks. In the water they appeared to be some sort of small landing barge, but as they approached the shoreline they climbed out on their tracks, and, by means of a small explosive charge, blew away the screens to appear completely ready for action.

Below: Churchill Mk IIs on a Southern Command exercise in October 1942. A 7.92-mm Besa machine-gun has been mounted in the hull to replace the 3-in howitzer in the Mk I

Below: A Carrier, Churchill, 3-in Mk I, a crude form of assault gun produced as a stop-gap home defence weapon. Surplus 3-in AA guns were mounted on a Churchill chassis, but the vehicle was unsatisfactory and they were never used in action

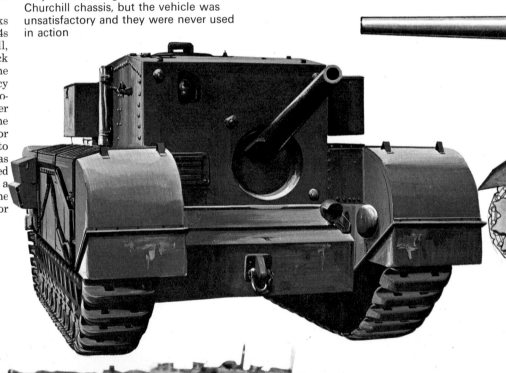

Left: A Churchill Mk I mounting a 3-inch howitzer in the hull and a 2-pdr in the turret. It was powered by a 12 cylinder Bedford horizontally opposed engine of 350 BHP which gave a top speed of 17 mph

Below: A section through a M-10 tank destroyer. It had an open turret, thick frontal armour and either a 76-mm gun in the US marks and a powerful 17-pdr in the British

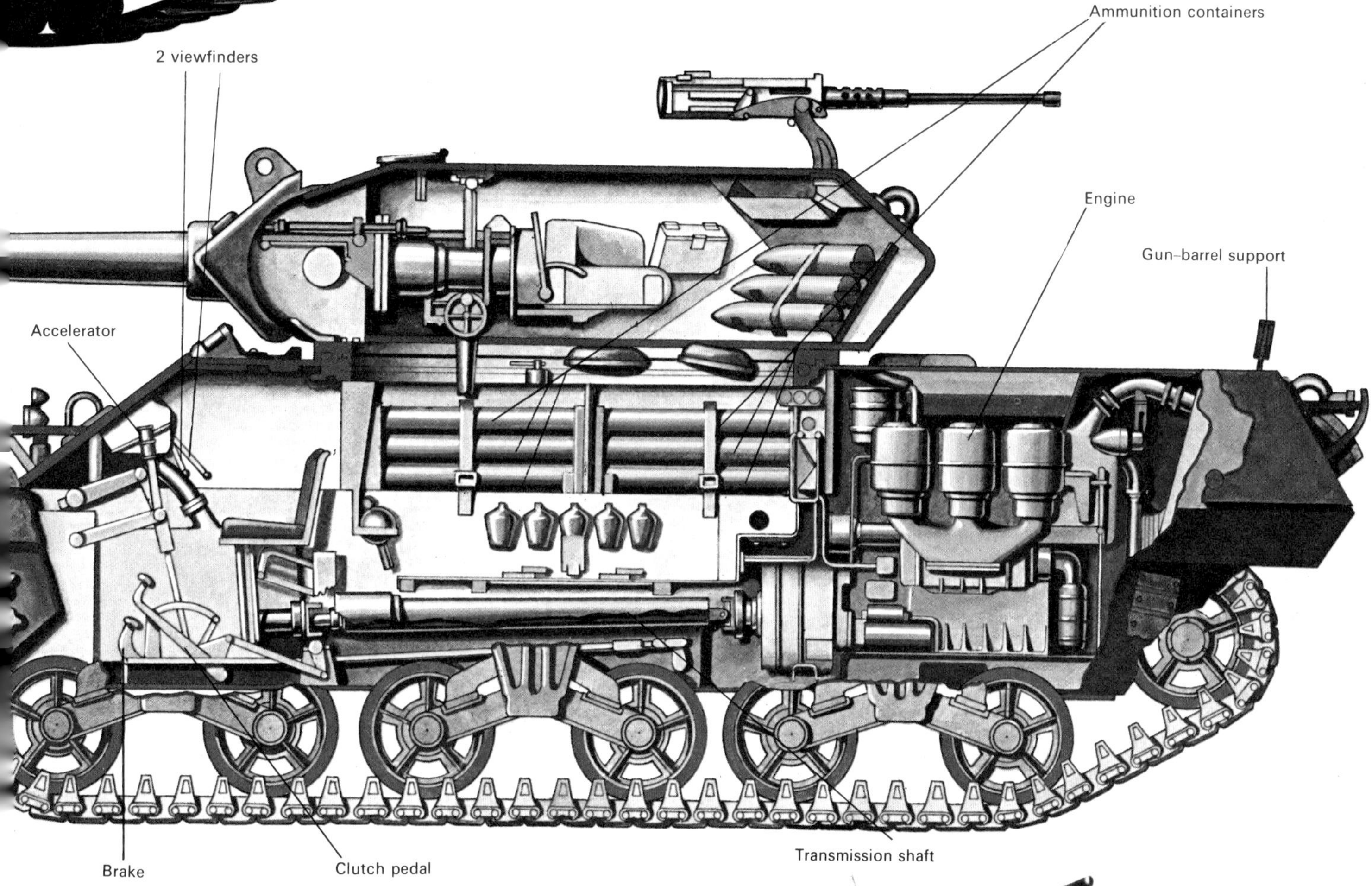

Ammunition containers

2 viewfinders

Engine

Gun–barrel support

Accelerator

Brake

Clutch pedal

Transmission shaft

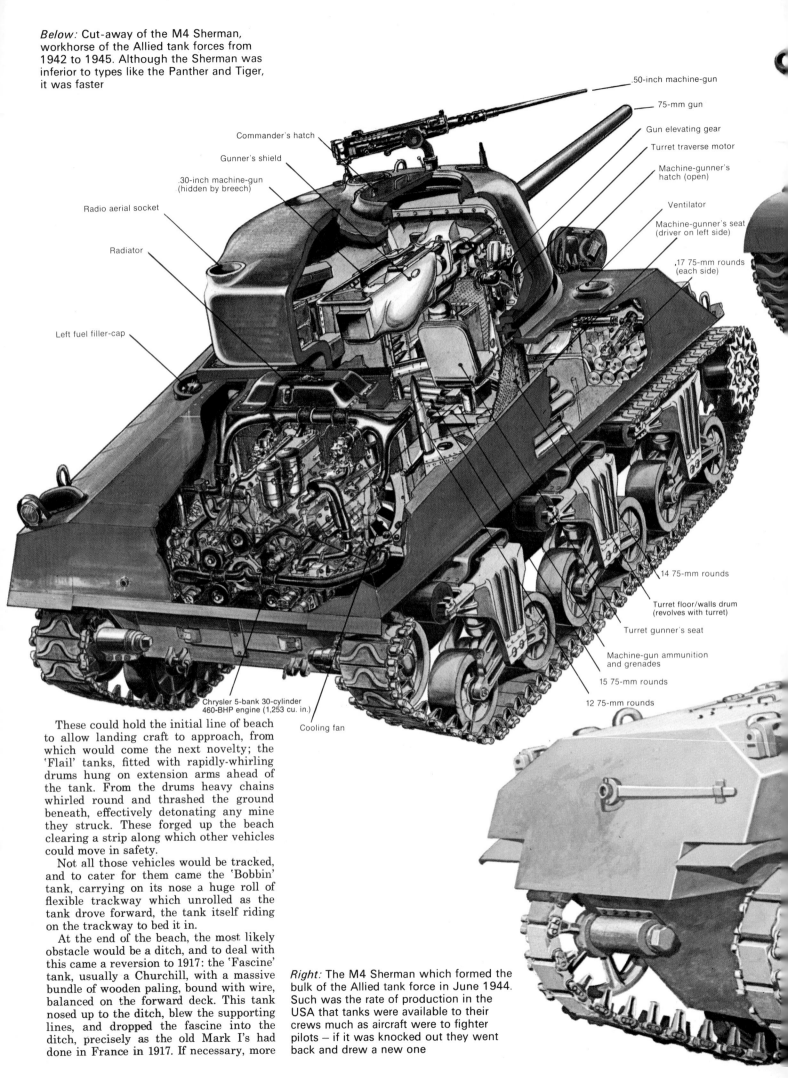

Below: Cut-away of the M4 Sherman, workhorse of the Allied tank forces from 1942 to 1945. Although the Sherman was inferior to types like the Panther and Tiger, it was faster

Commander's hatch

Gunner's shield

.30-inch machine-gun (hidden by breech)

Radio aerial socket

Radiator

Left fuel filler-cap

.50-inch machine-gun

75-mm gun

Gun elevating gear

Turret traverse motor

Machine-gunner's hatch (open)

Ventilator

Machine-gunner's seat (driver on left side)

.17 75-mm rounds (each side)

14 75-mm rounds

Turret floor/walls drum (revolves with turret)

Turret gunner's seat

Machine-gun ammunition and grenades

15 75-mm rounds

12 75-mm rounds

Chrysler 5-bank 30-cylinder 460-BHP engine (1,253 cu. in.)

Cooling fan

These could hold the initial line of beach to allow landing craft to approach, from which would come the next novelty; the 'Flail' tanks, fitted with rapidly-whirling drums hung on extension arms ahead of the tank. From the drums heavy chains whirled round and thrashed the ground beneath, effectively detonating any mine they struck. These forged up the beach clearing a strip along which other vehicles could move in safety.

Not all those vehicles would be tracked, and to cater for them came the 'Bobbin' tank, carrying on its nose a huge roll of flexible trackway which unrolled as the tank drove forward, the tank itself riding on the trackway to bed it in.

At the end of the beach, the most likely obstacle would be a ditch, and to deal with this came a reversion to 1917: the 'Fascine' tank, usually a Churchill, with a massive bundle of wooden paling, bound with wire, balanced on the forward deck. This tank nosed up to the ditch, blew the supporting lines, and dropped the fascine into the ditch, precisely as the old Mark I's had done in France in 1917. If necessary, more

Right: The M4 Sherman which formed the bulk of the Allied tank force in June 1944. Such was the rate of production in the USA that tanks were available to their crews much as aircraft were to fighter pilots – if it was knocked out they went back and drew a new one

Above: The Sherman Firefly weighed 32.9 tons, had a top speed of 24 mph and a range of 120 miles. It's chief asset was the 17-pdr anti-tank gun

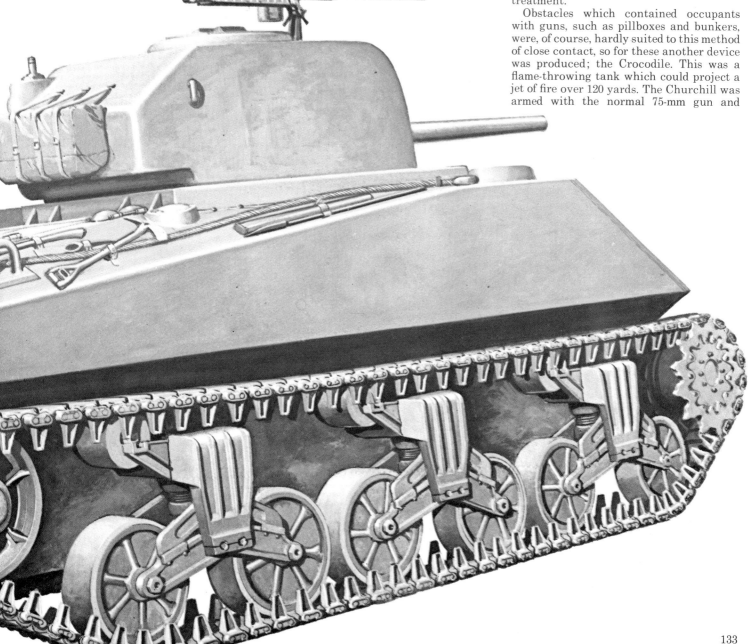

than one fascine went in, and then a Churchill, with a top deck reinforced with trackways, would drop into the ditch and sit on the fascines, making its top deck into a bridge for following tanks. If the ditch was too wide or deep for this technique, another Churchill, this time carrying a folding bridge, could drive up and unfold its bridge across the gap.

The vertical wall and concrete pillboxes were dealt with by the AVRE – Armoured Vehicle, Royal Engineers – a Churchill mounting a highly specialised short-range mortar which fired a massive 40-lb bomb designed to wreck concrete. Known officially as the 'Petard', and less officially as the 'Flying Dustbin', this could effectively breach most obstacles, but another approach was to bring up the next bridging tank and lay the bridge against the obstacle as a ramp, up which other tanks could drive.

If an obstacle could not be overcome by any of these methods, the 'Goat' was called in. This tank carried, on a framework out front, an 1800-lb charge of TNT. The tank, usually a Churchill AVRE, drove up to the obstacle until the charge made contact, whereupon it was released and forced against the obstacle. The tank then backed off, paying out an electric lead, to a safe distance and touched off the charge. Very little could withstand the effect of such treatment.

Obstacles which contained occupants with guns, such as pillboxes and bunkers, were, of course, hardly suited to this method of close contact, so for these another device was produced; the Crocodile. This was a flame-throwing tank which could project a jet of fire over 120 yards. The Churchill was armed with the normal 75-mm gun and

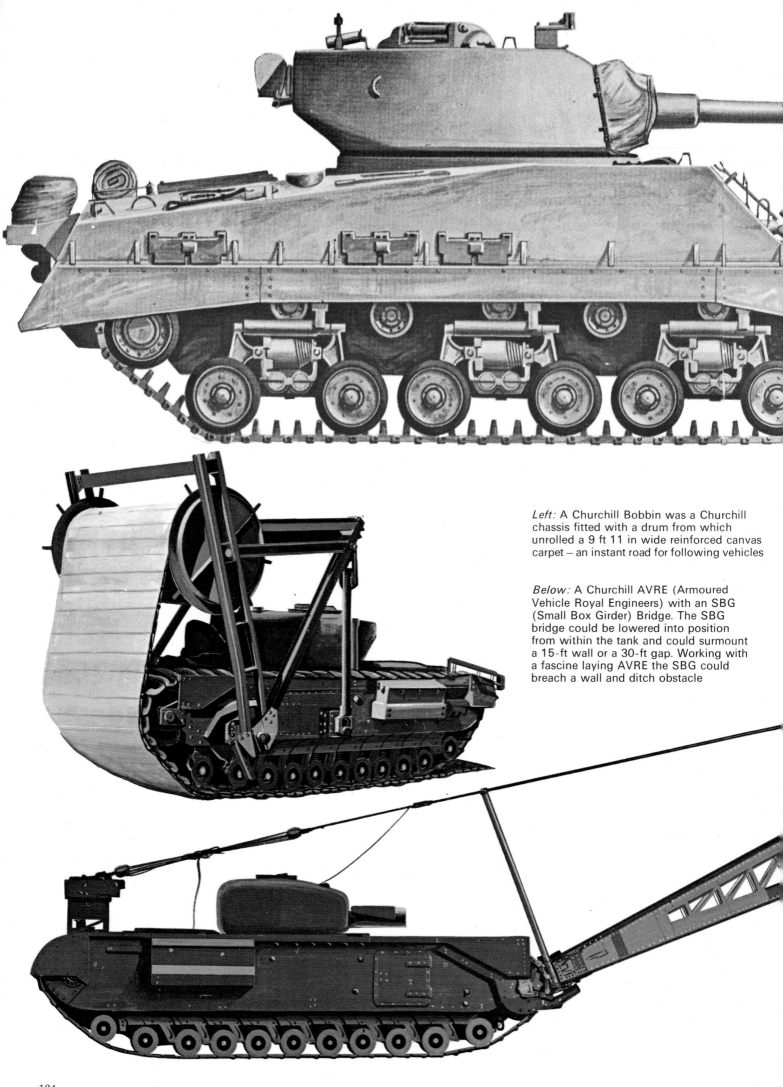

Left: A Churchill Bobbin was a Churchill chassis fitted with a drum from which unrolled a 9 ft 11 in wide reinforced canvas carpet – an instant road for following vehicles

Below: A Churchill AVRE (Armoured Vehicle Royal Engineers) with an SBG (Small Box Girder) Bridge. The SBG bridge could be lowered into position from within the tank and could surmount a 15-ft wall or a 30-ft gap. Working with a fascine laying AVRE the SBG could breach a wall and ditch obstacle

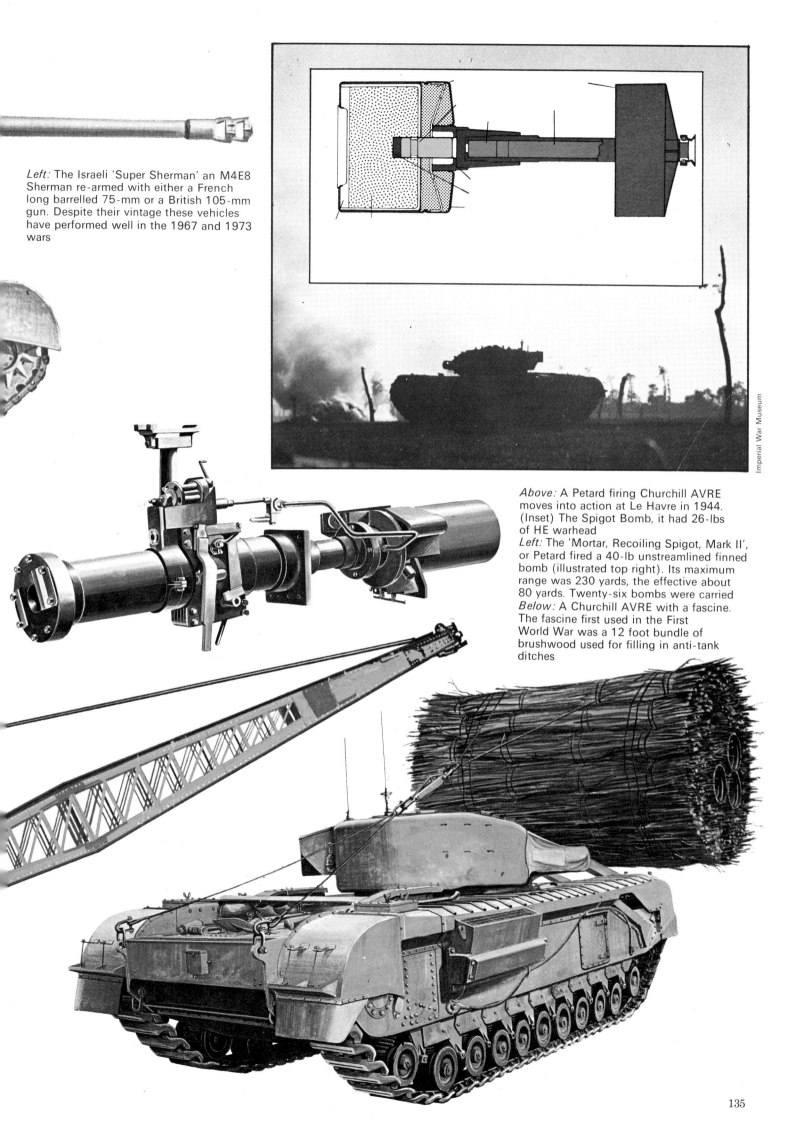

Left: The Israeli 'Super Sherman' an M4E8 Sherman re-armed with either a French long barrelled 75-mm or a British 105-mm gun. Despite their vintage these vehicles have performed well in the 1967 and 1973 wars

Imperial War Museum

Above: A Petard firing Churchill AVRE moves into action at Le Havre in 1944. (Inset) The Spigot Bomb, it had 26-lbs of HE warhead
Left: The 'Mortar, Recoiling Spigot, Mark II', or Petard fired a 40-lb unstreamlined finned bomb (illustrated top right). Its maximum range was 230 yards, the effective about 80 yards. Twenty-six bombs were carried
Below: A Churchill AVRE with a fascine. The fascine first used in the First World War was a 12 foot bundle of brushwood used for filling in anti-tank ditches

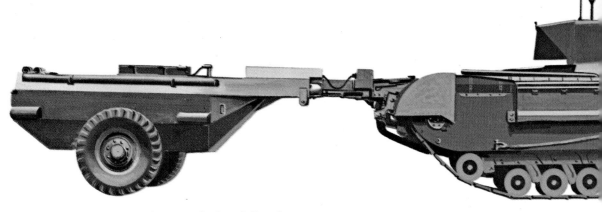

Below: A Churchill Armoured Recovery Vehicle Mk I. Its jib had a maximum lift of 3 tons. In the background are Canadian Ram and Kangaroo tanks

Right: A Sherman Crab, a flail tank designed to clear a path through minefields. Its loaded chains beat the ground detonating the mines in its path

Below: A column of Churchill Arks in Italy. The Ark could scale a 12 foot wall or span a 30 foot ditch

Centre: A tank commander checks his fascine during operations in northern Europe. The rope securing the bundle of brushwood is attached to the inside of the turret so that the crew can drop the fascine without having to leave the tank

Left and below: The Churchill Crocodile carried 400 gallons of napalm based fuel in an armoured trailer. Pressure of 280 lb p.s.i. projected 4 gallons per minute up to 120 yards. The fuel was ignited by a spark plug and carburated petrol jet. Crocodiles and AVREs made a very effective bunker destruction team

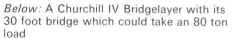

Below: A Churchill IV Bridgelayer with its 30 foot bridge which could take an 80 ton load

carried the flame projector in the hull, fuelled from a 400-gallon armoured trailer. In case the trailer was hit and set on fire it could be instantly jettisoned by an explosive breakaway charge in the trailer connection.

The whole collection was known to the rest of the army as 'The Funnies' and with their assistance the defences of Hitler's wall were breached in short order.

On the far side of Germany the Soviet Army had been preparing for their own invasion, though theirs was to be over land and did not involve the need for such things as bridgelayers and swimming tanks. What they faced was a simple slogging match, and in preparation for it they had been giving their tanks a last overhaul.

Below: A T-34/85, left over from the Second World War it was to prove a dangerous enemy during the Korean War

The first demand from the soldiers had been for a better gun than the 76-mm which formed the armament of the T-34 and the KV. This had been good enough in its day, but with the appearance of the Tiger and Panther, more punch was needed. The KV was accordingly given a larger turret and armed with an 85-mm high velocity gun, and shortly afterward the T-34 was re-designed so as to take the same turret and gun, becoming the T-34/85. This became the backbone of the Soviet tank force and was to remain in service for many years after the war.

The designers then turned their attention to the KV. There seemed to be little point in having a heavy tank which carried precisely the same armament as the medium, so the KV was completely re-cast, being made 5 ft longer, the armour doubled in thickness to a maximum of 4.7 in, and the turret enlarged. The first models of this new 'Josef Stalin' were given an 85-mm gun, but this was soon superseded by a 100-mm weapon and this, in turn, was replaced by a 122-mm gun. The JS-1 went into service in 1944 and over 2000 were built. It was almost unstoppable and its gun could dispose of any German tank, but even then, the designers were not completely satisfied.

They next threw out virtually everything except the suspension and tracks, built a new cast hull with its surfaces acutely sloped to deflect shot and to give a very low silhouette, made a new turret which is generally likened to an inverted frying pan, being low and well sloped, and put a new and improved 122-mm gun into it.

Weighing 45½ tons, with a crew of four, it was powered by a 520-hp diesel engine to give it a speed of 23 mph, and had a maximum of 4.7-in armour. It went into service early in 1945; few actually saw battle, but their appearance in Berlin after the fighting was over was as big a surprise to the Western Allies as it had been to the Germans.

And so eventually the Shermans and Comets and Cromwells and T-34s and KVs and Josef Stalins defeated the Tigers and Panthers and PzKpfw IVs and the war was over. The analysis has been going on ever since and will go on for many years yet, but, on balance, it was quantity that won the war, not quality. The German Panzers who had sown the wind, reaped the whirlwind not because they lost their skill but because they lost tanks faster than they could replace them. The figures speak for themselves; the German factories produced 23 487 tanks from 1939 to the end of 1944; Britain produced 27 000; the USA 88 276; and the USSR the staggering total of 109 700.

Although the shooting stopped in 1945 the search for tank supremacy was to go on, and continues to this day. By now, though, complications have crept in; guns have reached new degrees of sophistication, missiles have appeared, new types of armour replace the traditional steels, electronics

proliferate, lasers and rangefinders, radars and infrared help the commander to find his target. New and deadly weapons have been devised to deal with the tank, for the old-time anti-tank gun has disappeared, foundered under its own weight like some prehistoric monster. But the basic parameters are still there; the tank is a combination of firepower, speed and protection, and what you get depends on how you

shuffle those three cards. The game is the same as it was in 1916; one thing that has changed, however, is the size of the pot. The original British tanks of 1917 cost £5000 apiece; a recent press report announces that the new Swiss battle tank will cost £550 000.

Novosti Press Agency

Above: Tank riders leap from their T-34s during fighting in southern Russia. The combination of tanks and infantry allowed a haphazard but effective form of close support. Casualties were high, but the tanks could destroy enemy machine-gun posts while the infantry took out the anti-tank guns

Below: The Soviet JS-3 mounted a powerful 122-mm gun. It was introduced in 1945 and caused a stir at the Allied victory parade in Berlin

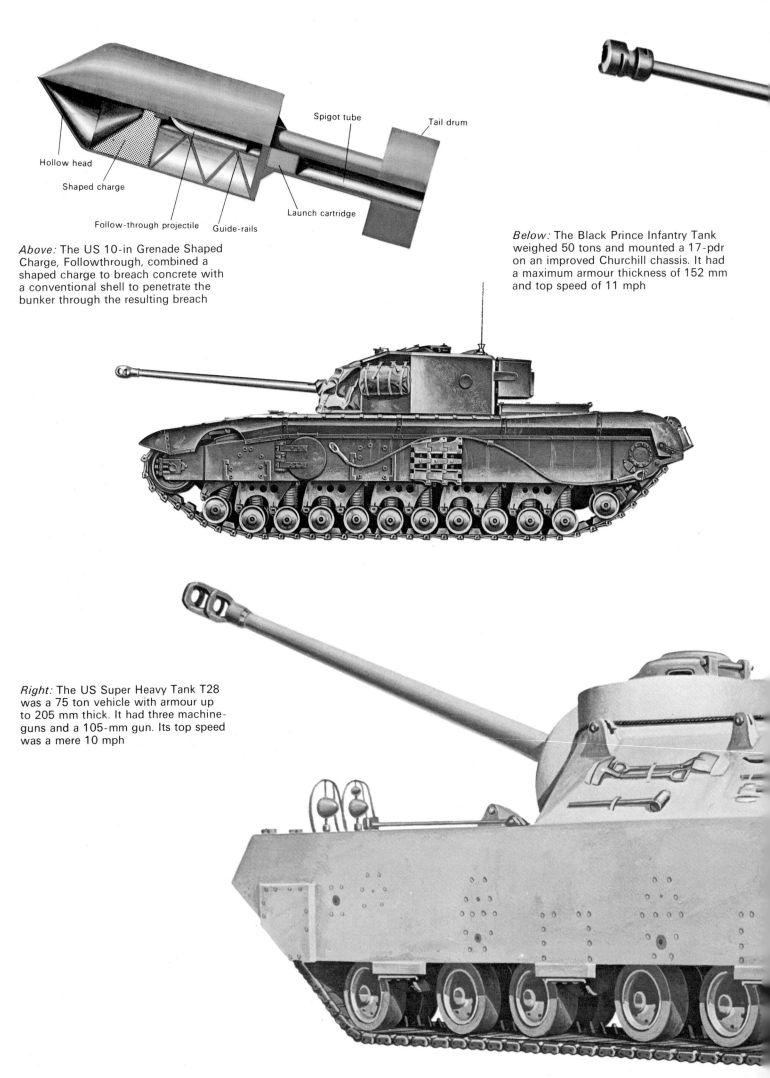

Above: The US 10-in Grenade Shaped Charge, Followthrough, combined a shaped charge to breach concrete with a conventional shell to penetrate the bunker through the resulting breach

Hollow head

Shaped charge

Follow-through projectile

Guide-rails

Launch cartridge

Spigot tube

Tail drum

Below: The Black Prince Infantry Tank weighed 50 tons and mounted a 17-pdr on an improved Churchill chassis. It had a maximum armour thickness of 152 mm and top speed of 11 mph

Right: The US Super Heavy Tank T28 was a 75 ton vehicle with armour up to 205 mm thick. It had three machine-guns and a 105-mm gun. Its top speed was a mere 10 mph

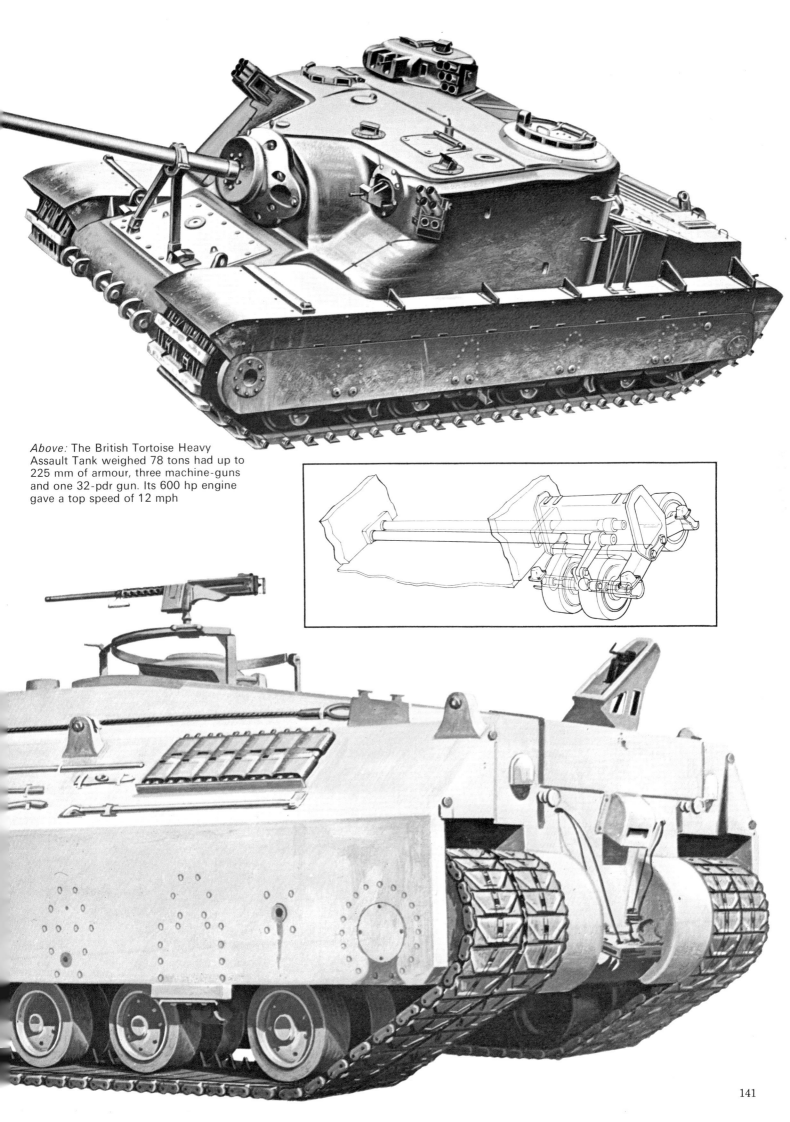

Above: The British Tortoise Heavy Assault Tank weighed 78 tons had up to 225 mm of armour, three machine-guns and one 32-pdr gun. Its 600 hp engine gave a top speed of 12 mph

Maus

The German super-tank *Maus* was designed by Dr Porsche from 1942 onwards. This monster weighed 183 tons and carried a 12·8-cm gun and a 7·5-cm auxiliary gun. A 1375-horsepower engine drove through an electric transmission to give a top speed of 12 mph. The layout of the vehicle was unusual in having the engine compartment in the middle and the fighting compartment at the rear. Armour of up to 9-in thickness was fitted. The whole concept was out of date before it ever began, since every other nation had abandoned the idea of super-tanks due to their immense bulk, slow production, and vulnerability in the battle-field. Although construction of one or two specimens was under way when the war ended, no *Maus* tanks were ever completed, and even had they reached the field they would probably have disappointed their backers

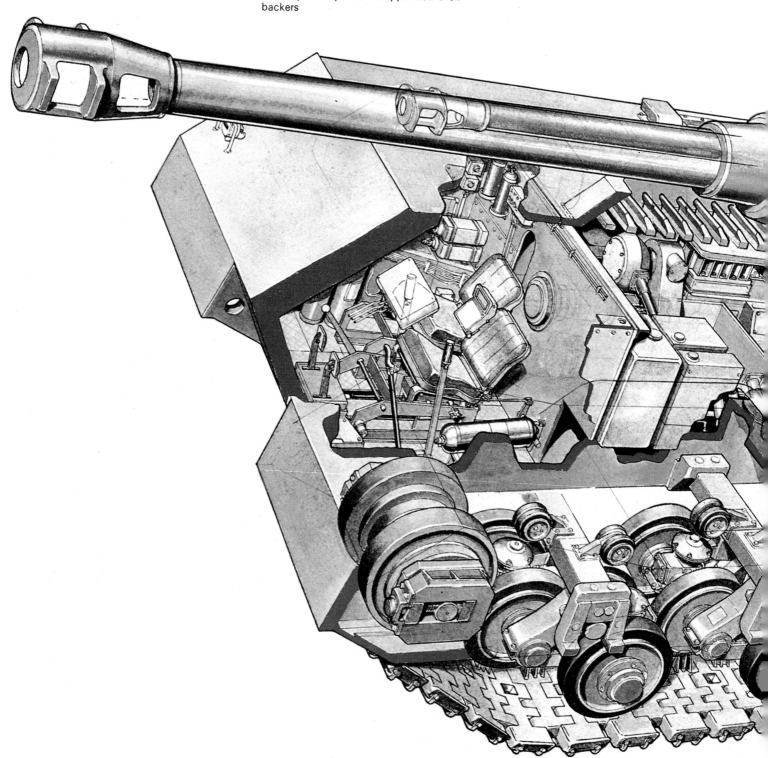

A weapon which surprised the Allies was this 38-cm Rocket Launcher. The blast from the rocket was turned around and vented through the ring of holes surrounding the muzzle

J. B. King

AFTER THE VICTORY
new tanks same principles

After the end of the Second World War the initial financial policies of the Western Allies were much the same as they had been in 1918. Contracts were slashed overnight and thousands of tanks scheduled for production were cancelled. In spite of this, some projects, which had gone so far that scrapping was impractical, were allowed to run to their completion, so that theories could be proved or disproved and design concepts carried to the functioning conclusion. In this fashion such vehicles as the British Black Prince and Tortoise and the American T29 series went as far as pilot models.

The British had been well aware that their final cruiser tank, the Comet, was far from being the best solution, and in 1944 work had begun on a new 'universal' tank, finally doing away with the 'infantry' and 'cruiser' demarcation. This project managed to produce six pilot models in time for troop trials in Germany in May 1945 but the end of the war prevented them being tried in combat. The troop trial results, however, were sufficiently good for the design to be accepted as the postwar standard and it entered service as the 'Centurion'.

These first models carried a 17-pdr turret gun as the main armament, with a 20-mm Polsten automatic cannon mounted independently in the left front of the turret. Weighing 47 tons, it had a 620-hp engine, up to 6 in of armour, and could travel at 22 mph. The Christie suspension was abandoned for a highly modified Horstmann system which mounted six road wheels on each side in coupled pairs, and for the first time in British armour the front hull plate was sloped to deflect shot.

In the USA there was not only the expected run-down in equipment contracts, but also a sudden change of heart about the whole subject of armour. Tanks, it was now contended by some sections of the US Army, were best suited to the role of exploiting success achieved by other branches, and not actually best utilised as a striking force. This peculiar opinion seems to have gained ground in spite of, and not because of, the record of US tanks in Germany in 1944–45. There was also an exaggerated opinion of the worth of such wartime anti-tank weapons as the Bazooka and Panzerfaust, leading to the view that the anti-tank weapon threat was now so great that the tank itself was no longer the master of the battlefield. Add to all this the euphoria due to sole ownership of the atomic bomb, and the collapse of the United States Armored Force was almost certain.

The over-rapid demobilisation of the wartime army was the final factor, and in a very short time the 16 US Armored Divisions had been reduced to one. Large numbers of tanks were dispersed to infantry divisions, each division acquiring a tank battalion and each infantry regiment a tank company, an astonishing reversion to the old system of tying tanks to infantry which, one might think, had been sufficiently discredited by that time.

Not all was lost, however. One lesson of the war which was correctly read was that the systematic pre-war development of engines, transmissions, tracks and suspension systems had paid off in a degree of mechanical reliability which was unmatched in the tanks of any other nation, and so a long-term programme was set up to continue this trend and develop a fresh generation of engines and mechanical components. At the same time, development of three new tanks to replace the current light, medium and heavy designs then in service was begun. Another wartime lesson

was assimilated here; the division between tank and tank destroyer was abandoned, the Tank Destroyer Command was abolished, and a policy was adopted of fitting tanks with guns capable of dealing with other tanks.

In 1947 the development of the three new tanks got under way. The light tank project began with the T37, which was essentially an improved M24 Chaffee. It carried a new 76-mm gun and a stereoscopic rangefinder, and on each side of the turret was a .30 machine-gun in a protected casing, operable by remote control from inside. This design gave way to the 'Phase Two' model which incorporated a relatively advanced (for that period) fire control system. The rangefinder was changed to a split-image type, and its output was automatically fed to a stabilisation system and an automatic lead computer coupled to the sights.

Gun stabilisation was a feature which had been tentatively explored during the war, the first reasonably effective model having been fitted to the turret gun on the M4 series of tanks. The system involves coupling a sensing device to the gun's elevating gear so that once the gunner has pointed the gun at a given target it will stay on that aim irrespective of how the tank bounces and dips while travelling across country. Without a stabiliser, firing from a moving tank with any hope of hitting is virtually impossible except on a smooth and level surface. The stabiliser fitted to the T37 Phase Two improved on earlier ideas by stabilising the gun in azimuth as well, automatically turning the turret to keep the gun pointed at the selected target.

More changes were made and the T37 became the T41, and the decision was taken to begin limited production. The Cadillac Division of General Motors were asked to take on manufacture, but since their existing factory wasn't big enough, a wartime aircraft plant at Cleveland, Ohio, was taken over and converted into the Cleveland Tank Arsenal. By this time the Korean War had begun, which stimulated production. The design was now standardised as the M41, christened the 'Little Bulldog', and 1000 were built. In 1951 the name was changed to the 'Walker Bulldog' in memory of General Walton H Walker, killed in a jeep accident in Korea.

The M41 initiated a number of features which were to become standard in tank

Below: A British Chieftain MBT, its 650 hp engine gives a top speed of 26 mph. It has a crew of four, armament of two machine-guns and one 120-mm gun

Below: The US M41 Light Tank Walker Bulldog on display at the Aberdeen Proving Ground. Developed in 1950 along with the M47 it was one of a new generation of post-war tanks

design. It was the first US tank to use a fume extractor on the gun barrel, to prevent the turret filling with smoke when the gun breech was opened after firing. It was the first to have any sort of integral fire control system; and it was the first to have an automatic loading system which selected, lifted and rammed the cartridge into the breech, and then caught and ejected the empty case. It also formed the basis for a number of self-propelled guns. But for all that, it was not the complete success for which the designers had hoped. At 23 tons it was too big to be a light tank and too small to be a medium, the 76-mm gun was outclassed by weapons in use by other countries, and the tank was too heavy to be used in airborne operations, which it had been hoped would be a useful bonus.

The medium tank programme became somewhat chaotic. Work began in 1946, but in the following year, when little had been done apart from studies of various design projects, the parlous political state of the world demanded some rapid action in order to provide the army with an efficient tank quickly. Some 2000 M26 heavy tanks, held in 'mothballs', were overhauled and fitted with new engines and transmissions and issued as the M46 'Patton', an interim measure. Work then continued on the new medium, by this time known as the T42. Before the design was completed the Korean War began and another 'interim measure' had to be adopted; the T42s turret was put into production and then fitted to the existing M46 tanks, the result being standardised as the M47.

By 1953 the T42 design had been completed and tested, and went into production as the M48, and a number of M47s were stripped of their turrets to supply the new chassis. So that eventually all the 'interim stages' and modifications caught up with each other and a complete new tank appeared. It included similar technical improvements in fire control as in the M41, weighed 44 tons and carried a 90-mm gun as its main armament. It subsequently gave rise to a number of variant models, differing in such features as the engine and transmission, and additions such as infra-red vision equipment. The US Marine Corps also owned a variant known as the M67 in which the 90-mm gun was replaced by a powerful flame-thrower.

The third American project was a heavy tank, in spite of the fact that the Armored Board were far from convinced that there was any need for such a vehicle. The first heavy tank project, which had begun in 1944, was concocted from parts of the M26 Pershing and the M4 Sherman, built on to a lengthened hull and with a raised superstructure carrying a powerful 105-mm gun. It was similar in concept to the German Ferdinand or British Tortoise, and shortly after being built it had its name changed to 'Gun Motor Carriage T28'. It weighed 93 tons and had up to 12 in of armour protection, which is why the 410-hp Ford engine could only propel it at 8 mph.

Two of these monsters were built; it has long been believed that one was destroyed by fire while on test and the other cut up for scrap in 1951, but early in 1977 one

was found in a corner of an abandoned ballistic range in the USA and efforts are now under way to restore it as a museum exhibit.

But the T28 wasn't a tank, because it didn't have a turret. So, using a similar design of chassis, a more conventional hull and turret were designed and built as the T29. This weighed 62 tons and mounted the same 105-mm gun as the T28; armour was up to 7 inches thick and it was powered by a 650 hp engine. This seemed to be a good design, but there was a school of thought which considered it to be a lot of tank for not much gun. Consequently the T30 was developed, more or less the same tank but mounting a 155-mm gun T7. Although of the same calibre as the artillery's 'Long Tom', this was a completely new weapon using a cartridge case and fitted with a muzzle brake to try and reduce the recoil force on the turret. This project came very close to production; 504 were authorised in July 1945, but were cancelled in the following month when the war ended.

Two T30s were fitted with 120-mm AA gun barrels to become the T34. This project was also closed down at the war's end, though the actual tanks were later built at the Army Tank Arsenal.

Out of this protracted development came the T43, in 1948, which in general terms was a scaled-up M48 medium. Weighing 56 tons it carried the 120-mm gun in the turret, had a five-man crew and could travel at 21 mph. It was standardised as the M103 in 1954 and went into production, but only in relatively small numbers. There was still no conviction that such a heavy vehicle had a place in modern war, and, as one critic shrewdly put it, only the continued presence of the Soviet Josef Stalin tank with its 122-mm gun kept the M103 project alive.

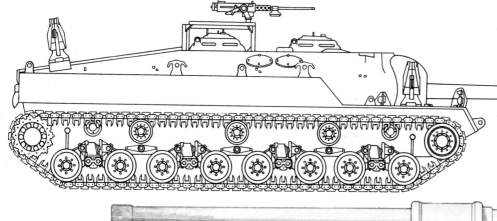

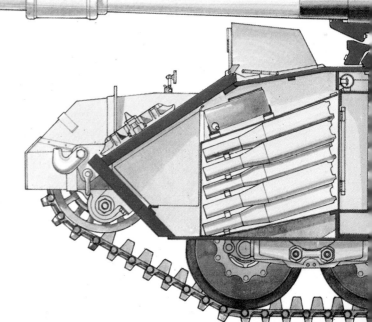

Left: The US T28 was developed in 1943. Like the British Tortoise tank it never saw action

Above: The US T30 Heavy Tank mounted a 90-mm gun and was evolved from the T29. The T30E2 had a 155-mm gun and weighed 65 tons

In 1948 the British Centurion was improved by fitting a new 3.3-in 20-pdr gun allied to full stabilisation, and in 1951–52 it proved itself in combat in Korea. But there was still room in the British Army for a heavy tank, it was felt. After looking at the American T43 project, a 120-mm gun of similar characteristics to the American model was developed and a 65-ton tank to go with it. This became 'Conqueror' which entered service at about the same time as the M103.

Shortly afterward came 'Caernarvon', an even heavier tank with a massive 183-mm gun. This potent weapon could reduce any tank in the world to a heap of smoking wreckage with one shot, but it was using a sledge-hammer to crack a nut. There were also mechanical problems with the tank, and in the end it never entered service.

The Centurion, in the late 1950s, was improved yet again by the adoption of a completely new 105-mm gun of great power and extremely high accuracy. This weapon so impressed the rest of NATO that it was adopted as standard tank armament, and the US Army fitted it to their new M60 medium tank in 1961. This was simply an improved and up-gunned M48, the greatest change being the large turret with a good 'ballistic shape' – i.e. the sides were well-sloped to deflect shot.

The 1950s saw some major developments

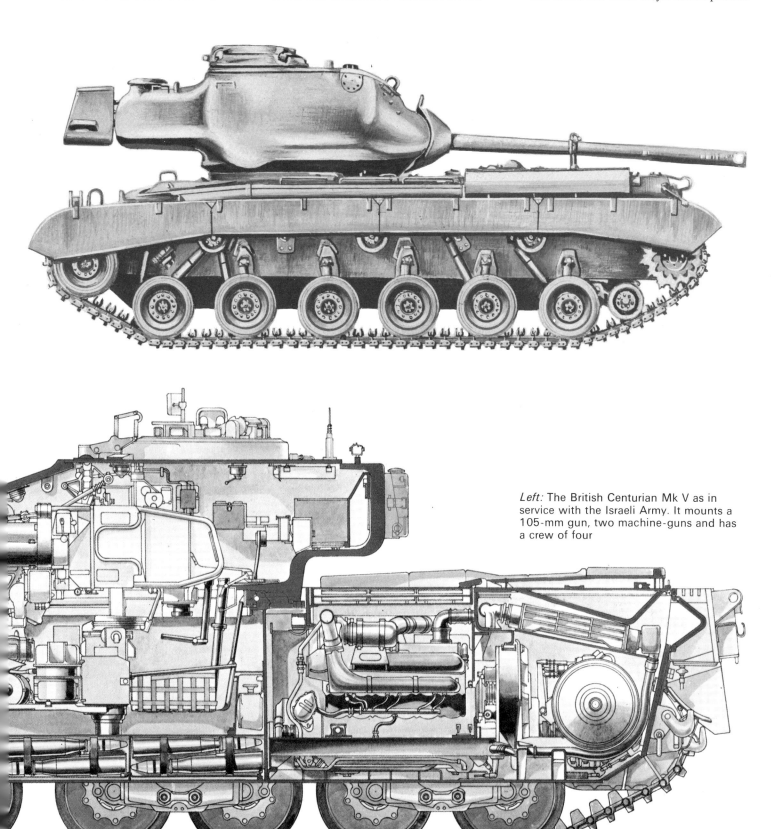

Below: The M-47 Patton used the M-46 hull with a new turret and a 90-mm gun. It had a crew of five up to 115 mm of armour and a top speed of 35 mph

Left: The British Centurian Mk V as in service with the Israeli Army. It mounts a 105-mm gun, two machine-guns and has a crew of four

coming from countries which had, up till then, not been notable as tank producers. Until 1939 most of the smaller nations had bought tanks, or at least tank designs, from Britain, the USA or Germany, following this up with minor modifications to suit their own preferences. The war years had thrown them back upon their own resources and, while there was still a certain amount of outside buying going on after the war, these nations were now beginning to show signs of original thought.

The most innovative design came from Sweden, with the Stridsvagn 103A or 'S-Tank', development of which began in 1956. In this design, all preconceived ideas were discarded and the designers went back to first principles and asked what the vehicle was expected to do. With that defined, they began from scratch and produced what is undoubtedly the most unorthodox tank ever seen in military service.

The most significant feature is that the gun is fixed to the hull and incapable of elevation or traverse. In order to point the gun it is necessary to move the whole tank, and since gunlaying demands precision, this meant the development of new and extremely sensitive steering so as to be able to point the gun accurately. Elevation was taken care of by a complex hydro-pneumatic suspension system which allowed the hull to be tilted on the wheels through an arc of 25°.

The result of this was to do away with the complexities of a turret and lower the silhouette. The tank stood slightly over 7 ft high to the top of the commander's periscopes, a considerable difference from, for example, the 10 ft 6 in of the US M60 tank. On the other hand, of course, one set of mechanical problems has been saved at the expense of another – the steering and suspension.

Another innovation was the use of dual engines, a Rolls-Royce diesel and a Boeing gas turbine, coupled together; either is capable of moving the tank, but both have to be running in order to slew the tank so as to traverse the gun. This is something of a disadvantage since the engines must be run constantly when the tank is expecting attack, a process which is wasteful of fuel and which tends to reveal the tank's position by a plume of exhaust emission in cold weather.

Further important features of the S-Tank include the ability to travel equally well in both directions, with duplicated driving controls and gun controls so that either the commander or the driver can drive the vehicle or fire the gun or both – which effectively makes the S-Tank a one-man system. The third crew member is the rear driver who faces backwards and controls the tank when travelling in reverse; at other times he doubles as the radio operator.

After prolonged trials the S-Tank was put into production in 1966 and now equips the Swedish Army. In spite of several tests by other countries, it has not been adopted elsewhere. Two reasons advanced for this are firstly that it seems to be purely a defensive tank, due to its inability to engage targets while on the move, and secondly its very high cost.

One consequence of the S-Tank's fixed gun mounting was that an automatic loading gear could be built into the breech area, since the gun would always be in the same place relative to the rest of the vehicle.

The automatic loader in the American M-41 was much less involved and was faced with the complication of having to cope with the gun at different angles of elevation. It was the adoption of this loading mechanism in the S-Tank that allowed the crew to be reduced to three men, the commander/gunner being able to do his own loading simply by pressing a button. A selector switch allowed him the option of either armour-piercing or high explosive ammunition; if smoke was required, this had to be removed from a magazine and dropped into the auto-loader by the rear driver, a task he could do quite easily without leaving his seat.

This advantage of using an auto-loader to save a man had previously been adopted by the French. Their postwar tank design had, in fact, begun clandestinely while the war was still going on and while France was still under German occupation; a 48-ton tank armed with a 90-mm gun, known as the ARL44, was the result. The intention was to build 600 of these to stock the postwar French Army, but finance reduced this to 60, which went into service in 1950. Meanwhile ex-German Panthers were refurbished and placed into service and in 1946, in return for financial aid from the USA, the French Government agreed to build a light tank within five years. After testing prototypes from three companies, a production contract was given to the Atelier de Construction d'Issy-les-Moulineaux (AMX).

Above and Right: The Swedish S Tank is in effect a superior self-propelled gun. The engine is the same as that in the British FV432 series but there is a Boeing gas-turbine as an auxiliary. Its hydraulic suspension enables the hull to be raised and lowered. It also allows the whole vehicle to be turned quickly to face a target. The 105-mm gun has an automatic loader. The low hull and well sloped armour make the S Tank a very difficult target and the crew of three have the consolation that the vehicle is designed with crew safety in mind. However the fixed gun means that the S Tank cannot fight from a hull down position and if one of the many complex parts fails the immobilised vehicle is worse than useless. A conventional tank can still fight on even if it is immobilised – becoming a turreted pill box

Left: The French AMX 50 with its 90-mm gun and rear decking which resembled the war time German Panther tank — the 1000-bhp injection engine was based on the best features of German designs of that period

The AMX13 (13 because the specified weight was 13 metric tonnes; in the event it weighed 15) used a conventional hull and running gear, innovation being found in the turret. The upper portion of the turret, together with the 75-mm gun, could oscillate up and down on the lower portion, so giving the gun its elevation. Traverse was produced by the usual form of rotating turret, but since the gun breech and the upper section of turret were in a fixed relationship, an automatic loader could be fitted, thus reducing the turret crew to two men, the commander and gunner.

The AMX13 was extremely successful, several thousand being built and sold across the world. The first production models appeared in 1952. In 1958 a new version appeared, mounting a 105-mm gun, but here the designers over-reached themselves. The chassis was too light to take the full recoil of a high velocity 105-mm, and so the ammunition had to be 'de-tuned' to reduce the muzzle velocity to 2625 ft/sec. Moreover the turret was now extremely crowded due to the bigger gun and its ancillaries, and only 32 rounds of ammunition could be carried. The 105-mm idea was, therefore, abandoned in favour of a new model mounting a 90-mm gun. This gave a velocity of 3120 ft/sec and a far better combat performance, and it has remained the standard ever since.

Once development had begun on the light tank, the French Army turned to the question of a heavy tank capable of standing up to a Josef Stalin. After a number of prototypes had been examined, another AMX design was chosen for development as the AMX 50. Armed with a 100-mm gun it was quite a conventional design, with a good performance due to the adoption of a 1000-hp engine. It was improved even more by fitting a 120-mm gun, similar to that in use on the American M103 and British Conqueror. But it was an expensive vehicle, and the ready availability of American M46 tanks led to the AMX 50 being dropped on purely financial grounds.

But soon after that decision had been taken France and West Germany agreed to develop a new design of medium tank between them. Their priorities were in the order Armament — Mobility — Protection, and the result reflects this quite clearly. The main armament was a 105-mm gun, though for reasons best known to themselves the French elected not to adopt the British 105-mm, as had the rest of NATO, and developed one of their own. The engine, a Hispano-Suiza flat-12 supercharged diesel developed 720-hp and moved the tank's $35\frac{1}{2}$ tons at 40 mph, with extremely good cross-country performance. But in order to keep the performance up, the weight had to be restricted, and this was done by cutting down on armour, to the point where the AMX 30, as the tank is known, is only proof against light weapons up to 30-mm calibre.

What lay behind all this activity was, of course, the threat to the West posed by the Soviet Army's ever-increasing tank strength. Their experiences in the war had convinced the Soviet leaders that tanks were the cutting edge of the army, and in the postwar years the aim was to maintain their quantitative superiority while working towards a qualitative superiority over the West.

Bearing in mind that the Soviets had finished the war with what were probably the best tanks in their respective classes, the T-34 and JS-3, they were able to concentrate on production of those models for some time before having to build replacements, and this time was spent on design studies and in assimilating the results of German research during the war years.

Right: The AMX-30 a 34 ton tank has a 105-mm gun, crew of four, and a top speed of 40 mph. The power/weight ratio is excellent, but suspension does not give a smooth ride when moving across country at speed

Right: The original AMX-13 with its 75-mm gun mounted rigidly in a trunnioned turret. The whole turret is tilted to elevate the gun, and the rigid mounting enables an automatic loading gear to be used

Above: An AMX-13 with its 90-mm gun showing how the turret tilts to elevate the gun

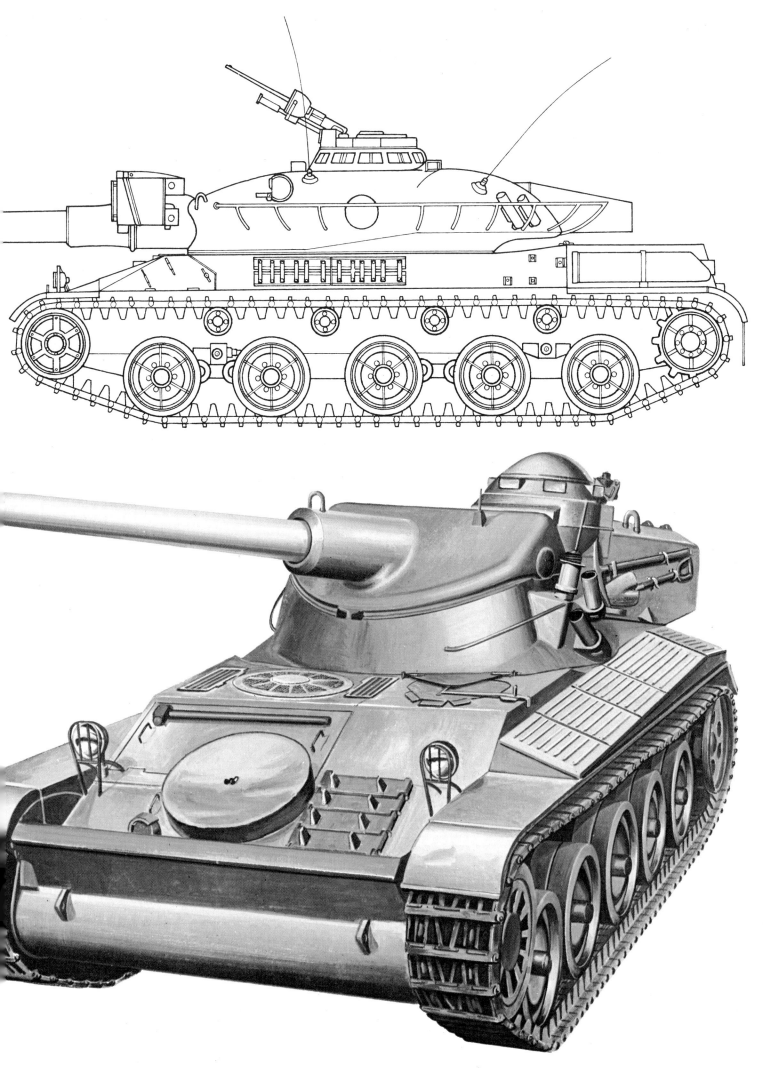

Above: The PT-76 is the first combat vehicle to have water-propulsion and needs no special preparation before it takes to the the water. It is intended to spearhead river crossings and has a top speed in water of 6 knots

The first new Soviet design to appear was the T-54, which went into production in 1948. It was an improved T-34 with better armour and a new and better turret, but its most important feature was its new 100-mm gun, extremely powerful armament at that time for a tank weighing 35½ tons. Although below Western standards of sophistication, it was an improvement on their wartime models, having electrical turret traverse and, eventually, such things as infra-red driving and sighting, stadiometric rangefinder and full stabilisation of the

Novosti Press Agency

Above: The amphibious Soviet PT-76 has a crew of three, weighs 14 tons, has a top speed of 27 mph and is armed with one 76-mm gun and one machine-gun

Below: The Soviet T-54 weighs 36 tons has a 580 hp engine giving a top speed of 34 mph. The crew of four are protected by a maximum armour thickness of 105 mm and the tank has two machine-guns and one 100-mm gun

Right: Soviet infantry in snow smocks during winter training. They are accompanied by JS-3 tanks

gun. Some 30 000 of these are believed to have been built between 1948 and 1963, and they were liberally distributed to Soviet satellites.

The next new design to appear was the PT-76 amphibious tank in the early 1950s. This used a totally new design of chassis and hull, bearing no resemblance to any previous design. It could drive straight into water without any preparation and, once afloat, propelled itself by two steerable water-jet units at the rear of the hull. With a well-sloped turret mounting a 76-mm gun, it weighed 14 tons and could move at about 30 mph on hard surfaces and 6 mph in water. Highly successful as a reconnaissance vehicle, it was less use as a fighting tank since armour protection had been sacrificed in the interests of flotation, and the gun cannot now be considered any sort of threat.

In 1957 the West first saw the T-10 heavy tank, though in all probability it had been

in production for some years by then. This was an improved Josef Stalin 3, with a better 122-mm gun with fume extractor, a large turret, better engine and thicker armour. About 2500 of these are believed to have been built, and while their technical features are poor in comparison with Western designs, the powerful gun and the 250 mm of armour on the front make it an extremely dangerous tank on the battlefield.

The T-10 production was, it seems, curtailed since the Soviet Army preferred a medium tank as its primary fighting machine, and some time in the early 1960s a new model, the T-62, went into production. It was publicly revealed for the first time in May 1965. Again, it was the T-34 overhauled in the sense that it had a similar suspension and general layout. But the hull was longer and wider, the track had greater ground contact and there was a new 'inverted frying-pan' turret. But the

Soviet 115-mm gun suggests that it wasn't quite as good as its designers had hoped. Accuracy was poor until the ammunition was modified so as to impart a small degree of spin to the shell.

Another new feature was the introduction of an automatic spent case ejector which threw the empty cartridge cases through a special hatch at the back of the turret, so as to reduce the build-up of gases inside and keep the turret floor clear of the clutter of spent cases in action. This device is also reported to have given trouble, the cases sometimes missing the hatch and being bounced back into the turret, injuring the crew members. Nevertheless, the T-62 was taken into service and remained the Soviet main battle tank until the early 1970s when a new design was seen.

At present the exact nomenclature of this new vehicle is in some doubt. It is believed that the Soviets call it the T-64, though British and US authorities refer to it as the T-72 and the West Germans as the T-70. Broadly speaking it seems to be the T-62 turret on an improved chassis, mounting a new 125-mm gun with automatic loader. The gun is reported to be partly rifled in order to impart a small amount of spin to the projectiles, the major part of the bore being smooth. The provision of an automatic loader does away with one crewman, as usual, leaving the tank with a commander and gunner in the turret and a driver in the hull. Beyond the belief that it weighs 40 tons and can move at 50 mph, little more is known, and it is not yet possible to say whether it has entered Soviet service in large numbers.

Above: Russian T-62s ford a river during the Odra-Nysa exercises in 1969. These tanks are fitted with snorkel gear and can submerge to a depth of four metres. Preparations for submerging take 15 minutes

big change lay in the gun, a completely new 115-mm smoothbore which fired fin-stabilised projectiles.

Little solid information has ever reached the West about this gun, but it seems likely that the object behind it was to achieve high velocity in order to improve the first round hit probability by reducing the error due to mis-estimation of range. The ammunition consisted of hollow-charge shell, the effect of which is always improved by fin-stabilisation and the absence of spin, but it also included discarding-sabot armour piercing shot, another reason for requiring high velocity. But APDS shot in a smoothbore gun is a dubious proposition in many people's view, and there are those who are still waiting to be convinced that the present-day rush to adopt smoothbores is anything but a trendy gimmick. Be that as it may, the subsequent history of the

Returning now to the West, the British Army had, in 1956, issued a specification for a new tank to replace the Centurion as the main battle tank. This became 'Chieftain', the first issues of which took place in 1965. The nine-year interval had been well-spent, and at the time of its introduction and for several years afterwards Chieftain was the most formidable tank in the world. For once the British designers had put gun-power at the head of their list and had developed a new 120-mm gun.

This was not simply a refinement of the US-originated gun in Conqueror but a totally new weapon which broke new ground by using a bagged charge loaded separately behind the projectile. Since the bagged charge is completely consumed on firing, there is no longer the problem of disposing of a hot and large cartridge case in the confined space of the turret, though there were problems associated with the storage of these bagged charges in fire-proof containers. Chieftain weighs 53 tons, is driven by a 730-hp engine, attains 30 mph and has an excellent cross-country performance. A notable feature is the comparatively low silhouette (just over 9 ft) which is achieved by having the driver operate from a prone position instead of the more usual sitting position.

Internally the Chieftain must rank as one of the most sophisticated and complex fighting machines ever produced. The turret is crammed with fire control equipment and electronic devices: a laser rangefinder, electronic fire control computer, infrared sights and driving aids; infrared detectors, devices for measuring wind angle and speed and applying the values to the fire

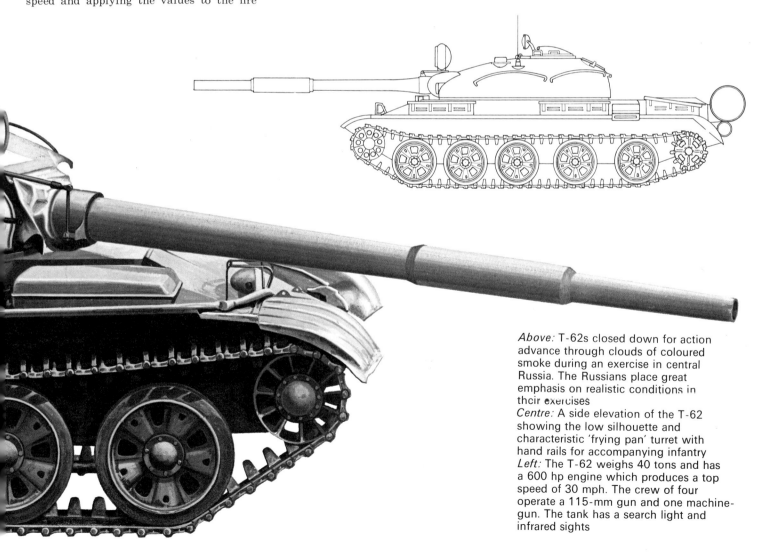

Above: T-62s closed down for action advance through clouds of coloured smoke during an exercise in central Russia. The Russians place great emphasis on realistic conditions in their exercises
Centre: A side elevation of the T-62 showing the low silhouette and characteristic 'frying pan' turret with hand rails for accompanying infantry
Left: The T-62 weighs 40 tons and has a 600 hp engine which produces a top speed of 30 mph. The crew of four operate a 115-mm gun and one machine-gun. The tank has a search light and infrared sights

Above: A Centurian AVRE Mk 5 with a specially designed 15-ton trailer for a Giant Viper, an explosive rocket propelled mine clearing device. The Viper is an explosive filled hose which is detonated across a mine-field to clear a path for small vehicles and infantry

Left: A Centurian AVRE showing its bull-dozer blade and fascine carrier as well as the 165-mm low velocity demolition gun

Right: A Centurian AVRE crosses an air-portable bridge. The Centurian replaced the Churchill AVRE in the mid 1960s

Below: A Chieftain MBT in a training area in southern England. The Chieftain has its 120-mm ammunition wet stowed to cut down the risk of explosions and fire if it takes a hit in action

RAC Tank Museum

COI

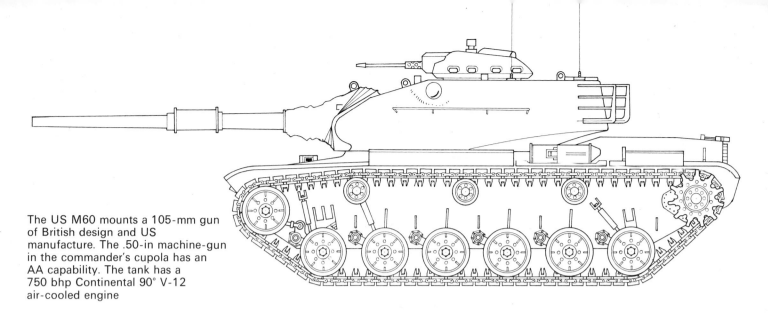

The US M60 mounts a 105-mm gun of British design and US manufacture. The .50-in machine-gun in the commander's cupola has an AA capability. The tank has a 750 bhp Continental 90° V-12 air-cooled engine

The joint West German and US tank the MBT-70 which failed when the West Germans rejected the Shillelagh missile weapons system, and Congress vetoed the project on cost. The British Chieftain costs £105,000 – an MBT-70 would have cost £215,000

control computer, and doubtless many other things not publicly revealed. As well as equipping the British Army, Chieftain has been sold to Iran, in an improved version which uses a newly-developed highly resistant armour, details of which are not yet publicly disclosed.

In the USA things have not gone so smoothly. In 1960 the M48 was improved by equipping it with the British 105-mm gun, and by this move it became the M60. At the same time, development of a new weapon, a 152-mm gun which could also launch a 'Shillelagh' guided missile, was under way, and this weapon first appeared in an 'Armoured Reconnaissance Airborne Assault Vehicle' – in other words a light tank – called the 'Sheridan', in 1962.

This vehicle introduced several new features including aluminium armour, aluminium and magnesium transmission, and various other equally advanced technical details, but it failed to live up to its promise. In the attempt to produce a vehicle which could be air-dropped, the designers had virtually to design a light reconnaissance vehicle with the fighting ability of a medium tank, and something had to give way. The guidance of the missile is affected by ground reflections and the 6-in gun, even though a low-velocity weapon, is still powerful enough to shake the vehicle so badly that the crew have to hang on to something when it fires. It is also more expensive than a Chieftain tank, and has little long-range fire capability.

But in spite of all this the 152-mm gun-launcher looked as if it might do well in a heavier vehicle, and it was decided to fit this into a new turret on the M60, turning it into the M60A2 and giving the medium tank a new lease of life. Three hundred new tanks were built to this specification, but they turned out to be unusable, as did the 243 new turrets built for fitting into old M60s. It took several years to sort out the problems, largely concerned with stabilisation and fire control, before the M60A2 could get into service, which it eventually did in 1975.

While all this was going on a new project had begun and was moving ahead. In 1956 a new 105-mm-gun tank project, the T95, was started, and in the next few years the pilot models were modified back and forth, fitted with this gun and that, until it finally exceeded the specified weight by far too much. In 1963, when the designers were probably wondering what to do next the US and West German governments decided to join together to develop a new main battle tank, the MBT-70. It was to be the most advanced tank in the world, capable of remaining in service for the rest of the century, and it was to go into production in 1970.

The prototype which appeared was, without doubt, the most complex tank ever built. At the same time it also claimed another record; it was the most expensive, the cost of a production model being estimated in 1971 as $1 million. The suspension was hydro-pneumatic and could be controlled so as to make the tank 'squat' on its belly when stationary in a firing position, reducing the silhouette. The 152-mm gun-launcher was provided with an automatic loader, the design of which was complicated by the fact that the gun could elevate from −10° to +20°, and the loader had to cope with any angle and with either gun ammunition or missiles. All the three-man crew were in the turret, the driver controlling the vehicle electrically from a contra-rotating seat and cupola which always faced the front, irrespective of where the turret was pointed. Extremely sophisticated fire control systems were fitted and the turret could be sealed against nuclear, biological or chemical attack. A 20-mm cannon in an independent cupola could be remote-controlled to fire against air or ground targets. The engine was a V-12 multi-fuel, supercharged and turbo-charged, and with a variable compression ratio, developing 1475 hp.

On trials it turned out that the poor driver soon became disorientated when trying to control the vehicle from a swinging turret; the powerful engine had considerable teething troubles; and there were arguments as to whether the vehicle were not being under-employed in mounting the 152-mm system which, in Vietnam, had now shown that it had problems. And, looming over all, was that $1 million price tag.

An attempt to produce an 'austere version' by cutting out some of the more exotic features reduced the price to about $850 000, but even this wasn't good enough, and in December 1971 the project was cancelled by the US Congress, the Army being told to start again with a fresh design which should be ready for production by 1980. This is currently known as the XH-1 programme and prototypes by

General Motors and the Chrysler Corporation are now being tested.

The Germans had bowed out of the MBT-70 project when they saw what it was going to cost and because they wanted no part of the 152-mm weapon, preferring a conventional 120-mm gun of their own. But by the time the MBT-70 project collapsed, they had completed development of an excellent design which suited them better, so the decision was not the setback to them that it was to the Americans.

The German tank industry had, of course collapsed completely at the end of the Second World War. At that time there were a number of projects in progress, including two which deserve mention as the final attempts at giantism in the tank world. These were the 'Maus' and 'E-100'. Maus was designed by Dr Porsche, with Hitler's enthusiastic backing, to be a super-tank capable of outgunning and outfighting any tank in existence. Weighing 180 tons it had frontal armour of 240 mm and carried a 150-mm gun in the turret. A prototype was built and tested early in 1944 and orders were given for the manufacture of six pilot models, but they were never completed.

The E-100 project was made by the Henschel factory to an army specification. Effectively, the High Command were saying that if they had to have a super-tank, they would prefer to have one in which they had had some say. The E-100 was, in general terms, a grossly enlarged Tiger; it weighed 137 tons, had 250 mm of armour, a 150-mm and 75-mm gun in the turret and a 1200-hp engine to move it at 25 mph, twice the speed of Maus. The prototype of this tank was not completed by the end of the war.

German postwar tank development began in 1957 with the previously-mentioned agreement with France to develop a medium tank. As usual with these combined developments, each party had their own ideas and gradually they moved further apart until they finally agreed to go their own ways, the French going on to the AMX30 and the Germans developing two prototypes. One of these was selected for further development under the code-name 'Leopard' in 1962, and in 1965 the first production model left the factory of Krauss-Maffei at Munich. It is of interest that the Leopard was designed by Dr F Porsche, the son of the wartime designer.

Leopard is an excellent battle tank. The

British 105-mm gun was adopted, an 830-hp multi-fuel engine fitted to give a speed of 40 mph and the welded hull and cast turret offer good protection. It is now in service with the West German, Belgian, Netherlands, Italian and Norwegian armies, over 3000 having been built. The design has not stood still during production, improvements having been added from time to time; the 'A3' model, for example, has a new spaced-plate turret and track aprons, while later improvements include a new type of track and a light alloy thermal gun-jacket to prevent distortion of the hot gun barrel during action due to atmospheric changes.

When MBT-70 went out of the window, the Germans decided to fill the gap by an improved Leopard, now known as Leopard 2. This is now under trial, numerous prototypes having been built. Much of the advanced technology pioneered by the MBT-70 project has been adapted to Leopard 2, but the principal bone of contention at the moment is the question of armament. A 120-mm smoothbore gun has been developed in Germany, but although the German hope is that Leopard 2 will be adopted as the future standard NATO tank, there are mixed opinions among the other partners about this new gun. Britain would prefer to see a conventional rifled 120-mm, while the Americans argue for retention of the existing 105-mm weapon. The debate is continuing and it will probably be some time before agreement is reached.

Although the shooting stopped in 1945 the search for tank supremacy will continue. By now, though, complications have crept in, as we have seen. Guns have reached new heights of sophistication, missiles have appeared, new types of armour replace traditional steels, electronics abound, lasers and rangefinders, radar and infrared help the commander find his target. New and deadly weapons have appeared to deal with the tank, for the old-time anti-tank gun has disappeared, foundered under its own weight like some prehistoric monster. But the basic requirements are still the same; the tank is a combination of firepower, mobility and protection, and what you get depends on how you shuffle the cards. The game is the same as it was in 1916; the only thing that has changed is the size of the pot. The first British tanks in 1917 cost £5000 each; the MBT-70 would have cost $1 million.

The West German Leopard mounts a British 105-mm gun. It has a top speed of 40-mph, weighs 40-tons and has a crew of four. A white light/infrared search light can be fitted on the gun mantlet for night vision and the commander and driver's positions can take IR viewers

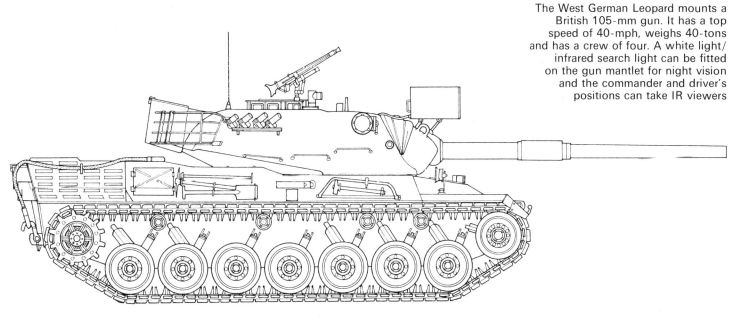

A sectionalised view of the Chieftain. It is fitted with an NBC system and has infrared driving and fighting aids. It can be fitted with a dozer blade. It has a range of 280 miles